Ber!in

YOU ARE LEAVING
THE AMERICAN SECTOR
ВЫ ВЫЕЗЖАЕТЕ ИЗ
АМЕРИКАНСКОГО СЕКТОРА
VOUS SORTEZ
DU SECTEUR AMERICAIN
SIE VERLASSEN DEN AMERIKANISCHEN SEKTOR

contemporary writing
from East and West
Berlin

Bandanna Books   1983   Santa Barbara

Copyright ©1983 Mitch Cohen. Upon publication all rights revert to the individual artists, writers, translators.
All rights reserved. Alle Rechte vorbehalten. For permission to reproduce all or part of *Berlin*, other than in reviews or brief quotations, please contact the publisher at 209 W. De la Guerra, Santa Barbara, California 93101, USA.

Cover art (silkscreen) by Reinhard Zabke
Endpaper maps by Tom Huston
Back cover photos by Jochen Melzian
The bulk of the translations in *Berlin* were done by Mitch Cohen; other translators are Prof. Stuart Hood (for Peter-Paul Zahl), Ulrich Danielowski (for Bodo Morshäuser and Reinhard Komor), Michael Meinicke (*P.* and *Fantasy* by Lutz Rathenow), and Johanna Bahne (co-translator of Michel Boiron).
Special thanks are due to Jochen Melzian for his photographs and reproductions of pieces from several artists.
This publication of *Rockbottom* 11&12 (LC 77-642342) was made possible in part by a grant from CCLM.

Library of Congress Cataloging in Publication Data
Main entry under title:

Berlin, contemporary writing from Berlin.

(Rockbottom, ISSN 0146-1419 ; 11-12)
English and German.
Bibliography: p.
Includes index.
  1. German poetry—Berlin (Germany) 2. German poetry—20th century. 3. German fiction—Berlin (Germany)—Translations into English. 4. German fiction—20th century—Translations into English. 5. English fiction—20th century—Translations from German.   I. Cohen, Mitch, 1952-
II. Title: Berlin, contemporary writing from Berlin.   III. Series.
PT3807.B4B38   830'.8'0943155   82-4015
ISBN 0-930012-23-2   AACR2
ISBN 0-930012-22-4 (pbk.)

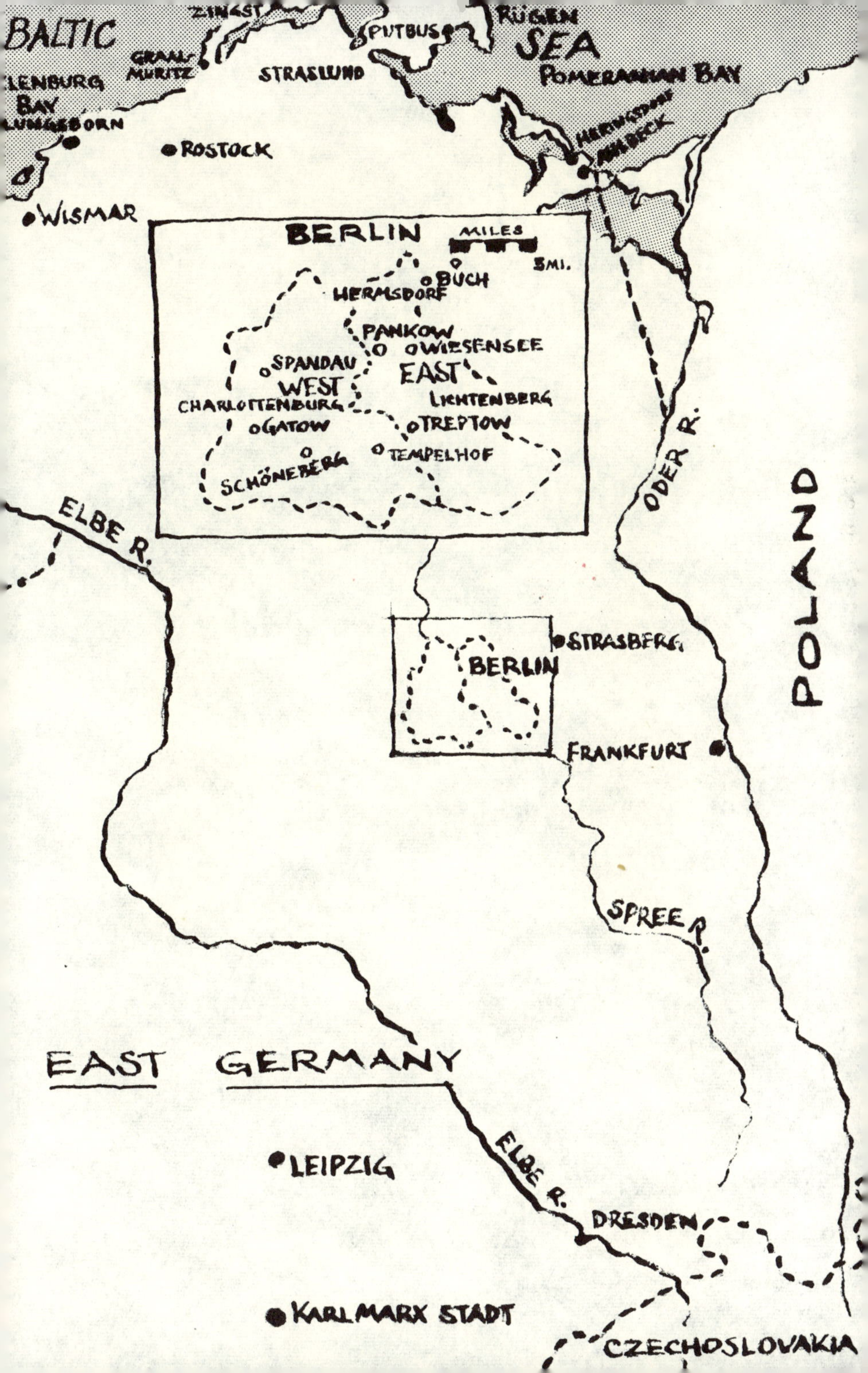
BALTIC
SEA
ZINGST
RÜGEN
PUTBUS
GRAAL-MURITZ
STRASLUND
POMERANIAN BAY
LENBURG BAY
KUNGSBORN
ROSTOCK
WISMAR
BERLIN
MILES
3 MI.
BUCH
HERMSDORF
PANKOW
WIESENSEE
SPANDAU
EAST
WEST
LICHTENBERG
CHARLOTTENBURG
GATOW
TREPTOW
TEMPELHOF
SCHÖNEBERG
ELBE R.
ODER R.
POLAND
STRASBERG
BERLIN
FRANKFURT
SPREE R.
EAST GERMANY
LEIPZIG
ELBE R.
DRESDEN
KARL MARX STADT
CZECHOSLOVAKIA

CONTENTS

Michael Meinicke	Foreword	13
Mitch Cohen	Introduction	15

I   LIFE

Jürgen Theobaldy	A Kind of Charity	24
	Furnished Apartment	26
	My Young Life	28
	Pictures from America	32
	Like This Summer Dress	34
Uwe Kolbe	the guilty	36
	Sacco & Vanzetti	36
	I Was Raised in the Name of a Weltanschauung	38
	We Live with Cracks	40
	Metamorphosis	42
	Melanie	44
Uli Hirschfelder	Like the Movies, like Life	46
	High Noon	50
	At the Bus Stops	52
	For Thomas, on the Thirteenth	54
	A Few Minutes of March	56
	Poesy & Praxis	58
Hans J. Scheurer	Your Father's Pants	60
	what they make of you	62
Alfred Miersch	Kicks in the Head	64
	The Attempt is What Matters	68
Jörg Fauser	At the Butcher's	70
	Requiem for a Goldfish	72
	Fame	80
Bernd Schmich	1977—but not for the files	84
	After Work	88
	"the still rooms . . ."	88
Michael Speier	"subwaysmell . . ."	90
	Ice Age III	91
	Statement	92

II   PEOPLE

Michael Meinicke	Your Kiss	94
	People—Fairy Tales	95
	Prison	97
Peter Bolster	Fairly Confused	98
	Walls	100
	Storm over a Chestnut Tree in the Afternoon	102
	Driving Back in November	102
Lutz Rathenow	Fantasy	106
	P.	108
	Prompt	111
	Change of Location	112
	The Applause	113
Silvo Lahtela	Places 1	114
	The Escalator at Pont de Sêvres	115
	from "Foreword for those who don't get it afterward"	116
Herbert Witzel	Letter Found in a Bottle	118
Stefan Keller	The Coal-Handler's Warmth	122
Gerd Böltz	landscapes	124
Peter Lackner	"Ick been ein Brrr leaner" says this Santa Barbarian solemnly	126

III   INTERIORS

Tillye Boesche-Zackarow	It was Your Coldness	134
	Change of Life	134
Karl Mickel	Summer in Petzow	136
	Linden Forum	136
	Orderly Hair	138
	Beer: for Leising	140
	The Modern Quarter	142
	German Woman '46	142
	Dresden Houses	144
Gerd Springborn	"Our landlord schlepps the pails . . ."	150
	The Good	152
Paul Gerhard Hübsch (Hadayatullah)		
Monica Streit	i dwell in me	160
	Processions	166
	Violent Habituation	168
	"I love you. . . ."	169

IV   RELATIONSHIPS

Sabine Techel	"of him it's said he . . ."	172
	baby it's great to be back home	172
	felix coniunctio	174
	unsettled, quietly and softly	174
	no poem	175
	family life	176
	no mail today	176
Michel Boiron	The Lonely Road	180
	little mornings of habit	181
Katja Tiel	Portrait 1970	182
Bodo Morshäuser	Flight in the Morning	184
	One of Those Letters	186
Ingeborg Middendorf	The Miscarriage	189
Ursula Rühle	Watertight Argument	196
Holger Schenk	Flourish	198
Maria-Stefanie Stern	you	200
Josepha Gutelius	The Idolaters	202

V   WORK

Ralf Rothmann	Memo	206
	What a Day	208
Sibylle Klefinghaus	The Other Side	210
	Werkkreis Literatur der Arbeitswelt	214
Joachim Steffenhagen	thoughts about the zehlendorf spinnery	216
	Mornings	220
	the basic fact	222
Reinhard Komor	The Release	224
Volker Wohlfahrt	Hot Coffee	228
	On the Anniversary of the Death of Hans Martin Schleyer	233
Jutta Bartus	Frau Mitschuleit's Survey	236

VI   IDEAS

Jan Koplowitz	Positive Provocation	245
	The Initials of the Seigneur	249
Künstlergruppe Ratgeb		252
Volker Braun	On Brecht, the Truth Unites	258
	On Climbing High Mountains (after Lenin)	260
	New Purpose of Hadrian's Army	262

Volker Braun (cont.)	The Myth of the Cave	264
	Newspaper Poem, Edited	265
	The Pleasure in the Creative	266
	Goethe's Leaseholders	266
	Going All the Way	267
Uli Becker	I Want My Money Back!	268
	The Suffering of the Fugitives	270
	Defeatist Depression	272
Bert Gorek	but primarily	274
	alkfowl rapt dripping	276
	you shielding & wielding	276
	Adder Earth Let It Be I Picture Me Something	278
	moocher pays	280
Knud Wollenberger	Design for a Monument	281
Thomas Brasch	Oedipus	282
	Rita's Fantasy	283
	Eulenspiegel	285

VII CONFRONTATIONS

Jürgen Fuchs	Feb. 18, '77	292
	The Turning Point	295
	The Child	296
	"That is exaggerated . . ."	297
	"I don't believe that . . ."	298
	9/1/'78	298
	"Always I see you in prison . . ."	300
Siegfried Heinrichs	Smoke Signal	302
	Sketches from a Socialist Prison, The Book	303
petition for Peter-Paul Zahl		307
Peter-Paul Zahl	february sun	308
	doors	310
Thomas Neubauer	The Request	328
Jochen Melzian	Realistic Curriculum Vitae	332
	The Predilection of the German Thinker	335
	Aktion Widerstand	336

VIII HISTORIES

Alfons Köhler	Cooling Towers	342
Stefan Döring	poem about my grandfather	344

Norbert Tefelski	Old Typewriter	346
	Nostalgic One	348
	The Constitution	350
Joachim Meyer	while watching the demolition of an old apartment building	352
	at the loading ramp	356
	tender bonds through off-colors	358
Ernst Wichner	fragment	362
	sleeping tablets	364
	no man's land	366
Hella Joanni	Christmas Outside	373
Hans Schumacher	Slow Motion	376
Index of authors and artists		383
Index of titles		385

IX GRAPHICS

Reinhard Zabke	silkscreen	cover
Tom Huston	pen	endpapers
Jochen Melzian	photo	title page
Mitch Cohen	photo	10
Jochen Melzian	photo	35
Jochen Melzian	photo	59
Jürgen Beissert	Malli Kneeling	77
Jürgen Beissert	Malli Sitting	79
Jürgen Beissert	Mitch	96
Jochen Melzian	photo	110
Jürgen Beissert	Bettina	117
Reinhard Zabke	oil	121
Wolfgang Gersch	Encounter	159
Jochen Melzian	photo	178
Mitch Cohen	Kreuzberger Prospekt	195
Werkkreis symbol	pen	215
Jürgen Beissert	Study of a Hand	219
Werner Steinbrecher	"When they marched in . . ."	253
Nil Fricke	Bundschuh	254
Nil Fricke	Ralph the Crow	255
Werner Brunner	Scheißspiel	257
Jochen Melzian	photo	299
Jochen Melzian	photo	305
Jochen Melzian	photo	331
Jan Huber	Buildings in Snow	354
Christine Arweiler	Abandoned House in Dahlem	375

Ber!in

Foreword

Soviet American French English occupation zones / special independently administered political entity within the territory of the German Democratic Republic / Capital of the German Democratic Republic / province of the Federal Republic of Germany / former capital of the German Empire / West- / East- / "the spark for the powderkeg of Europe" / "the stake in the flesh of socialism" / Berlin—the divided city.
—*that* is the name of a city in Germany. Here two extremely different powers confront each other face to face, closer than anywhere else in the world. Here soldiers look directly into the eyes of the enemy. At no time can they fight. Here neighbors look in each other's windows. At no time can they visit. Always there is the "Mauer"—a 6-meter-high concrete wall, a 30-meter-wide land mine zone, towers with gun-notches, sentries with heavy weapons, trained dogs. The irreconcilable views of two world powers.
Trains, bus lines, streets, sidewalks all end after a curve, behind the next building, unexpectedly. There are houses with two entrances, one in socialism, the other in capitalism. Between these, the border—dangerous and deadly, crossing and surrounding the city.
After the second world war, that border was agreed upon by the Allies. Investments under the Marshall Plan rapidly reconstructed the western part of the city. The living standard recovered. East and West adopted different currencies. East Berliners working in the West exchanged their western earnings on the black market in the East at 5 to 1.
The war-devastated Soviet Union had no capital for supportive investments in the East. East Germany was dependent on its workers. That was the main reason for closing the border. On August 13, 1961 began suddenly the separation of families, lovers, and friends. This was the real division of the city.
Twenty years afterward, this reality has become a symbol of impossibilities in people's private lives. Information about "the other side" comes mostly through the mass media. A dream is exchanged for a vision, a vision for a dream.
This means the total influence of politics, right into the intimate spheres of people's lives. Decision is constantly demanded. In the

East, consciously. In the West, often concealedly, masked by the doubtful accomplishments of the modern consumer society. Those who lose themselves in ways out sometimes find themselves in small closed rooms.

The truth for the inhabitants of the city is called freedom within close limits. It's through insight into necessity, or through compulsion. The unchecked flight of birds is forgotten. One person's Robinson Crusoe fantasy doesn't end with the arrival of the good ship "Hope." The desires of another are not satisfied with a Sunday drive away into the countryside.

For now, the hindrances can be described but not overcome. This powerful presence educates us, presses in upon us, destroys us. It's hard to speak of any future.

The possibility remains to learn from both parts, to keep eyes and ears open to collect experience, to search to improve the situation. That search should be respected and rewarded, not punished and condemned. The example of Berlin can show people in other countries the unhappy, unending effects of war, the possibility of peaceful coexistence.

Michael Meinicke

Introduction

Berlin, as focus.* All that most Americans seem to know about Berlin is that it is divided by a wall. Berlin is NOT on the border of East and West Germany, rather, it is entirely inside East Germany, and closer to the present Polish border than to the East German-West German border. East Berlin is the capital of East Germany. West Berlin is like an island; officially, an allied occupation zone (still!), practically, a noncontiguous enclave of West Germany. West Berlin has slightly more than, East Berlin slightly less than 2 million inhabitants. Together, 4 million = about the population of Detroit or the San Francisco Bay Area.

In America we can travel for days within our own borders. We can read the newspaper and not read of anything outside until the last page. We act as if foreign languages were other universes.

In Europe it's different. Two hours' train ride is the next country, and you need to speak the language to buy your return ticket. "National news" is local news, so interest is international.

All the more so in Berlin. On my way to the Kinderladen where I earn my living working with children—over ⅔ of them the progeny of Turkish, Yugoslav, or Arabic *Gastarbeiter* (foreigners with work permits)—I ride the subway, the *U-Bahn*, passing under a promontory of East Berlin before crossing back into the West: and the same coming home. Or: from my flat it's twelve minutes to the border. Without quickening step.

The literature and, for that matter, the life of East Berlin is even more unknown to us in the States than is that of the West. This need not remain so; as a tourist you can cross the border to visit the East for a 5 mark fee, plus a mandatory exchange of 25 marks, plus a bit of time and standing in line for the border and customs police to check your papers (and, sometimes, your bags or person). If you abide by their rules and procedures, you won't have any problem. In the East is

---

*But: (1) Some texts here are from other parts of Germany—Cologne (Scheurer), Düsseldorf (Bartus), Munich (Fauser), and Wuppertal (Miersch); (2) Not all Berlin residents are Germans—see Boiron (French), Lackner (American), Lahtela (Finnish), Wichner (formerly of Romania's German minority), and, in East Berlin, Wollenberger (Danish).

much worth seeing. In the East, books and records are much cheaper than in the West, though the selection is also more limited. There are good reasonably priced restaurants. Good opera, cabaret, and theater are easily affordable, and there are great museums. And, more important, you can make friends. I have.

Most of the younger authors in East Berlin seem to form a loose, warm community. The Writers Association is an important factor in their life—it influences publication possibilities and provides mentors and stipends to many. Publishing houses in the East are willing to print very large editions of poetry—and the editions often sell out. Paid readings by authors are organized in Youth Clubs and Cultural Centers.

The trouble and expense of visits to East Berlin, and the impossibility for most East Berliners to visit me in the West has limited the number of East Berlin authors who submitted texts. But even in this small sample it is clearly useless to speak of a "school" of East German writing, to try to find common denominators between Rathenow's Kafkaesque parables, Kolbe's directness and lyricism, Braun's dialectical sailboat-tacking, Gorek's forays into the dense undergrowth of the tongue. Jan Koplowitz, at 71 years of age the oldest writer in the collection, shows in "Positive Provocation" his efforts to use art and writing to break down the isolation of giant modern apartment complexes—maybe his ideas would work elsewhere too.

I also have texts from former East Berliners. Similarity of background is not always similarity of outlook. Jutta Bartus and Jürgen Fuchs are communists: Siegfried Heinrichs is conservative. Fuchs was forced to leave the East though he wanted to stay, Meinicke left illegally in a car trunk, the rest left by application (see Neubauer, "The Request"). It's not always in the one direction, either: Bartus has emigrated back and forth a number of times, and Koplowitz could have remained in English exile after the end of the last world war.

Fuchs, Meinicke, and Heinrichs all depict prison experience: in the West, Zahl is still doing time. The latter's sentence was extended in a situation we might, in the U.S., call double jeopardy. West Berlin has just finished building yet another prison facility, complete with isolation cells.

Each part of Berlin, East and West, pulls literary talent from its respective hinterland, but West Berlin's relation to West Germany is a real "quantum jump," perhaps because of its physical isolation. It is a magnet for people who want to lose their provinciality. The culturally cosmopolitan city has state-subsidized film festivals, music festivals (jazz, non-European, and others), its "alternative projects" scenes, its theater groups (from the opulently subsidized "Schaubühne" to the salty, quasi-guerrilla "GRIPS" and "Theater Manufaktur"), its annual "Art Days," and hundreds of galleries and movie theaters. Two thick program magazines, "TIP" and "Zitty" compete to present West Berliners with organized lists of what they could do this fortnight.

The city is a haven for West Germany's subcultures: artistic, political, homosexual, and hip. A sizable portion of the male inhabitants are West Germans who came because West Berlin, under the "Four Power Treaty," has no compulsory military service.

With no possibility of driving into the countryside, West Berlin is a bit like a gas whose atoms vibrate with more energy when it is compressed. As in New York, there is more going on than anyone can think of keeping track of.

Writers in West Berlin can join the Writers Association of the International Paper and Printing Union and/or the National Society for Literature. The latter actively works at getting state money for a number of writing projects and stipends. There are many small presses, mostly politically oriented. Each month there are dozens of poetry readings, often with payment for the author. There are several workshops where writers can test their products on each other. At the Free University, the first course in Creative Writing has begun.

On translating: German is closely related to English; not all the Saxons sailed with the Angles, some remained behind in Sachsen or Niedersachsen, and the Saxon dialect is still going strong. Even much German wordplay can be directly translated. Nevertheless, one of my hobbies since starting to seek material for *Ber!in* is collecting different *kinds* of untranslatability.

And even the translation of words for which all dictionaries give a simple, single equivalent involves a "loss in translation": words aren't mathematical symbols but forms of life, and the things the words denote play different roles in the life of different peoples. For example, anything that is "bread" in America is "Brot" in Germany, and vice versa. But what part of this spectrum do you *find* on the table in each country? In America, "white bread"—or have things improved since I left? In Germany this kind of "bread" is called "American Toast," with English spelling. When they say "Brot," Germans think of going to the corner baker's for a very hard-crusted, dense, chewy thing that an American would have to go to a "delicatessen" (from the German) to find.

Even a word that requires no translation at all plays a different role, or a role with a different dimension, in national life. Imagine, for example, a political activist in, say, 1968, calling his parents, the holders of or aspirants to political office, the administrators of his school or university, or the police, etc., "fascists." This epithet was often thrown around in both the U.S. and Germany (in West Berlin it's still quite a favorite), and the denotation is identical, but the context is quite different, and so the set of emotions aroused is more complex in Germany.

It is hardly possible to live in a foreign country and still preserve an uninfluenced mother tongue, as is made clear to me when I visit the States and try to make myself understood. Some grammatical and psychological aspects of German sentence construction are satirized by Jochen Melzian in "The Predilection of the German Thinker."

As far as time, opportunity, and an author's at-least-rudimentary bilinguality allowed, I have tried to translate with the direct help of the author, or at least to have him/her check through the English version. This seems to me an obvious and fruitful expedient when the author is living and nearby. Where I find no adequate translation, I have usually chosen to run the risk of pedantry by using a footnote, rather than to falsify a text.

Having done both, I can testify that editing is quite a different thing from taking a University course in Contemporary Lit. In the latter you feel you're getting an ever-clearer overview of the subject; and I'll share my university overview. Those medieval maps, distorted as they are, were a hell of a lot better than nothing. The trouble with university courses is that nobody notices how much of the space is white and unexplored. In editing it's all exploration, you don't have to explain *why* the museum piece is precious, you have to decide *whether* an object you find is good. You have to keep asking yourself if there aren't whole ranges of the spectrum to which you aren't sensitive.

Plenty goes on that never turns up in the Academy. There is for sure plenty which I haven't picked up either, and I make no claim that *Berlin* is a bird's-eye-view. Call it a core sample and examine it yourself. Still, a bit of the lay of the land, what I can piece together of the historical background to this material:

With the collapse of the Third Reich, and with it the monumental kitsch of national socialist "literature," German writers began looking around for new foundations on which to build. Both parts of Germany, each in its own way, wanted to regard the present and the coming future as a complete break with the Nazi past. In the East this was simplified when McCarthyism drove Bertolt Brecht, till then living in exile in the U.S., to settle in East Berlin (with Austrian passport), where he was able to direct his own plays and to continue writing and providing a good example until he died.

In the West, Günther Eich wrote "Inventur," a down-to-earth list of the few material and spiritual possessions he had left, symbolic for the country as a whole. The poverty, but also the down-to-earth realism disappeared, mostly, with the *"Wirtschaftswunder"*—economic miracle. West Germany threw itself into the hard work and dream of a prosperous future, tried to avoid thinking about the recent past, and was suspicious of anything that smelled of "politics," which was regarded as the source of all the troubles.

The poetry of the 50's—Celan and Benn are good examples—sought roots in the hermetic "absolute poetry" of such turn-of-the-century writers as Mallarmé. It was intentionally difficult to understand, gave a kind of passive resistance to consumption in the new Consumer Society. At the same time, its static perfection, and its refusal to participate and exert influence, made it ironically rather like jewelry, the apotheosis of affluence. The currents of modern writing represented by Neruda or W.C. Williams were largely ignored. Brecht was honored (what else could they do) and ignored. Writers concerned with actual human situations or political themes, like Günter Grass or Hans Magnus Enzensberger, were few.

As in America, in Europe the political and (counter-)cultural upheavals of the late 60's marked a turning point, whereby in Europe the emphasis was more strongly political than in the States, more reminiscent of Berkeley than of San Francisco. People here are much more likely to have the 3 volumes of Marx's *Kapital* (cheap in East Berlin) on their shelves than a stashbox full of cannabis. But the counter-culture did find a lyrical spokesman in the late Rolf Brinkmann who returned enthused from New York and put together translations from the American entitled *"ACID"* and *"Gras."* Another, Paul Gerhard Hübsch, wrote a volume of poems called *"ausgeflippt"*—*"Flipped Out."* Hübsch has since converted to a mystical form of Islam and changed his first name to Hadayatullah: he still writes, and you'll find his work here. Bukowski (who seems to be *the* American author for many Germans under 40) finds a rough equivalent in Jörg Fauser.

The turn toward politics was even stronger though, and authors produced Agit-Prop—agitation propaganda—which ranged from Erich Fried's articulate protests against the Vietnam War, attempts to draw lessons from the bout with fascism, and stand-taking on domestic issues to dogmatic, simplistic slogans whose principles of composition are the same as those for the writing of detergent advertisements, and whose ability to provoke thought is about the same. This politicization went so far as to put into question every "non-political" or "bourgeois," i.e., personal, expression. This resulted in uniformly shrill and abstract writing and an extreme disparity between political pose and private reality.

In the mid-70's, as the euphoria of the late 60's wore off, writers who had grown through that period tried to find more personal, more realistic, more human ways of writing *without* giving up political engagement: succinct satire, documentation (see Wohlfart's "Hot Coffee"), and a new current, dubbed by the media "New Subjectivity," "New Inwardness," "New Sensitivity," or "Everyday Poetry."

The political challenge is reconciled with a personal, often first-person or autobiographical standpoint by explicitly, as Theobaldy wrote, "regarding the person as a social unit of measure." The turn is also toward the use of colloquial speech as author's voice, not merely as the voice of some "character."

The political preoccupation of German writing is common to European writing in general, and not just the present writing. Central Europe especially is full of borders, is crowded, and has had its lion's share of political traumas—thus political events and organization are a more pressing aspect of people's lives than in America, where our frame of mind was formed in the struggle with the land, rather than with each other (I oversimplify, but . . .). And Berlin is the extreme, the seam between two still mostly rivalling superpowers.*

Contemporary Germans and their literature are different from Americans and their literature in another way: where we seem to have a categorical imperative to "keep smiling," the Germans have one to "be critical." The twentieth century has been rough on the Germans (and vice versa)—see Schumacher's "Slow Motion." High population density, few natural resources, a long history to look back on, and, again, the political division all work against at least the simpler, naïver forms of optimism. There is next to no nature poetry. Even love poems are sober about the future—see Hirschfelder's "At the Bus Stops." Humor tends toward gallows humor and the shit-eating grin—see Brasch's "Eulenspiegel" for a literal example of both, drawn from that figure of German folk legend.

These are generalizations. A counter example to "At the Bus Stops" is Kolbe's "Melanie." And there are plenty of non-political or less directly political personal expressions: Sabine Techel's wry excursions in metaphor and character analysis, Middendorf's powerful portrayal of an intimate trauma, Tiel's turning her earlier concrete poesy and abstract sound combinations toward a kind of psychological cubism, Schmich's use of trivial detail to flesh out a larger arc of life, Lahtela's musicality.

A few more words on the collection: some of these writers are well known in Germany, and some appear here for the first time (in a land and language not their own!). Authors whose work I judge to be already readily available in English I have not sought out, so you won't find Grass, Böll, Handke, or Fried. I didn't hunt down names from existing anthologies or reading lists. Wolf Biermann is left out in

---

*The division of Germany is actually nothing new or unusual. Germanic tribes subject to the Roman Empire fought Germanic tribes resisting its expansion. The 30 Years War in the 17th Century, fought between the Catholic and Protestant versions of Christian Love, halved Germany's population. The central European crazy-quilt of duchies, free cities, and small kingdoms wasn't unified until 1870 and even then it took the impetus of a common enemy, France.

order to retain the writing of an East Berlin writer who refused to appear in the same volume. Since Biermann has extensive publicity already, I chose to stay with the lesser-known writer (and the already acquired and translated texts!). This decision leaves me uneasy; the least I can do is admit it.

What's missing: my method of collecting—approaching writers whose friends recommended them, being approached by those who read my notices and ads or who had heard of the project through the grapevine—has left a distressing gap. There are vast numbers of foreigners living in West Berlin—I don't mean the "artistic expatriates" so well represented here, but Yugoslavs, Greeks, Italians, Kurds, Turks, and, in the wake of all the fighting, Lebanese. These people work in the factories or in construction or have small stores catering to their own nationalities, they live in the tenements, worry about being expelled from the country, are the niggers, the garlic-eaters, now that the Jews and Gypsies are gone or no longer acceptable targets of prejudice. And some of them write. More contributions from them would have given a better picture of the city. Someone else or another project will have to remedy my failing.

There aren't enough women represented, either. Why didn't I get more submissions from them? The manuscripts I did get hold their own. I don't believe fewer women write.

Mitch Cohen, Jan. 1981

I LIFE

Jürgen Theobaldy
Born 1944 in Strasburg, grew up in
Mannheim. Apprenticeship as salescraft.
Studied education in Freiburg and
Heidelberg, then Literature and Political

JÜRGEN THEOBALDY

A Kind of Charity

You want to call me up to say
I should come by later, oh, around ten
but I'm already gone
coming to you
and there's this guy sitting around
totally stoned
grinning burbling
and when we've got him
outside about eleven
there are already two others there
not as stoned
but just as kaputt
someone calls up: he's
already slit his wrists
new excitement . . .
about twelve-thirty then this psychologist
and his talk about group therapy
when about three we get all of them
out of the room
I'm confused enough to leave with them
you bring me back
we open a can
smoke
drink
and lay happy at four in bed
I mean finally

Science in Heidelberg, Cologne, and West Berlin.

Books: *Sperrsitz* (Reserved Seating), poems, 1973
Blaue Flecken (Black and Blue), poems, 1974
Zweiter Klasse (Second Class), poems, 1976
Veränderung der Lyrik (Changes in Poetry), nonfiction, with Zürcher, 1976
editor of the anthology *Und ich bewege mich doch* (And I do move), 1977
Sonntags Kino (Sunday Cinema), novel, 1978
Drinks, poems, 1979

Eine Art Nächstenliebe

Du willst mich anrufen um zu sagen
ich solle später kommen so gegen zehn
aber ich bin schon weg
komme zu dir
und so ein Typ sitzt herum
völlig stoned
grinsend glucksend
und als wir ihn
gegen elf draußen haben
sind schon zwei andere da
nicht so stoned
aber auch kaputt
jemand ruft an: er habe
die Pulsadern schon geöffnet
neue Aufregungen . . .
gegen halb eins dann dieser Psychologe
und sein Gerede über Gruppentherapie
als wir sie alle gegen drei
aus dem Zimmer kriegen
bin ich konfus genug um mitzugehen
du holst mich zurück
wir machen eine Dose auf
rauchen
trinken
und liegen glücklich um vier im Bett
ich meine endlich

Furnished Apartment

All the Personals in the newspaper
call to you: Here's a room!
but when I get there
it's an out-of-commission bathtub
as expensive as the payments on a sportscar . . .
For three weeks now, full of hot breakfast-coffee, I've rushed
to the landlords every morning
I'm the friendliest person in the city
I put on creased trousers
lick spit
lick shoes slippers
Take pants-buttons in my mouth wedding rings and hair curlers
I pound my fist on the dresser: rooms
are getting smaller and more expensive
I make appointments arrive punctually
but the Herr had to go drink a coffee
Someone offers his shoebox
I slip out of my jacket
and try to step in: already he raises the rent
Yes I understand
here I am worth less than a room
but you won't get me to the point
where for 200 marks a month I can
defend with claw and tooth your separate tea tins
against all attacks on private property
where I swear
to be thin and quiet as my shadow
where I beg to be pardoned
for my shoes because they step on the stairs
for my suit because it doesn't go without me
for the air that I use up
finally for myself
because I live
and am not as clear and cold as my bank account

Mobliertes Zimmer

Alle Inserate in den Zeitungen
rufen dir zu: Hier gibt es ein Zimmer!
und als ich dort ankomme
ist es eine stillgelegte Badewanne
teuer wie die Raten für einen Sportwagen . . .
Seit drei Wochen trage ich jeden Morgen
den heißen Morgenkaffee zu einem Vermieter
Ich bin um diese Zeit der freundlichste Mensch in der Stadt
Ich ziehe gebügelte Hosen an
lecke Speichel
lecke Schuhe Pantoffel
ich nehme Hosenknöpfe in den Mund Eheringe und Lockenwickler
ich schlage mit der Faust auf die Anrichte: die Zimmer
werden kleiner und teurer
Ich treffe Verabredungen komme pünktlich
aber der Herr mußte einen Kaffee trinken gehen
Jemand bietet seine Schuhschachtel an
ich schlüpfe aus der Jacke
und versuche einzutreten: schon erhöht er die Miete
Ja ich habe verstanden
hier bin ich weniger wert als ein Zimmer
aber dorthin kriegt ihr mich nicht
wo ich für 200 Mark im Monat
mit Krallen und Zähnen eure seperaten Teedosen verteidige
gegen alle Angriffe auf das Privateigentum
wo ich schwöre
schmal und leise wie mein Schatten zu sein
wo ich um Verzeihung bitte
für meine Schuhe weil sie auf die Treppe treten
für meinen Anzug weil er nicht ohne mich geht
für die Luft die ich verbrauche
endlich für mich selbst
weil ich lebe
und nicht klar und kalt wie mein Bankkonto bin

My Young Life

I want to grow up as big
as the men, when they rub their
thumbs on their suspenders.
The smoke of cigarettes mixes
with the dust of torn-down ruins
and the blue swaths of gases from BASF*
that drift over from Ludwigshafen.
Near the fairgrounds the Traber family suspends
a line from house to house and shows how you come
gracefully through the postwar years.
Below wind-down gradually the songs
of the working class, the red flags
disappear in the crowd, and
the union leaders look at their watches.
The television runs without sound
the whole afternoon already, now it's
the chaste sheriff's turn and thank god
he doesn't let himself get hooked
by this artful lady from Boston.
If I'm ever born again,
I want to come to the world
as a cigarette and then
burn out slowly between your lips.
While the television is still on,
in the bedroom my cousin shows me
her pussy. The pink uvula
between its lips is a discovery
that I can't keep to myself.
A letter from the teacher, which
all my relatives read, threatens me
with reform school. Uncle Karl comes from nightshift,
eats his potato salad, plays the banker,
and wins for the first time in his life.
If this were a film, we would have
murdered him just after midnight. Dear Uncle Karl,
all in all we were a peaceful
family. Now we are pretty much apart,
my cousin got a divorce
and Cousin Willy too. Greetings

---

*BASF—"Badische Anilyn und Soda Fabrik," a chemical factory.

Mein junges Leben

Ich will so groß werden
wie die Männer, wenn sie die Daumen
an den Hosenträgern reiben.
Der Rauch aus den Zigarren mischt sich
mit dem Staub abgerissener Ruinen
und den blauen Schwaden der BASF
die von Ludwigshafen herüberziehen.
Auf dem Messeplatz spannt die Traber-Familie
ein Seil von Haus zu Haus und zeigt, wie man grazil
über die Nachkriegsjahre kommt.
Unten drehen allmählich die Lieder
der Arbeiter ab, die roten Fahnen
verschwinden in der Menge, und
die Gewerkschaftsführer schauen auf die Uhr.
Der Fernseher läuft ohne Ton
schon den ganzen Nachmittag, jetzt ist
der keusche Sheriff dran und Gottlob
er läßt sich nicht kriegen
von dieser raffinierten Lady aus Boston.
Wenn ich noch einmal geboren werde,
möchte ich als Zigarette
auf die Welt kommen und dann
zwischen deinen Lippen langsam verbrennen.
Während der Fernseher immer noch läuft,
zeigt mir meine Cousine im Schlafzimmer
ihre Muschi. Das rosa Zäpfchen
zwischen ihren Schamlippen ist eine Entdeckung,
die ich nicht für mich behalten kann.
Ein Brief vom Klassenlehrer, den
meine ganze Verwandschaft liest, bedroht mich
mit dem Jugendheim. Onkel Karl kommt von der Schicht,
ißt seinen Kartoffelsalat, übernimmt die Bank
und gewinnt zum ersten Mal in seinem Leben.
Wäre dies ein Film, wir hätten ihn
kurz nach Mitternacht erschossen. Lieber Onkel Karl,
alles in allem waren wir eine friedliche
Verwandtschaft. Jetzt sind wir ziemlich auseinander,
meine Cousine hat sich scheiden lassen
und Cousin Willi auch. Viele Grüße

from Austria, the weather is beautiful.
My mother brings me a ballpoint pen
on which a little ship keeps
sailing on Wolfgangsee. In BASF
a cauldron explodes, and each worker
gets his own grave, although no one knows
which pieces from whom lay in it.
Uncle Karl still lives and takes me along
to the grave-rows. They remind me
of the war, I decide
to become a pacifist and listen to records
from Pete Seeger. Beforehand is Kirmes festival,
we hide in the darker passages of the
funhouse and smooch the girls
who always come in twos. Today they work
at BASF or at Daimler-Benz in Waldhof,
their breasts are grown larger, their behinds,
their arms. I hear from the business section
of the FAZ* that the firm where I apprenticed has
gone bankrupt: Back then it seemed so much bigger than me,
and now I've outlived it. Dear cousin,
all together we are still poorer
than every one if its stockholders. They change
their investments, you change arch-supports
and look for a new job. I already
quit in 1963 and go for the first time
to Paris. It is a sensation.
Hans and I find two whores for 17 francs,
afterwards we drink red wine at the counter,
talk about Rimbaud and from now on imagine
how really far out our life will be.

---

*FAZ—"Frankfurter Allgemeine Zeitung," a large conservative newspaper.

aus Österreich, das Wetter ist sehr schön.
Meine Mutter bringt mir einen Kuli mit,
worauf ein Schiffchen immerzu
über den Wolfgangsee fährt. In der BASF
explodiert ein Kessel, und jeder Arbeiter
bekommt sein eigenes Grab, obwohl niemand weiß,
welche Reste von wem darin liegen.
Onkel Karl lebt noch und nimmt mich mit
zu den Reihengräbern. Sie erinnern mich
an den Krieg, ich beschließe
Pazifist zu werden und höre mir Platten
von Pete Seeger an. Vorher ist Kirmes,
wir drücken uns in die dunkleren Gänge
der Raupenbahn und knutschen die Mädchen ab,
die immer zu zweit sind. Heute arbeiten sie
bei BASF oder bei Daimler-Benz auf dem Waldhof,
ihre Brüste sind größer geworden, die Hintern,
die Arme. Ich erfahre aus dem Wirtschaftsteil
der FAZ, daß meine Lehrfirma bankrott gemacht hat:
Damals stand sie mir so groß gegenüber,
und heute habe ich sie überlebt. Lieber Cousin,
alle zusammen sind wir immer noch ärmer
als jeder ihrer Teilhaber. Sie ziehen
ihre Einlagen ab, du wechselst die Einlegesohlen
und suchst eine neue Stelle. Ich habe schon
1963 gekündigt und fahre zum ersten Mal
nach Paris. Es ist eine Sensation.
Hans und ich finden zwei Huren für 17 Francs,
anschließend trinken wir Rotwein am Tresen,
reden über Rimbaud und stellen uns ab jetzt
unser Leben ganz toll vor.

Pictures from America

Because I, hardly born,
was almost taken along by a soldier
over there to America in the last weeks
of the world war, I dreamed often
of waking up in America
with jeans and tennis shoes,
a baseball bat under my arm.
I dreamed of fresh lawns
in front of the high school, of pink toothpaste
and canned pineapple. I would have spoken
American very broadly
and later, so I dreamed, I would have
driven up to the big office building in the Cadillac.
But later I was still
here in Mannheim and rode every morning
on my one-speed bicycle
in the port to the export department.
And after that I saw young
Americans, as old as me,
taken away because they had
burnt their draft notices.
I saw the smoke-billowing houses
in the ghettoes of the blacks, and I saw
the National Guard in Combat Uniform
against barefoot students, saw the
billy clubs of the police, as big
as baseball bats.
Now I hardly ever dream
of America, not even anything bad.
But I often wonder how that land
may be, whose pictures
have changed so much, so swiftly
and so thoroughly.

Bilder aus Amerika

Weil mich, kaum geboren
in den letzten Wochen des Weltkriegs,
beinah ein Soldat mitgenommen hätte,
hinüber nach Amerika, träumte ich
oft davon, in Amerika aufzuwachen
mit Jeans und Tennisschuhen,
den Baseballschläger unter dem Arm.
Ich träumte vom frischen Rasen
vor der High School, von rosa Zahnpasta
und Ananas aus der Dose. Amerikanisch
hätte ich sicher sehr breit gesprochen,
und später wäre ich, so träumte mir,
im Cadillac vors Bürohochhaus gefahren.
Aber später war ich immer noch
hier in Mannheim und fuhr jeden Morgen
auf einem Fahrrad ohne Gangschaltung
in den Hafen zur Exportabteilung.
Und noch später sah ich junge
Amerikaner, so alt wie ich,
abgeführt werden, weil sie ihre
Einberufungsbefehle verbrannt hatten.
Ich sah die qualmenden Häuser
in den Gettos der Schwarzen, und ich sah
die Nationalgarde im Kampfanzug
gegen barfüßige Studenten, sah die
Schlagstöcke der Polizisten, die lang
wie Baseballschläger waren.
Jetzt träume ich kaum noch
von Amerika, nicht einmal Schlechtes.
Aber ich frage mich oft, wie das Land
sein mag, von dem sich die Bilder
so verändert haben, so schnell
und so gründlich.

Like This Summer Dress

I too would like to be light
light as this summer dress on the rack
It rustles when you go by
it responds to every breath
and the young women, they
handle it with love

I wish it were me, this summer dress
that you put on,
to turn back and forth before the mirror
In its colors I would be
so close to you I could forget that I
am supposed to act like a man:
tough enough to take it.

photograph by Jochen Melzian

Wie dieses Sommerkleid

Auch ich wäre gern leicht
leicht wie dieses Sommerkleid auf der Stange
Er raschelt, wenn man vorbeigeht
es antwortet auf jeden Hauch
und die jungen Mädchen, sie
fassen es an mit Liebe

Ich wäre es gern, dieses Sommerkleid
das du anziehst, um dich
vor dem Spiegel hin und herzuwenden
In seinen Farben wäre ich
dir so nahe zu vergessen, daß ich
wie ein Mann sein soll: stark
und hart im Nehmen.

UWE KOLBE

the guilty

    die, unfortunately, mostly

    of sniffles
    in a big bed
    near the airport
    that is

    of a natural death

Sacco & Vanzetti

    for J. Halle

We few millions demand
Demand just like a hundred years ago
              a thousand years ago
We few demand:
That the heavens fall.
We demand:
That the heavens fall.
That the heavens fall.

More we don't ask.
We are too few.
We few millions can
Demand no more.

Uwe Kolbe
Born 1957 in Berlin, Abitur, Army, work in
the Aufbau Verlag (Build-up Publishing
House). In 1980 a volume of poetry,
Hineingeboren (Born Into), appeared in
Aufbau.

---

die schuldigen

sterben, leider, meist

am schnupfen
in einem großen Bett
nahe beim flughafen
also

eines natürlichen todes

Sacco & Vanzetti

für J. Halle

Wir wenigen Millionen verlangen
Verlangen wie vor hundert Jahren
          vor tausend Jahren
Wie wenigen verlangen:
Daß der Himmel einstürze.
Wir verlangen:
Daß der Himmel einstürze.
Daß der Himmel einstürze.

Mehr verlangen wir nicht.
Wie sind zu wenige.
Wir wenigen Millionen können
Nicht mehr verlangen.

I Was Raised in the Name of a Weltanschauung

With closed eyes I remained a believer
I knew no other philosophy than the rul-
ing one I never thought that so many rul-
ing philosophies existed didn't understand this war.
Now I see the number of the heads:
                                        : understand
That war unavoidable play likewise
Paper tiger   Sand lion   Droplet tank smile
Gun-bore black and blood hound sweet I greet
The World Peace Conference, any at all; my parents
The pennant with Lenin's picture on Venus
The dust from which my Cosmos formed.
I see no chance to rescue my head
From the war for peace from the war
Between man and woman from that of the intestinal wall
And the blood with remnants of food from the osmotic
World War from the world-political pushbutton war.
Away from the chessboard, out of the pincers pulls
Me—only he with the scythe one of the friends
Who is reliable one of the greatest players
The feared bank breaker one of the winners.

Ich bin erzogen im Namen einer Weltanschauung

Mit geschlossenen Augen blieb ich gläubig
Ich kannte keine andere Filosofie denn die herr-
Schende ich dachte nie daß es so viele herr-
Schende Filosofien gibt verstand diesen Krieg nicht.
Jetzt seh ich die Zahl der Köpfe:
:verstehe
Daß Krieg unvermeidlich spiele ebenfalls
Papiertiger Sandlöwe Tropfenpanzer lächle
Mündungsschwarz und bluthundsüß ich grüße
Den Weltfriedenskongreß, irgendeinen, meine Eltern
Den Wimpel mit Lenins bild auf der Venus
Den Staub aus dem mein Kosmos geformt.
Ich sehe keine Chance den Kopf zu retten
Aus dem Krieg um den Frieden aus dem Krieg
Zwischen Mann und Frau aus dem der Darmwand
Und des Bluts mit Speiseresten aus dem osmotischen
Weltkrieg dem weltpolitischen Knopfdruckkrieg.
Vom Schachbrett weg aus den Zwickmühlen zieht
Mich nur der mit der Sense einer der Freunde
Auf die Verlaß ist einer der größten Spieler
Der gefürchteten Banksprenger einer der Gewinner.

We Live with Cracks

We live with cracks in the walls,
have you noticed?
We live on floorboards with paling colors,
under a movable ceiling.
The windowframe is long since
eaten through with rot, the draft
even in summer, the cold night air
comes in unhindered.

We live illegally, become
conscious each day anew that, otherwise
we'd both sit on the street.

We house in Prenzlauer Berg,
four flights up under the attic.
Pigeons go almost in and out.
The wood lice I kill, unnoticed by you,
in a flash on the window sill,
the black spiders under the sink,
fifty years old, in the kitchen
I slay them with extreme disgust,
although their sight is aesthetic
and shudders comb my spine.

I paint the doors black,
through them visitors, much too seldom,
reach us here, under question-glances
: a casket? in this way emphasizing
the unbearability? no no, loudly
I strike a string instrument,
play host for you with hot tea, you
friendly exhausted ones,
who've finally arrived up here.

and still laugh in the sound of hail,
if the heavens grow dark,
still laugh in the flood of tears
and in the coldness between us.
In the dust of the steam of bodies I laugh,
enjoying through much exertion
the security given us.

Wir leben mit Rissen

Wir leben mit Rissen in den Wänden,
ist es dir aufgefallen?
Wir leben auf sich entfärbenden Dielen,
unter beweglicher Decke.
Das Fensterkreuz ist längst
von Fäulnis durchgefressen, es zieht
im Sommer schon die kalte Nachtluft
hindrungslos herein.
Wir wohnen illegal, mach das
dir täglich neu bewußt, daß sonst
wir beide auf der Straße säßen.
Wir hausen im Prenzlauer Berg,
vier Treppen hoch unter dem Dach.
Tauben gehn fast aus und ein.
Die Asseln töt ich unbemerkt von dir
ganz schnell am Fensterbrett,
die schwarze Spinne unterm Becken,
fünfzig Jahr alt, in der Küche
erschlage ich trotz großen Ekels,
obwohl der Anblick sehr ästhetisch
und Schauer mir den Rücken kämmen.

Ich strich die Türe schwarz,
wodurch Besucher, viel zu seltne,
hergelangen, unter Frageblicken
: ein Sarg? auf diese Art betont
die Unerträglichkeit? nein nein, laut
schlage ich ein Zupfinstrument,
bewirte euch mit heißem Tee, euch
freundliche Erschöpfte,
hier oben wirklich Angelangte

und lache noch im Hagelrauschen,
wenn der Himmel finstrer wird,
lache noch im Tränenfluß
und in der Kälte zwischen uns.
Im Staub der Körperdünstung lach ich,
genießend unter Kraftaufwand
die uns gebotene Sicherheit.

Metamorphosis

I could be a wooden floor
No problem being a wooden floor or
Cobblestonecolors as street as its dirt.
I could be the man too in the suit
Would have the stiff knee and chalk in the face
Were the running girl, away from him
I could fall asleep in the subway
And would be the official in colorful uniform
In the service of a higher power and throw
The bum out and occasion the cleaning
Of the cleaning woman on the up-chuck.
I could be the plastic floor, I dunno,
Would you still recognize me?
The man from Borges' story with the brain
Into which all out of which nothing more goes.
I'd be happy with it and would fly away
From the windowsill along the street, then
After I passed along a friendly picture
To a friendly womanly voice.
I tried to live with it black
To paint like all the devils under the cross.
I were this great master whose hand
Hardly the notion attainable I'd have
Myself in my power would use all fashions
Of all tyrants' wisdom I Uwe Kolbe
Have all these possibilities open
Those of the little daily fascist
Those of the confused of the sculpture of the stage.
Happily too happily the fairytale figure too
Instead of three golden hairs the hard phrase.
Everything could be won through me
So much I know already so much
I forget like the fly the dragonfly-dream.

Metamorfosis

Ich könnt doch ein Parkett sein
Kein Problem ein Parkett zu sein oder
Pflastersteinfarben als Straße als Dreck drauf.
Ich könnt auch der Mann sein im Anzug
Hätte die steifen Kniee und Kalk am Gesicht
Wäre ein laufendes Mädchen, vor ihm davon
Ich könnt einschlafen in der U-Bahn
Und wär der Beamte in farbiger Uniform
Im Dienste höherer Gewalt und schmiß
Den Penner raus veranlaßte das Wischen
Der Wischfrau am Hingekotzten.
Ich könnt der Plasteboden sein, weiß nicht
Würdst du mich noch erkennen?
Der Mann aus Borges' Geschichte mit dem Hirn
Worein alles woheraus nichts mehr geht.
Ich wäre glücklich damit und flöge ab
Vom Fensterbrett die Straße lang danach
Nachdem ich ein freundliches Bild weitergab
An eine freundliche weibliche Stimme.
Ich versuchte zu leben damit schwarz
Zu malen wie alle Teufel unterm Kreuz.
Ich wär dieser Große Herr dessen Hand
Kaum der Ahnung erreichbar ich hätt
Mich in der Gewalt benutzte alle Moden
Aller Tyrannen Weisheit ich Uwe Kolbe
Hab alle diese Möglichkeiten offen
Die des kleinen täglichen Faschisten
Die des Verworrenen der Plastik der Bühne.
Gern zu gern auch die Märchenfigur
Anstelle drei goldener Haare den harten Satz.
Alles könnt gewonnen sein durch mich
So viel weiß ich bereits soviel
Vergesse ich wie die Fliege den Libellentraum.

Melanie

*for the girl
and the beloved friends*

We build the house
We will build the house
Also the garden
We will plant
From our city
They'll come back laughing
Our children will be well-loved

The garden
The garden will
Have to be in the house
And the city
In the house
And the house is a room
A room full of music

This room
This beautiful chamber
Is often under open sky
Has room now and then
On a fingertip
When we hold us tight
It is the whole world

Melanie

*dem Mädchen
und den geliebten Freunden*

Wir bauen das Haus
Wir werden das Haus bauen
Auch den Garten
Werden wir pflanzen
Aus unserer Stadt
Wird man lachend zurückkehren
Unsere Kinder werden beliebt sein

Der Garten
Der Garten wird
In dem Haus sein müssen
Und die Stadt in dem Haus
Und das Haus ist ein Zimmer
Ein Raum voll Musik

Dieser Raum
Dieses schöne Zimmer
Ist oft unter freiem Himmel
Hat auch mal Platz
Auf einer Fingerspitze
Wenn wir uns festhalten
Ist es die ganze Welt

Orangen ("Oranges") 1980, Verlag Harald Schmid, poems.

ULI HIRSCHFELDER

Like the Movies, like Life

    I believe this
    landscape
    too is again only
a backdrop. Are there still
    not-yet-wide-angled places

    I mean
    blended-out regions
    that is

    from our wide-screen gaze
    not yet worn-out
                nature?

What I really mean is
    are there still
    blades of grass before which no
    cosmetician kneels
    and puts on their make-up?

I sit in the cinema next to softly
drawn cardboard
extras and see what
I otherwise don't see
              light ref-
lections, broken, on tempestuously shaken
plastic sheeting.

Uli Hirschfelder
Born 1954, lives in West Berlin, studies
German literature and Drama. Assorted odd
jobs, published in magazines, anthologies,
broadcast in radio. "... I'm trying to start
my rocket to world stardom in
America..."

Wie im Kino, wie im Leben

Ich glaube diese
Landschaft
ist auch nur wieder
eine Kulisse. Gibt es noch
nicht weitgewinkelte Orte
ich meine
schwarzgeblendete Gegenden
das heißt
von unseren Breitwandblicken
nicht abgefahrene
                    Natur?
Was ich wirklich meine ist
       gibt es noch
Grashalme vor denen nicht schon
ein Maskenbildner kniet
und sie schminkt?
Ich sitze im Kino neben weich
gezeichneten Papp-
statisten und sehe was
ich sonst nicht sehe
                Lichtspie-
gelungen, gebrochen, auf stürmisch bewegter
Plastikfolie.

                    The perfect illu-
mination in a winterfilm (art
ificial snow) and in the moviehouse
                                    a built-in
                                    cooler!
            What I really see
            I have all seen before
            once (at least)
            in the movies, for example
women, especially nude ones.
    When you lie next to me, I could
        swear, I have already
            once in a movie
                loved you! Do you know
                what appears between your
                lips when you smile?
                    THE END!
                                Or
sometimes I go through streets and
suddenly right in the middle of a step
a hand shoves itself in from below on the right
with a scene-clapper
                into the picture: Those are the winks
                    of an eye, in which I
                        say to myself, that I ought to
                            go more often into the life.

              Die perfekte Illu-
    mination in einem Winterfilm (Kunst
    Schnee) und im Saal
              eine eingebaute
              Kältemaschine!
    Was ich wirklich sehe
    habe ich alles schon
    einmal (mindestens)
    im Kino gesehen, z. B.
Frauen, vor allem nackte.
    Wenn du neben mir liegst, könnte
    ich schwören, ich habe dich
    schon mal in einem Kinofilm ge-
    liebt! Weißt du
      was zwischen deinen Lippen
      erscheint wenn du lächelst?
          E N D E !
                    Oder
manchmal gehe ich durch Straßen und
plötzlich mitten in einem Schritt
schiebt sich von rechts unten eine Hand
mit einer Szenenklappe
      ins Bild: Das sind die Augen
        Blicke, in denen ich
          mir sage, daß ich öfter
              ins Leben gehen muß.

49

High Noon

As I come out of "Quelle,"* the
street is empty. The next duel
with a personnel manager is nothing I'm

keen on. Other States seem better
organized, or did anyone ever
hear of an unemployed ant? Ten

rejections in seven days, the sun
sticks on my body, one-thirty P.M., I read
Motor Works, Room 28 "Sincerely

yours," and the real motors
stand still in the corridors of the Bureaus!
Construction workers sit drinking on a

pile of wood, but at least they have
work. They call something after me, as
I hear, I should go get a job.

---

*Quelle: spring or source; the name of a department store and mail-order business.

12 Uhr mittags

Als ich aus der "Quelle" komme, ist
die Straße leer. Auf das nächste Duell
mit einem Personalchef bin ich nicht
scharf. Andere Staaten scheinen besser
organisiert zu sein, oder hat jemand je
von arbeitslosen Ameisen gehört? Zehn
Ablehnungen in sieben Tagen, die Sonne
klebt mir am Körper, 13 Uhr 30, lese ich
Motor Werk, Zimmer 28 "mit freundlichen
Grüßen", und die wirklichen Motoren
stehen still in den Fluren der Ämter!
Bauarbeiter sitzen trinkend auf einem
Holzstapel, aber immerhin, sie haben
Arbeit. Sie rufen mir etwas nach, wie
ich höre, soll ich erstmal arbeiten gehen.

At the Bus Stops

Thick snowdriving and fat
muffled-up figures, that still
pull cigarettes from the machine
for a flickering evening, show-
case window lights are switched
on and overheated cars
drive past. In them
I recognize old class-
mates, beside them fresh-linened
women, to whom,
when they're at home, they'll explain
who I was.   They've learned
something practical, have
made something of themselves, they
earn well, more than me, sure,
I can make a poem from
anything, but not from every
poem money. If I pick you up, I
come always just myself, in cars they
drive up and through life and
with gallant hand movements past
us, we who closeembraced
wait for the next municipal bus.

An den Haltestellen

Dichtes Schneetreiben und dick
vermummte Gestalten, die noch
schnell Zigaretten ziehen
für einen flimmernden Abend, Schau-
fensterbeleuchtungen werden ein-
geschaltet und überheizte Autos
fahren vorbei. In ihnen
erkenne ich alte Klassen-
kameraden, neben sich frischbezo-
gene Frauen, denen sie, wenn
sie zuhause sind, erzählen
wer ich war. Sie haben etwas
Ordentliches gelernt, haben
es zu etwas gebracht, sie verdienen gut, mehr als ich, der
ich zwar aus allem ein Gedicht
machen kann, aber nicht mit jedem
Gedicht Geld. Hole ich dich ab, komme
ich immer nur selbst, sie fahren
mit Autos vor und durchs Leben und
vorbei mit galanten Handbewegungen
an uns, die wir engumarmt
warten auf den nächsten Linienbus.

For Thomas, on the Thirteenth

(This is how poems come to be:) Next to
a woman in the U-Bahn,
on a newspaper margin I note

this, of which I don't know how
it will end. "Poesy
has nothing to do with the poems"

says Brinkmann, that could be what
it adds up to. Two, drunk, put the make
on the woman next to me, if the

men knew how ugly they are
when they want to be good looking! What
did I want to say? We used to have to

have the poems in our heads, that
was it; nothing about the life
of the poems, about the feelings

in our bellies like with the baddest blues.
Come close your eyes and
read! Do you feel the warmth of the skin

next to you? That's it: what
I mean: A poem is simply
a poem like this girl

here is simply a girl
which is not to say that it
is simple. I wanted

to tell you that, but there was
not enough time, so
now I write it on

a newspaper margin in the U-Bahn
next to this woman. (Is this how
poems come to be?)

Für Thomas, am dreizehnten

(So entstehen Gedichte:) Neben
einer Frau in der U-Bahn
auf einem Zeitungsrand, notiere ich

dies, von dem ich nicht weiß wie
es enden wird. "Die Poesie
hat nichts mit den Gedichten zu tun"

sagt Brinkmann, darauf könnte es
hinauslaufen. Zwei Betrunkene machen
die Frau neben mir an, wenn die

Männer wüßten wie häßlich sie sind
wenn sie schön sein wollen! Was
wollte ich sagen? Früher mußten wir

die Gedichte im Kopf haben, das
war es: nichts über das Leben
der Gedichte, über die Gefühle

im Bauch wie bei einem satten Blues.
Komm mach die Augen zu und
lies! Spürst du die Wärme der Haut

neben dir? Das ist es: was
ich meine: Ein Gedicht ist einfach
ein Gedicht wie dieses Mädchen

hier einfach ein Mädchen ist
was nicht heißt daß es
einfach ist. Das wollte ich

dir noch sagen, aber es blieb
keine Zeit mehr, deshalb
schreibe ich es jetzt auf

einen Zeitungsrand in der U-Bahn
neben dieser Frau. (Entstehen so
Gedichte?)

A Few Minutes of March

You come, like you are, to meet me
halfway, a light wind blows
us a weak sun
      (the short shadow
         of your young life, I say)
so begins the Spring, opening
the uppermost buttons of your
blouse, bringing out the first
tables in the street cafés; how
does it continue, the story
of this moment, I mean, standing
still, embracing each other, a few
minutes, that are a beginning
of our story
      (without much of a past
         with little future, you say)
we go on, out of
these lines, in which we stand
and don't want to stay

Ein Paar Minuten März

Du kommst, wie du bist, mir
entgegen, ein leichter Wind weht
uns eine schwache Sonne zu
   (der kurze Schatten
     deines jungen Lebens, sage ich)
so fängt der Frühling an, offen
die obersten Knöpfe deiner
Bluse, herausgestellt die ersten
Tische in den Straßencafés; wie
geht sie weiter, die Geschichte
dieses Augenblicks, meine ich, still
stehend, einander umarmend, ein paar
Minuten, die ein Anfang sind
unserer Geschichte
   (ohne große Vergangenheit
     mit kleiner Zukunft, sagst du)
wir gehen weiter, aus
diesen Zeilen, in denen wir stehen
und nicht stehen bleiben wollen

Poesy & Praxis

After he had written
the poem
it rose up
went onto the street
and called the people
together to a
demonstration.

Frightened by
this fixity of purpose
he preferred to look on
from the window.

Poesie & Praxis

Nachdem er das Gedicht
geschrieben hatte
stand es auf
ging auf die Straße
und rief die Leute
zusammen zu einer
Demonstration.

Erschrocken über
diese Entschlossenheit
sah er lieber
vom Fenster aus
zu.

photograph by Jochen Melzian

HANS J. SCHEURER

Your Father's Pants

I want to be close to you
with my poems
so I can tailor them to you
like those light swim suits
that always fit
that's how they have to be, my poems
tight and revealing
under the armpits and on the elbows
and between the legs
no place for old double meanings
But in my head
wait finished newspaper sentences
that flutter about your legs
like your father's pants

Alfred Miersch
Born 1951 in Cologne, learned business, then different jobs, now Zivildienst (the civilian alternative to the draft in W. Germany). Editor of the literary mag *TJA*, will open the Dichterland (Poet land) store to sell books, records, poetry tape cassettes, photography. Planning a new mag, *First Avenue*, whose first issue will treat the Naropa Experiment. Published in newspapers, magazines, anthologies. Loud readings.

Tritte in den Kopf

Das Leben verlangt Großes von Euch,
sagen sie & sie meinen sich & ihre Stellungen
& sie schauen uns von ihren VERANDEN zu,
wie wir an den Kleinigkeiten scheitern

    an Amtsärschen mit zugenähten Gehirnen
    an Verträgen voller Kleingedrucktem
    an winzigen Paragraphen, die nur mit
    dem Gewehr zu fällen sind . . .

Und sie lassen dich laufen,
mit einem Stempel hinter dem Ohr
und einer Kanüle in den Gedanken
& dein Nebenmann hat den Draht zu ihrem Computer

    deine Nummer im Notizbuch
    deinen Briefkasten im Auge
    dein Konterfei im Sucher

& zielt mit vorgehaltener Hand zwischen Deine Augen.

"Was ist denn noch wichtig?"
Sie führen die Hunde und die Kinder spazieren
    sag Guten Tag Guten Tag Guten Tag
Die Schweine, die Schweine
von heute

    hier setzen wir ein Theaterstück ab
    den da entlassen wir aus dem Vertrag
    & sowas kommt erst gar nicht in unseren Vertrieb.

Your Freedom, slippery as margarine
Tolerance as far as your garden gate
Imagination is only a solution
in the TV Quiz Show
. . .

& still the great appearances
with the 8 inch smiles
and 3-button coats.
Of course they know nothing about it again,
because the system is the cause
of the good side of life
the bad things
are your own damn fault . . .

The headlines are brushed smooth
bad statistics are photocopied for internal use only
the loud fellows from the sixties
polish their rhetoric,
crouch in the starting blocks of politics
and we beat ourselves off
    with bottles, with needles
    stereotowers and videotapes
    fixed to death and drunk to sleep
stranded in banality
taking off into the next decade . . .

With the whack on your ass
they bring you into life
with every kick in the head
they bring you into their oversized heart
and their candied existence
    at the fireplace with too sweet drinks
    and too beautiful women
    as court jester at Chancellor Receptions
    or as a wild bonbon for the Goethe Institute

and it functions it functions it functions . . .

Eure Freiheit, schlüpfrig wie Margarine
Toleranz bis zu Eurem Gartenzaun &
Phantasie ist nur ein Lösungswort
aus dem Fernsehquiz
. . .

& immer noch die großen Auftritte
mit dem 20 Zentimeter Lächeln
& den 3 Knöpfen-Jacketts.
Sie wissen natürlich wieder von nichts,
denn für die guten Seiten des Lebens
ist das System verantwortlich
an den schlechten Dingen
ist jeder selber schuld . . .

Die Schlagzeilen sind glatt gebürstet
schlechte Statistiken werden nur intern fotokopiert
die lauten Burschen aus den Sechzigern
schleifen ihre Rhetorik,
hocken in den Startlöchern der "großen Politik",
& wir murksen uns ab
  mit Flaschen, mit Spritzen
  Stereotürmen & Videoband
  zu Tode gefixt & ins Lallen gesoffen
im Banalen gestrandet
auf dem Sprung ins nächste Jahrzehnt . .

Mit dem Schlag auf den Arsch
holen sie dich ins Leben
mit jedem Tritt in den Kopf
schaffen sie dich in ihr übergroßes Herz
& in ihre kandierte Existenz
  ans Kaminfeuer mit zu süßen Drinks
  & zu schönen Frauen
  als Hofclown bei Bundeskanzlerfesten
  oder als wildes Bonbon fürs Goethe Institut

& es funktioniert es funktioniert & funktioniert . . .

Es Kommt auf den Versuch an

Das alles lag hinter uns
und das alles wird noch auf uns zukommen, sagte er
und er hatte schwarze Haare oder rote,
war auf einem Auge blind oder auf beiden.
Manchmal morgens, nach einer regnerischen Nacht
zog er das linke Bein nach, wenn er zum Kiosk ging,
um sich Zigaretten zu kaufen und die Morgenzeitung.

The Attempt is What Matters

All of that lay behind us and all of that lies ahead of us, he said, and he had black hair or red, was blind in one eye or both. Sometimes, mornings, after a raining night, he'd drag his left leg behind him to the newsstand for cigarettes and the paper. We did a hell of a lot, but when someone sees us go by it's all become worthless. Why travel anymore or think about important things if it won't change the way we look.
He received a small pension or didn't, didn't think about tomorrow, and if anybody spoke of homes for the aged or senior citizens clubs, he'd snort contemptuously. I didn't go through all that just to end up in kindergarten again, drinking coffee with the ladies or pushing them across the hall to slow waltzes. I wanted to end in dignity, with gray or white hair and rooms full of books. I thought that sometime it would all come to an end, that wisdom would roost in like being in love or growing up.
Nothing stops, he mumbled in his smoke, it's always the same, you always try to be better than yourself and to step on perfection's toes. Whenever I thought I'd made it, came these deep holes, and I always fell into them and always I'd look at myself in the mirror and know: that's you, or maybe not, maybe a piece of you. And that's how it'll continue till my heart stands still. Others will take your place and it was senseless or the underexposed passport photo of an attempt.
It hurt and it was fun. There were too many sunsets on foreign postcards. Too few shoulders on which I laid an arm and too many eyes that I didn't really look into. It was a hundred lives and only one. No more, no less.
He pushed back the chair and brought me to the door. I went down the stairs and into the street, and I knew that he was right or wrong. No solutions or too many. The attempt is what matters.

Wir haben verdammt viel mitgemacht,
aber wenn uns jemand vorübergehen sieht,
ist das alles wertlos geworden.
Warum noch reisen oder an wichtige Dinge denken,
wenn sie sich nicht in unserem Aussehen niederschlagen.
Er bezog eine kleine Rente oder auch keine,
lebte in den Tag hinein und wenn jemand von
Altersheimen oder Seniorenklubs sprach,
schnaubte er verächtlich durch die Nase.
Ich habe nicht all das auf mich genommen,
um wieder im Kindergarten zu enden,
mit alten Damen Kaffee zu trinken oder
sie beim langsamen Walzer durch den Saal zu schieben.
Ich wollte einmal würdevoll enden,
mit grauen oder weißen Haaren und Zimmern voller Bücher.
Ich dachte, daß irgendwann alles ein Ende haben würde,
daß Weisheit sich einstellen würde wie verliebt sein oder
erwachsen werden.
Nichts hört auf, murmelte er in den Zigarettenrauch,
es ist immer dasselbe, immer versucht man,
besser zu sein als man selbst und der Vollkommenheit
auf die Füße zu treten. Immer, wenn ich dachte, es
geschafft zu haben, kamen diese tiefen Löcher,
und immer bin ich in sie hineingefallen und immer
habe ich mich im Spiegel angesehen und gewußt:
Das bist Du, oder auch nicht, vielleicht ein Stück davon.
Und immer wird es so weiter gehen bis das Herz stillsteht.
Andere werden dich ablösen und es war sinnlos oder nur
das unterbelichtete Paßbild eines Versuchs.
Es hat weh getan und es hat Spaß gemacht.
Es waren zuviele Sonnenuntergänge auf fremden Postkarten.
Es waren zuwenige Schultern um die man den Arm
gelegt hat und zuviele Augen in die man nicht richtig
hineingesehen hat.
Es waren hundert Leben und nur eines.
Nicht mehr und nicht weniger.
Er schob den Stuhl zurück und brachte mich zur Tür.
Ich ging die Treppe hinunter und trat auf die Straße
hinaus und ich wußte, daß er Recht hatte oder Unrecht.
Es gibt keine Lösung oder es gibt zuviele.
Es kommt auf den Versuch an.

Jörg Fauser
Born 1944. Dropped out of the U, worked as hospital orderly in London, night porter in Istanbul, airport worker in the Rhein-

JÖRG FAUSER

At the Butcher's

This evening in the butcher shop
an old man stood before me
threadbare winter coat
a wart on his neck
blackish border on his shirt collar
worn out shoes
remnants of cotton in his ears
cartilaginous hands
clamped on a plastic bag
and as his turn came
he ordered in a quiet voice
2 ounces of blood sausage
2 ounces of jellied meat
and a bottle of cheap beer
paid hesitantly from an old beat-up purse
and went quickly without a word
into his winter

and suddenly it was clear to me
how old
and beaten and destroyed they are
my fathers

Main Airport. Now earning his living as free-lance writer. Co-editor of "Gasolin 23" literary mag. Books: *Aqualunge*, 1971. *Tophane* (a novel), 1972. *Die Harry Gelb Story* (poems), 1973. *Marlon Brando* (biography), 1978. *Der Strand der Städte* (The Beach of the Cities, essays), 1978. *Trotki, Goethe, & das Glück,* (poems), 1979. *Alles wird gut,* (story), 1979. *Requiem für ein Goldfisch* (novellas), 1979. Plays & radio plays.

Metzgerei
(Oder: A Man Can Be Destroyed and Defeated)

Heut abend in der Metzgerei
stand ein alter Mann vor mir
fadenscheiniger Wintermantel
eine Warze im Genick
schwärzlicher Rand am Hemdkragen
ausgetretene Halbschuhe
Reste von Ohropax in den Orhen
verknorpelte Hände
an eine Plastiktüte geklammert
und als er an der Reihe war
bestellte er mit leiser Stimme
50 Gramm Blutwurst
50 Gramm Sülze
und eine Flasche Vollbier
zahlte zögernd aus einer abgewetzten Börse
und ging rasch und ohne Gruß
in seinen Winter

und mir wurde plötzlich klar
wie sie alt
und besiegt und vernichtet sind
meine Väter

Requiem for a Goldfish

The alarm rattled at eight, right when Carl saw the Queen of Sheba dancing in the Spitfire Bar in Alexandria.
The Queen of Sheba had golden hair and green eyes and strings of pearls around her wrists and ankles, and she danced with peculiar partners, with snakes, birds, and fish, and the man next to Carl, who had a slight similarity to Carl himself, said: "Nuts, too bad they are all nutty," and as Carl wanted to go for the man's throat, the man said, sadly smiling, "I'm sorry, the payroll office has cancelled any further use of the expense account," and then Carl felt around for the rattling alarm and knocked over the wine bottle next to the bed and then the alarm stopped rattling.
For a moment it was still, and Carl lay motionless and tried to remember the Queen of Sheba, and then the streetcar rattled below at the stop and it stopped and then rattled further, and Carl saw a stripe of light where the curtain didn't quite touch the wall, and then he smelled the wine and the dream oozed away and he took the bottle to his mouth and drank.
Of course he was too late again. At ten AM the corridor of the employment office was swamped, like everywhere else. He thought for a moment whether he should try in the Office for Oven Scrubbers and Dishwashing Assistants again, but thought better of it in time, remembering the incident fourteen days ago when he knocked the wig from the scalp of the head lady as he tried to give her a light. "It's no use," Carl said to himself, "she'd have an attack and call the paddywagon."
The head lady was bald under her wig.
Carl went instead to the Department for Temporary Work. He waited until a Turk, who actually wanted a job in metalworking, and a boy, who still fell under the ban on child labor, were finished; and then he stalked in.
He knew the two girls who distributed the jobs to a hair. Nevertheless he always acted as if he were there for the first time. Unacquaintedness was easier for him to play than some kind of acquaintance that would have had some small measure of outward justification, but which corresponded to no inner reality. Besides, the two girls also acted as if they had never seen him. Maybe they had never seen him.
He turned, as always, to the one who sat closest to the door—she had curled locks and a pale, dumb face—and brought his usual speech: "Yes, I'm looking for something for a few weeks, but it has to be something solid . . . as close as possible to where I live . . .

Hans J. Scheurer
Born 1953, lives and works in Cologne, studied Drama and German, free lance journalist, interest in photography as art, published the Photo Magazine "Glasherz." Published in: Akzente, Literaturmagazin, Sender Freies Berlin, Gasolin, Nervöse Blätter, and in the anthology "Und ich bewege mich doch . . . ," edited by Jürgen Theobaldy.

Die Hosen Deines Vaters

Ich möchte nah bei dir sein
mit meinen Gedichten
um sie auf dich zuzuschneiden
damit sie dich überall berühren
wie diesen leichten Badeanzüge
die immer sitzen
So müßten sie sein meine Gedichte
nah und ehrlich
unter den Achseln und an den Ellen
und zwischen den Beinen
ohne Platz für alte Zweideutigkeiten
Aber in meinem Kopf
sind fertige Zeitungssätze
die an deinen Beinen flattern
wie die Hosen deines Vaters

what they make of you

They pull you in off the street
take your beer away
send you for a haircut
give you little tips
about how to dress
get you enthused about Art
take you along into bed
whip up stormy nights for you
twist your head around
help you get an honest
job
make it clear to you that one
writes essays
and not poems
see to it that you
have the right tone
so that your boss likes you
lay out the appropriate shirt
bring you away from the french fry stands
give you a can of armpit spray
drink Beaujolais with you
get you a subscription to a newspaper
and sooner or later take you
for a talk about the future

Was sie aus dir machen

Sie holen dich von der Straße
nehmen dir das Bier weg
schicken dich zum Frisör
geben kleine Tips
in Kleidungsfragen
begeistern dich für die Kunst
nehmen dich mit ins Bett
bereiten dir stürmische Nächte
verdrehen dir den Kopf
helfen dir anständige
Arbeit zu finden
machen dir klar daß man
Essays schreibt
und keine Gedichte
sorgen dafür daß du
guten Umgang hast
daß dein Chef dich mag
legen dir das passende Hemd raus
bringen dich weg von den Frittenbuden
schenken dir Achselspray
trinken mit dir Beaujolais
abonnieren eine Zeitung für dich
und nehmen dich irgendwann mit
damit man über die Zukunft redet

ALFRED MIERSCH

Kicks in the Head

Life demands great things from you
they say and they mean themselves and their positions
and they look on us from their verandas,
how petty things ruin us

> things like office-asses with sewn-in brains
> like contracts full of small print
> like tiny laws that can only
> be felled with a rifle . . .

And they let you go
rubber-stamped behind the ear
with a catheter in your thoughts
and your neighbor has a line on their computer

> your number in the notebook
> your mailbox under observation
> your portrait hanging in the post office

and aims his outstretched hand between your eyes.
"What is still important?"
They take their dog and their children for a walk
> say Good day Good day Good day

The pigs, the pigs
of today

> we ban this play here
> there we cancel your contract
> and something like that is out of the question
> in our publishing house

preferably in the afternoons, then it wouldn't matter so much . . . well, you know what I mean . . . "

The girl didn't look at him at all and said to her colleague: "Wasn't there something there with waffles?"

The colleague put her nailfile away and, more disinterestedly than indolently, handed an index card across the desk. Curlilocks read aloud:

"Waffle Salesman wanted at Fischinger Bakery, Offenbach, for a stand in front of the store in Stuttgart Street. Working hours: from 8 till 6, 2 hours off for lunch, 6 marks 50 an hour. For two weeks. D'ya want it?"

"Uh, I don't know . . . isn't there anything else?"

"No. That's the only one that came in this week. D'ya want it?"

Carl thought it over. He was in a pinch. He had exactly 20 marks left and was 2 months behind on his rent. "Okay, I'll go there."

She filled out the card and gave it to him, still without looking at him. Next to her file cabinet lay an opened knitting magazine and a ball of green yarn. The other filed her right thumbnail. The taste of red wine came up in Carl's throat. He got out of there. Before the exit was the department for watchmen, rent-a-cops, guards, and professional sleepers. It can't hurt to take a look, thought Carl. Working nights was best anyway. In front of him stood two old men in overcoats that must have come from the Salvation Army. One babbled a monolog. The other read shortsightedly in a soiled but carefully-folded newspaper. Carl saw that he was reading the massage ads. He moved his lips. From time to time he turned around with a disapproving, almost hate-filled look to the other, who stood behind him and monologized. Carl listened:

" . . . Margot, I told her, you can't just sweep the caterpillars from the rug, they jump right away into the incinerator and then we can't heat and then the Head Doctor will be angry and my leg is in Stalingrad again, and of course he doesn't believe that the caterpillars crawl out of my leg and the locusts swarm out of the wall as soon as the light goes out, because Margot wants to save electricity again, and the landlord waves the notice out of the stove and then the garter snakes in the slippers, Margot, and the staff medic pressed one in my hand and says, take care you don't get a fragment in your throat, oh God, Herr Inspector, if only the caterpillars wouldn't devour my blanket, when my money isn't enough coming or going . . . "

Man, they're waiting for something else, Carl said to himself suddenly, lit a cigarette and went past the two old guys into the room. Inside sat a big guy in a checked suit fanning cigar smoke from his desk. "Are those crazies still out there? Sit down please."

Carl sat down. "No, there aren't any crazies," he said.

"Izzata fact." The big guy rubbed his nose. "Well they threw in the towel early, today, then . . . or else Kowalek found them a place with the city finally." He flicked ashes onto the floor. "And what do you want? Unemployment checks or something? Just don't get the idea . . . "
"No, no!" Carl rushed, "I'm looking for honest work."
The big guy looked disappointed.
"Work? Mister, everyone's looking for work. Can't you think of anything more original?"
Carl began to sweat. Why did he always have to run into sadists? He repressed a burp.
" . . . be glad to another time, boss, at the moment I'm a bit out of ideas, I really do need work, something perfectly normal, in your branch, as doorman or night watchman, I've done it often . . . "
The big guy waves him off. "You don't impress me, young man, not with the way you look . . . you checked the mirror yet today? Like leftover oatmeal, I tell you . . . well, you won't get work from me, looking like that."
He put out his cigar. Carl put out his cigarette. Why can't I be lying with a dark beauty on the beach in Tahiti, drinking rum on ice, and writing immortal poems in the sand? Okay, he thought, anyone can think that. In reality that's not what matters.
"Let me tell you something," he bent forward and swung smoke and garter snakes toward the big guy, "if you want to play crazy that's your business, but as long as you polish your ass here on taxpayer's money, you've got to look for work for me. You get me?"
The big man's eyes popped out, he giggled and opened his file.
When Carl came out ten minutes later, the two old men were gone; only the Turk who wanted to do metal work stood at the door and waited for the screeching of turbines, the roar of the blast furnace and the taxi to Ankara.
That afternoon Carl stood at the bar. He was drinking a Schnapps to keep warm, and the only other customer, a pensioner, threw another coin into the slot machine on the wall, pulled the lever, waited, pulled and lost again.
"Fraud," he said to Carl and spilled some beer on the counter, "the system is built on fraud. I came with nothing out of the East, I know it: every system is built on fraud." He gestured to the bartender. "Some more change, and give Carl another Schnapps, he looks like he's going back to the farm leagues!" They drank. The pensioner put his money into the automat.
"Do you have to shake out the caterpillars from your pillow each night, too," asked Carl, "or do the garter snakes wind around your neck?"
The old man let go of the machine, squinted, opened his eyes

halfway, eyed Carl sideways, and smiled. Then he motioned Carl to him and drew Carl's head to his shoulder. Carl felt a trembling. They both trembled and lay there a half a minute outside of space, head on shoulder, fear on fear, and then the old man said: "Just between us old salts, I see the Grim Reaper every time I open my eyes."
"And when you close them?"
"My homeland, buddy," said the man with a slight sigh.
"And how does it look?"
The man shoved him aside and reached for his glass. "What do you know about it," he said and spilled some more beer.
Carl shrugged his shoulders and drank his Schnapps. Then the door opened, and with a shot of cold and a swipe of rain, in came the Queen of Sheba.
The Queen of Sheba was a queen in exile, anyone could see that. Her long black coat was tattered and stained, the green dress underneath was torn at the arms, and she herself was getting soggy. But her legs under the black silk stockings were still slim and tight, and her blonde hair, even if it was a bit tinted, fell in natural waves onto her white shoulders, and her face, even if it was a bit marked with the coldness of an exile which had already lasted longer than youth, was still pretty, even if the shadow of a mild drunk lay on it now. In her dark green eyes were tears. She set a small vessel on the counter and next to it a silver-glitter handbag.
Carl went and sat next to her.
She looked at him, smiled, and asked, "What's your name?"
"Johnny Tristano," said Carl, "And yours?"
"Lola Love," said the Queen of Sheba.
Three Leonard Cohens and four Vermouths later, Carl couldn't restrain himself any longer. "What's in that thing there?" he asked and pointed with his empty glass at the vessel, which was covered with satin, so that you couldn't look into it.
"Shhh," said Lola, "he can't take it when people speak about him like that." She put her hand gently through Carl's hair.
"Who can't take it? Is someone in there?"
Lola emptied her glass, made a face, and looked like she would cry. "You are all alike: suspicious, ill-bred, unjust, you can't understand a single dream and have to dig everywhere in souls with your machines . . . men!" She wiped her eyes and hugged the vessel with both hands.
"Lola," said Carl, pushing the glasses to the bartender, "that's not how I meant it. I was just curious, it was no big deal."
"You're jealous, admit it!"
Behind them the slot machine tinkled with coins and the old man triumphed. "Didn't I tell you? System, everything's system, whoever doesn't figure it out goes under and deserves it too!"

"Let's go somewhere else," whispered Lola in Carl's ear, "if you promise you won't get jealous."
"Who should I be jealous of?"
"Promise me." Her face rubbed against his, he could smell her. Hell, thought Carl, the world owes me something.
"Okay," he said in her hair, "promised."
When they went out, it was still raining, and the wind slapped its fins in their faces, but to Carl it seemed as if he were walking in the sun on Tahiti.
"I really am fond of you," said the Queen of Sheba in the taxi and snuggled up to him. "I think I've fallen in love with you."
Carl tried to embrace her, but his hand bumped into the vessel, which she had pressed to her bosom. He twitched lightly away.
"Goddam," he said, "I really like you."
"But we can't go to my place," said Lola, "I don't have any place to live." Well of course, thought Carl, how could the Queen of Sheba have a stupid home, 2 rooms, kitchen, shower, balcony in the smog—she, a queen in exile?
"Logo," he said, "we can go to my place. It's a bit of a mess and I never can scrape the rent together, but the landlord won't just happen to come today, and anyway, what difference would that make? Love is where you find it."
The taxi took a violent curve and he felt Lola real close.
"Really?" she asked softly. "Do you really mean it?"
"Lola Love," said Carl, looking for her navel and bumping the vessel, "I really mean it."
"Johnny Tristano," said the Queen of Sheba ceremoniously, "I will let you in on my secret, I will love you."
Carl got rid of the biggest mounds of trash, cleared away the empty bottles, shook out the blanket from the bed, rinsed two glasses and opened his last bottle of whiskey. "Fine," he said, dropping a couple of ice cubes in each glass, "show me."
Lola Love sat in the armchair, and dreamily smoked a cigarette. She had placed the satin-covered thing on the table. Her eyes, these green eyes that almost drove Carl crazy, were closed. "I know what you're waiting for," she said.
"Cheerio," said Carl and pushed a glass over to her, "let's drink up to keep warm, my heater is in the pawnshop."
She opened her eyes. They were swimming with green tears. "If you can't wait, then I'll just have to show you now," she said and cried softly.
Damn it, thought Carl, no woman who's not nuts. You dream of the Queen of Sheba, meet her, even get her to come home with you, and what does she have in her head?—
Then he saw how Lola pulled the satin from the vessel. It was a small,

square aquarium with water and a bit of sand and greenery, and in the middle hung a fat goldfish.

Carl started to giggle. "And I thought you had a *mandrake* in there!" He picked up his glass and poured down his whiskey, filled it again, giggled some more, laughed. Then he saw her face and stopped laughing. He followed her glance. The goldfish had opened an eye. It was a pretty big eye, big for a goldfish, and the eye stared at Carl, and Carl recognized the clouded whitish shimmering cold hate in the eye and took fright and remembered the caterpillars and garter snakes from earlier today and asked himself if there was any connection—dream? delirium? insanity?

"He can tell you're jealous of him," said Lola, smiling, and blew her breath into the glass, and Carl saw how the goldfish shook and moved his gills harder and stirred the water with his short fat tail.

Carl drank down the next drink and all the rest without ice, half leaning on the bed, half lying down, he saw the Queen of Sheba dancing through his apartment, partly with and partly without clothes, in rhythm with a music that he heard, not in his ears, but in his nerves, and he saw how the goldfish in the glass observed the queen and finally seemed to breathe, to shake, to glide, and to dance in the same rhythm, and then the Queen of Sheba stood before Carl and tears flowed and she said, "You're dreaming, Johnny Tristano, you're finally dreaming," and he heard himself saying, "Come, Queen of

Malli Kneeling   by Jürgen Beissert   graphite

Sheba, come," and much later he woke up and fell out of the bed to drink a glass of water, and saw water, and in the water floated a goldfish belly-up, and he dipped a finger in the water and touched the goldfish and the goldfish was dead, and then he took it out and threw it in the garbage can and drank the rest of the whiskey, and then he fell back into bed with the Queen of Sheba.

The queen slept, and as he watched her face in the light of the lamp, he saw the defeated face of an old woman with grey hair and pouches under her eyes. He crept back in with her, and she said something, and he crept nearer and heard her whisper, "Don't be jealous . . . don't ever be jealous again. And now it's too late." He watched her for a little while, then turned off the light and lay there for a moment and saw nothing and then submerged and still saw nothing, felt nothing, dreamed nothing.

When Carl awoke the next morning he was alone.

He drank a glass of tapwater and slowly got dressed and tried to get any kind of a feeling, to feel anything at all, but he didn't feel anything. He drank some more water and washed down two aspirin and looked around again, but he didn't see anything worth seeing, and the goldfish in the garbage had disappeared too. At the streetcar stop as he rummaged for his fare, he found the two cards from the employment office: "Waffle Salesman" and "Assistant Bouncer at the Lido Bar." That doesn't sound bad, Lido Bar, he thought, but bad with other people. Today he didn't want to have anything to do with other people. Waffles were neutral. Two hours later he was at his stand and the man from the bakery unpacked the waffles and explained what he had to do. He sold waffles.

As he was going to the next bar in his lunch break, he passed a pet store. He went inside. A salesgirl with curled locks came to him.

"Can I help you?"

"I'm looking for a goldfish," said Carl.

She showed him all the goldfishes. "Are you looking for a special kind? We have . . . "

"I'll take a look around," said Carl. He looked at each goldfish. They stupored away cloudily in their aquariums. Then he noticed that he was thinking of the Queen of Sheba, and that he was sick with pain. The saleslady eyed him with suspicion.

"I think I'd better stick to caterpillars," said Carl and left.

Fame

A person travelling through calls up
and wants to know, what have
I written lately.

I want to know his name.
That's none of your business!
he shouts and hangs up pretty fast.

A filmmaker calls up.
My girlfriend is reading your book
now for the second time,
he says. Maybe we should meet sometime
and talk about a film.

I haven't had a girlfriend for a long time
and I try to imagine
how she lays in bed with my book,
the girlfriend of the filmmaker.
Would she sleep with me a second time too?

A man from the local Sponti* gazette calls up
and wants to know if I'm
contained in my last book.
For all eternity I answer heartily
and the Sponti-man hangs up.
The man from the Verfassungsschutz† hangs up too.
I still don't have a girlfriend
and I open a bottle of whiskey.

The doctor's forbidden me whiskey in the meantime.
A package comes into the house.
Handle with care! DO NOT THROW! written large next to the
   address.
Omigod, I think. So little written,
so gently spoken against the current,
and you're already worth a letter-bomb.

I open the package. From many layers of newspaper
I peel a bottle of Black and White. On the

---

*Sponti (colloquial): a leftist political activist who rejects the idea of theoretical concern or planned activity in favor of "spontaneous" activity and demonstration.

†Verfassungsschutz, literally Constitution-Protection, is the arm of the West German government corresponding to a combination FBI and House Committee on Unamerican Activities.

Ruhm

Ein Mensch auf Durchreise ruft an
und will wissen, was ich
in letzter Zeit geschrieben habe.

Ich will seinen Namen wissen.
Das geht dich gar nichts an!
ruft er und legt ziemlich schnell auf.

Ein Filmer ruft an.
Meine Freundin liest dein Buch
jetzt schon zum zweiten Mal,
sagt er. Vielleicht treffen wir uns mal
und reden über einen Film.

Ich habe schon längere Zeit
keine Freundin mehr
und versuche mir vorzustellen,
wie sie mit meinem Buch im Bett liegt,
die Freundin des Filmers.
Würde sie mit mir auch ein zweites Mal
schlafen?

Ein Mann von der örtlichen Sponti-Gazette ruft an
und will wissen, ob ich
in meinem letzten Buch
enthalten bin.
Für alle Ewigkeit, antworte ich wacker
und der Sponti-Mann legt auf.
Auch der Mann vom Verfassungsschutz legt auf.
Ich habe immer noch keine Freundin
und öffne eine Flasche Whisky.

Inzwischen hat mir der Arzt den Whisky verboten.
Ein Päckchen kommt ins Haus.
VORSICHT! NICHT WERFEN! steht groß neben der Adresse.
Donnerwetter, denke ich. So wenig geschrieben,
so sanft gegen die Strömung gesprochen,
und schon bist du eine Briefbombe wert.

Ich öffne das Päckchen. Aus mehreren Zeitungshüllen
Schäle ich eine Flasche Black & White. Auf dem

pasted-on note it says: HAVE READ YOUR
LAST BOOKS. THEY REALLY SPEAK TO ME!

I open the bottle, sniff. It's
whiskey all right. I pour
a fingerbreadth in a glass
and drink.

I drink to fans, Verfassungsschutz
and doctor.
It really speaks to me, the whiskey,
the fame.
If I just had a girlfriend now too
I would almost feel like
a human being.

angeklebten Zettel steht: HABE DEINE LETZTEN
BÜCHER GELESEN, HABEN MICH STARK
ANGESPROCHEN.

Ich öffne die Flasche, schnuppere. Es ist
zweifellos Whisky. Ich gieße einen
Fingerbreit in ein Glas
und trinke.

Ich trinke auf Fans, Verfassungsschutz
und Arzt.
Er spricht mich stark an der Whisky,
der Ruhm.
Wenn ich jetzt noch eine Freundin hätte,
würde ich mich fast fühlen wie
ein Mensch.

BERND SCHMICH

1977—but not for the files

> *Siehe da, habe ich mir gesagt,*
> *auch einmal wieder einer,*
> *der aus seiner Haut steigt,*
> *während die übrigen nur daraus*
> *fahren möchten!*
>   Raabe, Die Akten des Vogelsangs*

A whole year long done nothing but
drink tea
the winter over a bottle of rum
a jar or two of honey with it
and slunk through the apartment
listened to radio
fifty-eight year old oil paint
as childhood memory
so it wasn't even disturbing
that it was *verboten*
to photograph
Dix's whores
or Beckmann's gypsy woman
A few days at the sea
a dead seagull on the beach
crunched a shell underfoot
on a pier
red granite that I hid in the grass
and then had to leave behind anyway
sat on an overturned boat
and in my thoughts fist-fought
stabbed the white swollen fish-eyes

Bernd Schmich
Born 1952 in Heddesheim, studies German
literature, art history, and drama.

1977—aber nicht für die Akten

Ein ganzes Jahr lang eigentlich nur
Tee getrunken
den Winter über eine Flasche Rum
ein oder zwei Gläser Honig dazu
und durch die Wohnung geschlichen
Radio gehört
achtundfünfzig Jahre alte Ölfarbe
als Kindheitserinnerung
so hat es auch nicht gestört
daß es verboten war
die Nutten von Dix
oder die Zigeunerin von Beckmann
zu fotografieren
Ein paar Tage am Meer
eine tote Möwe am Strand
eine Muschel zertreten
auf einem Bootssteg
roter Granit den ich im Gras versteckte
und dann doch liegen lassen mußte
auf einem umgekippten Boot gesessen
und in Gedanken mich geprügelt
in die weißen aufgequollenen Fischaugen gestochen

*Wilhelm Raabe 1831–1910. *Die Akten des Vogelsangs* (Mr. Birdsong's Files) is a novel about different paths to self-actualization: the apparent failure as he who frees himself from convention and finds his way to himself; the author/narrator as the chronicler helplessly bound in societal imperatives who, in bureaucratic manner, keeps "files" when he tells of the life of the other. An attempt at self-criticism by Raabe, and a lament over the senselessness of literature. The novel was written between 1893 and 1895 in Braunschweig (Brunswick), and the city appears in this poem.

invented a mayonnaise
that maybe already existed
learned to play a middling Doppelkopf*
saw clouds to my heart's content
—before that, stumbled up and down the stairs
took a cello between my thighs
and tuned straight across to AFN†
and with that already on your nerves
that night, on a still-empty stomach
drinking beer and feeling conspiratorial
in the strange apartment
Ten hours later anxiety in the Elbe tunnel
like so often before on the streets of Berlin
that were stuffed full of thick headlines
that counted a person's days
no one said anything till we were through
Cats lured from a cutter at the harbor
"Die Akten des Vogelsangs" read aloud
a few days later in Brunswick
took a chestnut from the table
shrunk up, it's still there in my pocket
bringing luck and preventing rheumatism
Drinking
beer that ended with "—borg"
and fried herrings
wanted to catch a pheasant with bare hands
scared you with the throat-cutting gesture
Photographed the clouds evenings
and, laughing, we got wet
face to the wind to the rain
on the second day
wanted to do that
which I couldn't even imagine anymore
that I could do it
and made a story out of it.

---

*Doppelkopf is a card game for four players, in which two teams of two play against each other—teams are not chosen but are determined by the chance distribution of the cards and the run of play. The changing player-pairs aren't named, rather the fascination of the game consists in the tension of determining with whom you are paired.
†AFN—American Forces Network, the radio station of the U.S. troops which still occupy West Germany. In many areas of the country, AFN is the only station on which jazz or rock can be heard.

eine Mayonnaise erfunden
die es vielleicht schon gab
leidlich Doppelkopf gelernt
an Wolken mich satt gesehen
—vorher Treppen rauf und runter gestolpert
ein Cello zwischen die Schenkel genommen
und quer zu AFN gezupft
und da schon dir im Rücken gesessen
nachts auf noch immer nüchternen Magen
Bier getrunken und mich dabei konspirativ gefühlt
in der fremden Wohnung
Zehn Stunden später Beklemmung im Elbtunnel
wie vorher schon oft auf den Straßen Berlins
die zugestopft waren mit dicken Überschriften
die die Tage eines Menschen zählten
keiner sagte was bis wir durch waren
Katzen von einem Kutter gelockt am Hafen
"Die Akten des Vogelsangs" vorgelesen
ein paar Tage später in Braunschweig
eine Kastanie vom Tisch genommen morgens
verschrumpelt liegt sie noch in der Tasche
bringt Glück und verhütet Rheuma
Bier das am Ende "-borg" hieß
getrunken
und Heringe gebraten
einen Fasan mit bloßen Händen fangen gewollt
mit der Kopf-Ab-Geste dich erschreckt
Die Wolken fotographiert abends
und lachend sind wir naß geworden
mit dem Gesicht zum Wind zum Regen
am zweiten Tag
das tun gewollt
was ich mir nicht einmal mehr vorstellen konnte
daß ich es tun könnte
und eine Geschichte daraus gemacht.

After Work

Afternoons about five
appear the tattooed arms
of my neighbor
on the balcony balustrade
in front of the geraniums
and the sunflower of plastic

from his white undershirt
he watches the parking maneuvers

on the street sways a drunk
in white pants, white T-shirt
sunglasses
and shouts "James Bond!—James Bond!"

music drones out of an apartment
Pink Floyd between the houses

my neighbor scratches his blue girl
on his forearm
and flicks his cigarette
in a broad arc
to the street.

          The still rooms
          mornings around four
          things yet lying leaning against each other
          and sunk into themselves
          in the courtyard the lamps
          illuminate now only themselves
          birds flit over the roofs
          sing in the antennas
          I go in your room
          quietly pull back the curtain from the window
          and draw your still face.
          It is light.

Feierabend

Nachmittags gegen fünf
erscheinen die tätowierten Arme
meines Nachbarn
auf der Balkonbrüstung
vor den Geranien
und der Sonnenblume aus Plastik

da schaut er aus seinem weißen Unterhemd
den Einparkmanövern zu

auf der Straße wackelt ein Betrunkener
in weißer Hose, weißem T-Shirt
Sonnenbrille
und ruft "James Bond!—James Bond!"

Musik dröhnt aus einer Wohnung
Pink Floyd zwischen den Häusern

mein Nachbar kratzt sein blaues Mädchen
am Unterarm
und schnippt seine Zigarette
in weitem Bogen
auf die Straße.

        Die stillen Zimmer
        morgens um vier
        die Dinge liegen noch aneinander gelehnt
        und in sich zusammengesunken
        im Hof die Lampe
        beleuchtet nur noch sich selbst
        Vögel huschen über die Dächer
        besingen die Antennen
        ich gehe in dein Zimmer
        ziehe leise den Vorhang am Fenster zurück
        und zeichne dein stilles Gesicht.
        Es ist hell.

MICHAEL SPEIER

subwaysmell
the impatience of a landscape
wholly of metal
a beggar at the turnstile
his song whistles
no photomat
to preserve us
out of the chromeslit
noiseless the ticket
a little yellow tongue.

Metrogeruch
die ungeduld einer landschaft
ganz aus metall
der bettler am drehkreuz
sein lied pfeift.
kein fotomat
der uns aufnimmt
aus dem chromschlitz
geräuschlos das ticket
die kleine gelbe zunge.

Michael Speier
Born 1948, lives in Berlin. *Traumschaum*
(Dreamfoam), poetry, 1978. Editor of
PARK, Berlin.

Ice Age III

For Sarah Kirsch

Most were already gone
we remained at the kitchen table
I want to talk with you
like a woman but you are
another part of the city
first the couples went
into the cold
singles with glass teeth
they all asked for happiness
at the door
where the girl lay
with a mask of snow
a white paper that doesn't thaw
we were silent while all the others
laughed into their coats
the talk went without mechanism
and the city through our bodies
while it snowed on both parts
we smoked Golddollar.

Eiszeit III

für Sarah Kirsch

Die meisten waren schon weg
wir blieben am küchentisch
ich möchte mit dir reden
wie eine frau aber du bist
ein anderer teil der stadt
zuerst gingen die paare
einzelne mit gläsernen zähnen
hinaus in die kälte
alle fragten nach dem glück
vor der haustür
wo das mädchen lag
mit einer maske aus schnee
ein weisses papier das nicht taut
wir schwiegen als alle anderen
in ihre mäntel lachten
das gespräch ging ohne mechanik
und die stadt durch unsere körper
wir rauchten golddollar.

Statement

Forms: how they bend around the corner and become a loss. The consolations sleep in light / here: touch my shards, hands, moving, they are none. no objects in them / no skin-part over which you caress, it's just as with the words: only movements, a sun, red above the cemeteries, the landing strips / it is much easier to say what is not / as me.
New thought: dreamed-away colorful slip-knots, rooms in which nothing falls but snow / white like "white" / isn't it / 1 pounding knock / 1 folder / 1 knife of plastic (white too) / illuminations vibrate / transparent as a slide / the old films held up against the light / nothing moves any more / I can't get inside the movement of poem / the pictures are mute in the room / views / later thighs roast no you can't imagine it in the line in the supermarket where the pennies wander to small compartments with a view-pane / no the line with the old ones with their washed out faces / couples in mid-forties, buying charcoal for the grill, they have become modest later nothing more will occur to them / the woman at the register presses a hidden lever with her foot and the belt runs, on it what bought for the evening of the next day / sale zones / that is, in rank and file, bags are opened / plastic bags / the patient waiting till the money is taken / the dreary togetherness / the interchangeability / no that's my cart / next cow please / feelings=conveyer belt moving past the register / the last you see is the last / or how should I describe it to you / a supermarket which in the states would already be a relic / here they still stand like idiotic here they want to be rid of their pennies from life, want to get past the register / 1 ring through the nose, the smooth skin / Klaus Kammen in "Report for an Academy" / repudiations, days happen, look, shifts. on East TV they speak of banners, in West TV that's the name of a soap. wave a flag or foam in the armpits. that is the question. the wall thrown away I misunderstand your name from here to there / 1 candle in the window / then I translated myself into Spanish / my reading speed is 3 days to you / labyrinthine sentences, houses built one inside the other, from which the facing crumbles when you strike it / the shoulders the folds of the armpit their smell the cool of the upper arm on the back side the bump on the arm the 2 tomatoes going over the crossing one time to say I or ah

II PEOPLE

MICHAEL MEINICKE

Michael Meinicke
Born 1948 in the part of Berlin that would become "East." Became an electrician, worked as an exports salesman. Joined the Lyrik Klub Pankow (Pankow is a district in East Berlin). The club ceased to exist when

Your Kiss

You have gone. You gave me this kiss. At the door. Half open. Dark like a stairwell.
Now it comes and goes. Uninterrupted within me. Like stairs. Up and down. Arrival, destination or passing by.
It throws me against the lonely walls of my room, where my fingers search in vain for the bell with your name plate. Maybe I forgot your address? The way to reach you finally? Just how was it?
First in my thoughts, then in your eyes. Your mouth! The lips—small, red, partly opened as if for speaking. Full of tiny wrinkles. Firm and fissured like cliffs at a summer beach. Behind them the whiteness of your teeth—foam on the waves of the sea.
All this I experienced. Now it is within me.
Your kiss crescendos in my body and tears the most beautiful, sunniest day of my life into small snips of clouds that—absolutely calm, slowly and snow-white—snow in my thoughts.
I drink a little and feel tipsy.
Too bad that kisses can't be seen. Maybe every day there would be proud and happy people walking in the streets. Demonstrating to everyone their own happiness. For everyone to share. So they may dance, sing, laugh. Somebody got a kiss!
I go to bed. While in bed I whisper my experience with you into my pillow. Holding it in my arm . . .

most of the active members were arrested between 1968-1970 for dissent and political activity against the Soviet/East German occupation of Czechoslovakia. Some members got up to 8 years. Michael got 2 and lost his acceptance to the University as Econ student. After prison he worked as a warehouse man, salesperson, stage hand in a theater, elevator operator, assembly line worker, gardener, and "Bottle-return-taker." Unsuccessful application to study at the University. In October 1978 he fled to the West with his wife in the trunk of a Ford; he lives and studies German literature in West Berlin. In November 1979 he made a poetry-reading tour of West Germany.

People—Fairy Tales

And we are. We exist. We live. We dwell, laugh, eat, listen now to this music.
We look different and are exactly the same. We sit on chairs, on the floor. We watch as the record turns and our eyes flicker in the candle light.
We do everything together. Smoking as if insane. Guzzling red wine, schnapps, beer. Together we feel miserable. We whisper. Try to communicate within the belly of that beast, society.
Oh no! That's wrong! Not communicate, we have to confirm our existence. Nobody knows about the other. We touch our bodies. They are beautiful in summer and dreadfully white in winter.
We move. We laugh silently and never cry. We dream joy. We clamp on tightly lest we suddenly take off.
Sometimes we go right up to the window pane: Always a sun appears in front of it. If we hold our fingertips outside, they shine and our eyes begin to flicker again.
Then we lie on carpets in strange flats. We hold glasses and cigarettes. We wait. We breathe slowly. We turn our feet. So they may touch touchingly.
We call out. Actually we should be choking of our horror.
Filled with truth we sink into sounds. Then we notice our hands. They try carefully to find each other across the small pyres and sticky swamps of poisonous liquids.

We ask. We answer. We would like.
We imagine Life. We remember. We forget.
Our similarity is our hold. Our way is to be together. If only we had a park, our own big house. A street, where we could walk. Where we could say hello to one another, where all houses would be inhabited by ourselves. If only we had our shops, schools, pubs, sporting grounds.
Oh, and our own parents, relatives, and our own children. And all would have small and big dogs, cats, and budgerigars.
If only we had something. And if it were just a flower in some corner somewhere. And happiness!
Nothing, nothing, *nothing* is ours. We only are. We have to be. We are princes and princesses under a spell.
We are forever people.

Mitch   by Jürgen Beissert   graphite

Prison

I can't sleep—and put myself to bed anyway. Because They turn out the light.
I love music—but I'm unmusical. Because They've taught me to sing another tune. Whoever is forced for a long time, without interruption, to hear the same concert, he forgets, unlearns the songs.
I can neither drink nor eat. There was water. The animals guzzle. There is nothing to say about the food. Such a pig I've never seen before.
I can't see out the windows. There aren't any. Only the memory.
Naked—I can be only in dark rooms. But it's not dark enough anywhere. I was eternally undressed in the light past the limit. Nakedness exists only in paradise or in the grave for me.
And only there love. A difficult word.
I handed in a lot of words when I was brought in. Faster than I expected. When the ship sinks, the ballast gets thrown in the water. Everything—furniture, clothes, freight, masts, sails—just swimming, swimming—
Friends, too, drift off, no matter. It's no struggle any more, just hold on, just cling to the surface. Everything is forgotten. Only up and under remain, up and under on the waves—life.
The ship is long since a hollow, hungry belly. It floats.
I can't write. Am humble and plain. A filthy hog.
I'm no longer interesting. I'm not interested in myself any more. It doesn't interest me any more. Because they lost interest in me, I've made myself interesting.
It got silly.
I can't laugh any more. For the most part it was forbidden, and besides it sounded too uncanny. Criminal. Witch and devil. Medieval. Illusory burning at an imaginary stake.
I can't go on. I'm too deep in the shit. Head shut! Face to the wall. Hands behind your back. At corners stopping and waiting for the red light. Get moving—get moving. The iron doors slam shut and then The Rolling Stones—"we love you"—
They hung my own ass in my face.
Goddamn, oh goddamn . . .

PETER BOLSTER

Fairly Confused

On the streetcorners the newspaper vendors are standing again,
each one with his story—it's gotten colder.
Where were you,
I looked all over for you:
in the toy department, in books and lingerie,
between lobsters and Indian tea
and even in the mirrored hall of an auto dealer.
In the city they shook their heads,
breathed visibly while they waited in panic at traffic lights
and cursed about the weather.
Finally I did find you
between dolls and old pictures
and other stuff in a junk shop.
As I wanted to touch you, your arm broke off
and a saleswoman shrieked:
"That costs you at least 300 marks, man!"
Outside it occurred to me then, there must be something else
than these metallic dreams you go for so much,
cool—cool and gleaming
Later, as I bought oranges, I reminded myself
of the south,
where I look upwards so much oftener
if the sky is cloudlessly hazy
or black and full of constellations.

Peter Bolster
Born 1947 in Munich, studied German
literature, MA.

Ziemlich verwirrt

An den Straßenecken stehen jetzt wieder Zeitungsverkäufer,
ein jeder mit seiner Geschichte—es ist kälter geworden.
Wo warst du,
überall hab ich dich gesucht:
in der Spielzeugabteilung, bei Büchern und Wäsche,
zwischen Hummern und indischem Tee
und sogar in der Spiegelhalle eines Autosalons.
In der Stadt schüttelten sie die Köpfe,
hauchten sichtbar, während sie panisch an Ampeln warteten
und fluchten über das Wetter.
Schließlich fand ich dich doch
zwischen Puppen und alten Bildern
und sonstigem Krempel in einer Trödelboutique.
Als ich dich anfassen wollte, brach dir der Arm ab
und eine Verkäuferin kreischte:
"Das kostet Sie mindestens 300—Mark, Mann!"
Draußen fiel mir dann ein, es müsse noch etwas anderes geben
als diese metallenen Träume, auf die du so stehst,
kühl,—kühl und glänzend.
Später, als ich Orangen kaufte, erinnerte ich mich
an den Süden,
wo ich viel öfter nach oben schaue,
wenn der Himmel wolkenlos dunstig ist
oder schwarz und mit Sternbildern voll.

Walls

    An old drunkard
pisses against the cemetery wall
                      his laugh*
        disperses   biting and toothless
      in little brooks   is hard
                  runs over
              the street dirt

              word-tatters
                    but
                    how
  can anyone sink so low   many wars with the world
                                   does he have behind him
Mommy what is he doing there
and may he go in there too
    and what will   he sits down
our dear Lord say about it   on the fairly well-worn
                                lowest step of the stairs
        be still   to the church portal
            he knows no more questions
                about reality

only fluid contents remain
    everything else
        lands in the refuse   behind the wall

Lache is the German noun for laugh; a second meaning is pool or puddle.

Mauern

Ein trunksüchtiger Alter
Pißt gegen die Friedhofsmauer

        seine Lache

    zerfließt   beißend und zahnlos
in kleinen Bächen   ist hart

      und zieht her
    über den Straßendreck

     Wortfetzen

       aber
       wie

kann man denn so herunter kommen   viele Kriege mit der Welt
                                        hat er schon hinter sich
  Mami was macht der da
  und darf der da auch rein
    und was wird   er setzt sich
  der liebe Gott dazu sagen   auf die ziemlich abgetretene
                                    unterste Stufe der Treppe
     sei still   zum Kirchenportal

       er kennt keine Fragen mehr
        nach der Wirklichkeit

nur noch flüssige Inhalte

  alles andere
  landet im Abfall   hinter der Mauer

Storm over a Chestnut Tree in the Afternoon

All day long the radio plays country & western
and the expectation of great things keeps on.
The pigeons stoop under the rain gutters,
the tree shakes tempest,
lightning breaks through the black heavens:
the worry of the museum curators at five,
let no one succeed
in tempting one of the statues to dance in their absence
or in indulging in a little nap
on the bench before the "Fall Into Hell."
A bad wind blows the balloons
behind the post windows and in the editorial offices of the dailies.
Equanimity caresses the leaves
while heavy drops patter down on them.

Driving Back in November

Through the full moon night
past white stretches and light blue peaks of snow
or on the horizon:
as if the southern heavens were fallen down.
Now you speak of the day,
but here the times flow into each other anyway.

Don't you believe
that we're too small to be beyond astonishing
or to speak sentences that begin "Well, uh, ya know"?
These are bad times for emperors, kings,
and all-knowing judges of wisdom,
what if the cosmos were just
like the four tires under us on the asphalt, here and in moonlight?

Gewitter über einer Kastanie am Nachmittag

Das Radio spielt den ganzen Tag Country & Western
und das Warten auf die großen Dinge hält an.
Die Tauben hocken unter den Dachrinnen,
den Baum schüttelt Sturm,
ein Blitz durchbricht den schwarzen Himmel:
die Sorge der Museumswärter um fünf,
niemandem möge es gelingen,
in ihrer Abwesenheit eine der Statuen zum Tanz zu verleiten
oder ein Schläfchen zu halten
auf der Bank vor dem "Höllensturz".
Ein schlechter Hauch bläht die Ballons
hinter den Postschaltern und in den Redaktionen der Tagespresse.
Die Blätter streichelt Gleichmut,
während schwere Tropfen auf sie herunterprasseln.

Rückfahrt im November

Durch die Vollmondnacht
an weißen Flächen und hellblauen Schneegipfeln vorbei
oder am Horizont:
als wäre der südliche Himmel heruntergefallen.
Jetzt sprichst du vom Tag,
aber hier fließen die Zeiten ohnehin ineinander.

Glaubst du nicht,
daß wir zu klein sind, um über nichts mehr zu staunen
oder Sätze zu sprechen, die mit "Ach, weißt du . . ." anfangen?
Es sind schlechte Zeiten für Kaiser, Könige
und allumfassende Richter der Weisheit,
was nämlich, wenn der Kosmos so wäre,
wie die vier Räder unter uns auf dem Asphalt, hier und im
  Mondschein?

Even our car radio squeaks across many dimensions;
tenor saxophonists, St. Louis/Mississippi
dissolve themselves in waves of aether
nice to meet you again in the Alpine foothills nights in November.
We could make experiments
if you know how
chugging faster and faster over the concrete track
and suddenly
the pressing back—you fly:
here are the new spaces beyond the words.

You laugh—fitted out with psychoanalysis
and I believe you
all your nights,
in which trees like chewed-up fingernails
stretched themselves toward you,
in which you waved from the window, three in the morning, nude,
and below on the street someone got into his car,
in which you watched
how a moth grazed the candle,
a living room Icarus
like all of us.

I know someone who takes his glasses off
every time he enters a church,
only afterwards crossing himself.

What do you believe
in this moment
where without words and without memory
the moonlight falls on the strands of your hair
and the headlights wipe across the firs?

Selbst unser Autoradio überwindet krächzend mehrere
Dimensionen;
Tenorsaxophonspieler, St. Louis/Mississippi
lösen sich auf in Wellen im Äther
nice to meet you again im Voralpenland nachts im November.
Wir könnten Experimente machen,
wenn du das kennst,
immer schneller über die Betonpiste zu holpern
und plötzlich
der Druck nach hinten—man fliegt:
hier sind die neuen Räume jenseits der Worte.

Du lachst—psychoanalytisch beschlagen
und ich glaube dir
all deine Nächte,
in denen Bäume wie angeknabberte Fingernägel sich
nach dir streckten,
in denen du morgens um drei am Fenster winktest, nackt,
und unten auf der Straße stieg einer ins Auto,
in denen du zusahst,
wie ein Nachtfalter die Kerze streifte,
ein Wohnzimmer-Ikarus
wie wir alle.

Da kenne ich jemanden, der nimmt seine Brille ab,
sooft er eine Kirche betritt,
dann erst bekreuzigt er sich.

Was glaubst du
in diesem Augenblick,
wo ohne Worte und ohne Erinnerung
das Mondlicht auf deine Haarsträhne fällt
und die Scheinwerfer an den Fichten vorüberwischen?

LUTZ RATHENOW

Fantasy

> *Poetry, in smoke—*
> *there you shall stay*
> *Not yet ready*
> *becoming cured*
>
> *Be careful of the smoke*
> *for its bitterness*

In the gentle waving of leaves
a shadow drizzles to the ground
in the soft gliding of bodies
we see only the movement

We met us yesterday
we meet us today
we don't say: tomorrow

We are sitting in high branches
seeing faces through the leaves
seeing through dreams   dreams
being giddy in high places
never jumping down
never falling up
standing still huddled
huddled in a lashing wind

translated by Michael Meinicke

Lutz Rathenow
Born 1952 in Jena. Abitur, Army, 1965-70
studied education, history, and German at
the Friedrich Schiller University in Jena.
Worked as truckdriver, then as stage-
manager at a Berlin theater.
various lit-mags, incl. *Auswahl*, which
appears in E. Berlin.

Phantasie

Verse, im Rauch—
da sollt ihr dauern
Jetzt noch nicht brauchbar
werdet ihr haltbar
Habt acht im Rauch
vor dem Verbittern

Im sanften Wogen der Blätter
rieselt zu Boden der Schatten
Im sachten Gleiten der Körper
sehen wir nur das Bewegen

Wir trafen uns gestern
Wir treffen uns heute
Wir sprechen nicht: morgen

Wir sitzen auf hohen Ästen
sehn durch die Blätter Gesichter
Sehn durch die Träume die Träume
Taumeln auf hohen Spitzen
springen niemals herunter
fallen niemals hinauf
Bleiben so stehen im kauern
kauern vor Peitschen des Windes

P.

My friend
always knows better
and just smiles these days
when other people begin to rage
    about yet others, all the
    cold ones who don't want to understand
    what they should get angry about
So P.
    of whom I have spoken
    is no longer my friend
went
    not over the border
    not to jail
    not to his death
He went to the Television Tower
    took the elevator to the tower restaurant
    and stepped to the window
cried:
    Workers of the world, unite!

A lady looked askance
Ha, ha, went the waiter just to be safe

translated by Michael Meinicke

P.

Mein Freund
Der alles besser weiß
Und nur noch lächelt
Wenn andere wütend werden
    über wieder andere, die alles
    kalt läßt oder die nicht begreifen
    über was sie wütend werden sollten
Also P.
    dem ich gesagt habe
    daß er nicht mehr mein Freund ist
Ging
    niche über die Grenze
    nicht in den Knast
    nicht in den Tod
Er ging zum Fernsehturm
Fuhr mit dem Fahrstuhl in das Cafe
Und begab sich zum Fenster
Schrie:
    Seid umschlungen Millionen!

Eine Dame guckte pickiert
Ha, ha, machte vorsichtshalber der Kellner

Prompt

He flew swiftly over the notice and then passed it on, the secretary should arrange everything.

As usual the persons in question were ordered into the appropriate room, he used the time to drink a cup of coffee. With three pieces of sugar and an open-faced sandwich. They were out of salami, so he took liverwurst.

Quite empty, the canteen, as usual around this time, and he wondered why they were nevertheless out of salami. Then he thought of the remaining paperwork of the day and went back punctually. Everything was prepared. All had formed up without the use of force. The secretary handed him the document.

As authorized official, he began to read aloud the order. His voice remained unconcerned, but he had to repress the suddenly appearing itch behind his right ear. As prescribed, the names were repeated, more hurriedly now, one seemed familiar to him, but he didn't detain himself with thinking about it—just get the business out of the way without delay. He wanted to be home earlier today, and first he wanted to have the new postage stamps cancelled at the post.

When he was finished, the secretary looked at him.

He nodded, folded the paper together, put it in the envelope and gave it to the secretary.

He expressed his thanks.

Then they came toward him. At first he didn't understand what it was all about. The situation was explained: after all, he had read out the sentence himself.

He was led out of the room.

Five rooms down the hall, the building was designed so practically. There wasn't time enough to believe in a mistake.

Shortly before the execution, the secretary came running: reception and completion of the directive must first be confirmed.

He signed receipt.

The secretary took his leave.

by Jochen Melzian   photograph

Change of Location

Town K. is off the beaten track. Town P. is no different. Herr L. always writes from K. to P. To an old friend: long letters full of contents. Almost daily. Herr L. is already older, that squares every distance. So he doesn't drive away anymore, especially not as far as P.
K. is a small town. There there is one mailbox one mailbox emptier one Post Outbringer (into the larger neighbor town, where the yellow car from the district town stops) one Post Inbringer one Post deliverer. This all in one person. In Herr S.
One doesn't write much in K. Except for L. One hardly ever gets mail in K. Except for Herr L. Regular answers.
S. knows everyone in town—everyone knows him. Actually he is content. Only that there's nothing entertaining, is disturbing. Pretty disturbing.
S. knows a lot. L. knows some. L. writes a lot to P. about same. S. knows more. For example, that the friend in P. is long since dead, and therefore that no answers from P. to K. can come.
S. missed something and L. would miss something, if the Post Outbringer Post Inbringer Mailbox Emptier didn't receive all the letters to K, open them—and then write an answering letter.
The cancellation is always illegibly smeared.
S. corresponds thus with L. about this and that, which isn't talked about in town. As is usual. Aside from that they see each other every day, when L., while picking up milk, passes the Post Office forty meters away from his apartment.
"Good day!" "Good day!" Seldom more.
On his way back, L. is already in his thoughts about the expected letter from P.

The Applause

At the beginning, everything like always. The usual applause, who wants to be the first to quit. A few want to stand out, others move their lower arms zealously out of boredom.
So it goes awhile.
Great, this enthusiasm, thinks the speaker.
Slowly the volume swells. No one knows why.
The first palms get numb. Ears begin to hurt.
That doesn't stop anything, all clap as well as they can.
Two pass out. They are carried away.
With the next three, the stretcher bearers hesitate—and clap along.
The applause increases. Stronger strikes hand on hand. More ragingly.
In the future, gloves, thinks the speaker, before he falls unconscious onto the stage floor.
A few tear their clothing, pound wildly on their thighs.
Then on other body parts.
The blows hail thicker.
Always faster. And thicker.
Window panes crack. The first ones beat themselves to death.
Others can take more. To come through the steadily growing noise, they open their mouths as far as they can, like they learned in the army.
Doggedly it is continued. Nonetheless, in spite of it, especially now in the face of it. Doggedly and with impact.

And when the building falls down, too.
Living room mirrors begin to shake.
House walls in the neighboring city show the first cracks.

SILVO LAHTELA

Places 1

Open resting
on a mound of earth
the jaws of the power shovel

Stellen 1

Offen ruhen
auf Häufung von Erde
die Greifschaufeln des Baggers

Silvo Lahtela
Grew up in a late '60s student commune in
Berlin. Finnish background. Studies German
literature in Berlin.

The Escalator at Pont de Sêvres

Over ice, ink-veils, pale blues,
that nestle through themselves, so hanging across it,
that draw in, enclose the upward-guided becomer.
Clearly grown between them,
Ice! Opening!
and into it,
the brown of the tree, whose
shivering limbs softly blow leaves on
against the visage. Against it like a strange woman's
hands' snowy touch, there to where these hands'
breathy hold. Still holding forth, now,
the kissing me of all the leafage.

Die Rolltreppe von Pont de Sêvres

Über Eis Tintenschleier, blaßblaue,
die selbst sich überschmiegen, so es verhängen,
die saugend umfangen den hochgeführt Werdenden.
Klar dazwischen gewachsen,
Eis! Öffnung!
herein auch,
das Braune des Baums, dessen
zitternder Äste Blätter weich wehen an
gegens Gesicht. Dagegen wie der Unbekannten
Hände schneeiges Berühren, dort, dahin dieser Hände
hauchiger Halt. Verhaltend noch, jetzt,
das Küssen all des Laubs meiner.

from "Foreword for those who don't get it afterward" (from Spielmans Tod)

4. The bedspread over the eiderdown quilt looks as if someone had lain there. But in truth the bedspread has only followed the contours of the unsmoothed quilt underneath.

5. The old woman's rigid stare at the green light as she crosses the street. If she is run over now, at least no one can blame her posthumously for breaking the law (is this her thought too?)

21. While reading the postcard, the feeling that it was written for the mailman.

22. Now I've really gone and done it, instead of giving someone the book, I've thrown it away, and why shouldn't I do it more often: like one throws away empty cigarette packages.

23. As soon as a corner seat is free in the U-Bahn, the closest slides into it.

25. Some never let go of their shopping cart. If in the middle of the Saturday crowd they want to go back through the shelves for some little thing that they forgot at first to pick up—they don't leave their cart in some free corner; instead they push it through the crowd to the stick of butter, and then the same way again in reverse.

29. For Nicola: The construction workers shovel, push wheelbarrows of sand, one runs a jack hammer, girls are grinned at, and as always I watch it all and think it's beautiful that there are objects of perception.

36. With her thumb, she wears out the label of my notebook, whose cardboard is turned upward: her venture at communication.

41. When the people look out the windows, they have or find inner balance; most often a pleasant indifference—the society-regulating apathy at the windows.

42. The year-worn man shakes the locked doors of the post office. Angry as if he had been defrauded. It is Saturday afternoon.

43. Student generation with me in the middle: upon demand rustle the book pages.

44. I would now be capable of duelling.

47. Idea: as if philosophy would become bearable only through one of my own.

59. One speaks well when one wants to listen to himself.

Bettina   by Jürgen Beissert   pastel

HERBERT WITZEL

Herbert Witzel
I was born in 1949 in Braunschweig (Brunswick). There I attended school, delivered newspapers, got my Abitur, worked in construction and as a housepainter, and studied German literature and art education. In 1971 I moved to Kreuzberg in Berlin and remained a student until 1978. In May 1976 I tried to make a

Letter Found in a Bottle
solo for breaking female voice

Today I am fifty-two years old, but you wouldn't know it to look at me. Just a week ago my new park bench neighbor—his name's Hanne, by the way—asked me how many years I've been pensioned. This Hanne with his doggish-smelling, eternally barking cur, is of course no friend of mine, even if now and then he imagines he is. Basically he's a makeshift replacement for good old Willi Hohmann, who couldn't take our last winter. I could really talk with Willi, he understood me.

Sometimes in the evening we would sit at our regular bench, drink to Orion, hold God responsible for everything, invite the Man in the Moon to play a hand, a penny a point—ah! if only he'd relented, now it's too late. Freedom-loving squirrels we fed with Health Store peanuts, dormice got their Bridge Mix, and the raccoons who'd escaped the zoo and made themselves at home got their pickled herring.

What a time that was with Willi! Even when Autumn came there was no stopping our gossip in the twilight, and if it was really too cold, then a campfire crackled in a punctured jelly tub before our brogues, Willi set it and fed it with popsicle sticks, cement sacks, and newspapers. If, drawn by our puttering and kindling, children came, Willi plucked a bag of malt candies from his left coat pocket, distributed one sticky brown cubelet apiece, and asked them, for example, if they had heard of Paul, the petroller. He housed many such unhistorical persons in his long-lived memory; there were also Glenn, the gluemaker, Don the dockworker, and Wayland the smith, to name just a few.

If the children, demanded too much, shook their heads, then Willi stuck the malt bonbons back in the green cloth, pulled out paper and tobacco from his right pocket and showed his audience how Paul the living with literature and opened the "Kaventsmann Kulturgüterumschlag," or in English, "The Guarantee-ers Cultural Products Envelope," a literature store, which closed its doors in July. Since then I have taken odd jobs.

Published:
Das Gelbbuch (The Yellow Pages), Berlin, 1976
Kreuzberger Dreifaltigkeit (Kreuzberg Trinity), Berlin 1979

---

petroller rolled himself a cigarette when he got home—understandably, he wasn't allowed to smoke on the job.
Continuing: how the petroller during a longer inhalation suddenly hears that his lovely, hardly seventeen year old daughter is ruined, because the manager's son K., that scoundrel, seduced her in the company restrooms but rejected her proposal of marriage. At that, Paul, the hero of the story, grinds out his cigarette, goes home and paints "To live means to live through!" in oil paint on the foot of his marriage bed, where he can read it each morning like new and can impress it upon his memory.
If at this point in the story Willi's listeners had nothing else to say but the quietly murmured phrase, that they had to go home, then he reached again into his left pocket, ladled seconds, and went on describing Paul's adventures.
The latter tears forth an old wool stocking from under the bed, shakes it out, and buys a twenty-two and one cartridge to go with it. With this one shot in his fist he lies in wait for that cad K. in front of a brothel, aims, pulls the trigger—rrumms!!—, throws the gun in the next garbage pail and disappears to finish his petroller's workday. Paul remains undiscovered, K. uninjured, life goes on.
By now it was dark. Now the bonbon eaters really did have to go, so Willi rounds off the story: "When he sees that it didn't accomplish anything, Paul thinks better of it and joins the Communist Party. And with that, children, let's call it enough for today!"
After he entrusted another periodical to the custody of the fire, he surrounded himself with silence for five minutes, smiling.
Willi's silence always said more to me than Hanne's swollen talk.
This quarter of an hour when Hohmann opened his heart ruthlessly to the coming generations—and for that heart, Communism was

merely the common denominator for untimely dreams and longings—these moments full of lawlessness and cowboy songs are among my fondest memories. When I returned later to the women's home for the aged, that sanctuary of the moderate, where I am the only novice of the Order of the Streaming Blood, I took *Don Quixote* down from the shelf and spent the time before getting tired in that limitless freedom that only uselessness provides.

The unions with Willi, in front of, on, over, under, and behind the park bench are some of my most impressive experiences. Hohmann, whose strength of will, which in the final analysis ends in illegalities, made me into a moaning cuddle-kitten, and I . . .

Toward a woman in menopause he was the epitome of understanding. When in spring he caught me between crocuses and "Prohibited!" signs with the park caretaker, he restricted his acts of violence to sitting mutely next to me on the bench next day and scratching "donna e mobile" in the gravel with his maple walking stick.

Hanne told me again yesterday how his wife, now passed on, always came to the construction site Fridays to cash in "before the pay was even in its envelope," and only gave him a fiver a week for pocket money. He couldn't even keep his hands still, till I finally rapped him on the fingers. This old bore just better not get any false hopes. Besides, I don't like it when a person speaks about other women in my presence. If you ask me, it's impolite.

Now I drag fifty-two years around with me like a deck of cards, but I'll live to be twice as old, and you won't know it to look at me. When I was twenty-six, I slapped the paperboy on the back in the stairwell, in my late thirties I visited the man on the metal-punch machine, at forty-four I cooked stew for Hieronymus in the house. Yes, I've been around, but I've never been anywhere again since I've come to the women's home. Here I have my rest.

By the way, I'd make a good catch: I'm the widow of the man who invented the double-muffed inter-crosspiece, which is so taken for granted today, but which back then was a revolutionizing improvement of the socket-bearinged swing-fraise.

Nothing will develop between Hanne and me. I grow lonesome, that's why I seek acquaintanceship through this no longer so unusual means; I roll these sheets together, shove them in the green belly of a vermouth bottle which I recork—hopefully with enough care—and then throw into the fountain at the park crossroads.

Where will the message come to land? Who will find it? Maybe a fanatic with glowing eyes, whose corduroy pants carry traces of paste from nocturnal placard-pasting, or a bearded, messy, stoic philosopher, plagued with scabies, who knows?

untitled by Reinhard Zabke oil

STEFAN KELLER

The Coal-Handler's Warmth

    he thumps me on the shoulder
has in front wet and
in back dry briquets standing
for increasingly loyal customers
    on his spotless floor
you could wed or with clear conscience
let the best of your infants
play.
    one time I came shortly
after closing time right into the middle
of the soapiest store where they
embarrassedly, cordially
waited on me,
the coal-handler and his wife.
    tomorrow, he says, tomorrow you get
even drier briquets, tomorrow
you get really dry briquets
from the new delivery. tomorrow
you get some of them, because today we're
taking them down off the truck,
he keeps thumping me on the shoulder.

Stefan Keller
Born 1958, grew up in Heimenhofen,
Switzerland. Studied at the University of
Constance in West Germany: German
literature, history, and philosophy. Since Fall
1978 in Berlin. Work on magazines and
newspapers. Has published articles and
poems.

die wärme, die der kohlenhändler gibt

    mir klopft er auf die schulter,
hat vorne nasse &
hinten trockene briketts stehen
für immer treuer werdende kundschaft.
    auf seinem peniblen fussboden
könntest du heiraten oder ruhig
den besten deiner säuglinge
spielen lassen.
    einmal kam ich kurz
nach geschäftsschluss & mittenhinein
in den seifigsten laden, wo sie mich
verlegen herzlich
bedienten dann,
der kohlenhändler & seine frau.
    morgen, sagt er, morgen kriegst du
noch trockenere briketts. morgen
kriegst du ganz trockene briketts
aus der neuen lieferung. morgen
kriegst du davon, weil wir sie heute
vom lastwagen runterholen,
    er klopft mir dauernd auf die achsel.

GERD BÖLTZ

landscapes

white wall with a thousand books
all full of wisdom, knowledge
linen bed with stain-sheets
ground away by the truth

I see lakes on it,
or islands,
nameless landscapes,
seas;
poorer than the moon,
full of promise

—as a child says:
"I've been in America;
—on the map"—

I go through and say to myself
—I was with you;
come look, my
—blessed isles—

Gerd Böltz
Born 1947 in Ravensburg. Studied philosophy, theology, languages. Much travel.

landschaften

weiße wand mit tausend büchern,
alle voller weisheit, wissen;
linnenbett mit fleckentüchern,
von der wahrheit ganz verschlissen.

ich sehe seen darauf,
oder inseln,
namenlose landschaften,
meere;
ärmer als der mond,
voller verheißung

—wie ein kind sagt:
'in amerika bin ich gewesen;
—auf der karte'—

gehe ich durch und sage mir:
—ich war bei dir,
komm schau, meine
—seligen inseln—

Peter Lackner
Born in Santa Barbara, California of Third Reich-refugee parents, spent his youth in both California and the German-speaking world. He studied creative writing and after winning a playwriting

PETER LACKNER

"Ick been ein Brrr leaner"
says this Santa Barbarian solemnly

> "When I go to bed at night,
> I try not to think of Berlin."
> —Dean Rusk

1
I sought my father's Fatherland
in literature and gallery
in histrionic memory
in young touristic odyssey
and found Berlin.
The cloven city tempted me.

In the parks of her broken heart
a gutted opera whispered an aria:
    "You are my fallen husband fallen son."
Hit right in my Teutonic Prussian Bureaucratic ancestry
I retorted in anti-operatic East Santa Barbara blues:
    "Mother Courage Father War,
    Ain't your soul a little sore?
    Mother Money Father State,
    Call your kiddies Fear and Hate—
      Widow, why did you let him go?"
On the strip of empty outlawed embassies,
craving the former capital splendor
of absolute respect at home and abroad,
Germania soothed her pain with silent rain,
made the unkempt earth between the grass-crowned marble
shells smell like the sacred Sierra—
on purpose, to give me home pangs.

award became the first Playwright Major at Pomona College, where two of his plays were produced. He switched to stage directing for his MA work at UC Santa Barbara, but continued writing plays, poetry, and music during professional theater work in San Francisco. Since 1975 he has been living in West Berlin, is creating a family, and working in many aspects of theater—from directing to dramaturgy to theater journalism.

Against a shrapnel-pocked pillar
leaned Lorelei
showed me her thigh
and said "You wanna buy?"
I was aflame: Here in the halls where they kissed Hitler's name?
International diplomacy has never known shame.

2
"Santa Barbara's a great place to live—
if you're an orange," I quoted decidedly
and planted myself in Berlin's stirring center.
Friendships became irrevocable,
the winters were a curiosity,
I met another Saint Barbara,
We bought landscapes of potted plants from Amsterdam,
grew closer than We thought We could trust,
gave birth to God's son,
I got paid for my art,
and couldn't complain,
although I bitterly tried.
In the traffic-rimmed playground
my son cooks with sand.
We buy clothing sewn in the surrounding enemy land
by the prisoner's hand.
We eat avocados from Israel and Spain
and make love in the parks in the summer rain.
But here the moon is surprisingly small;
We follow the birds in the Fall with our hearts.
The winters are colder and longer each year,
and sometime some storm will uproot us,
to bear us to blue roofs by the blue sea.

3
The martial plan rebuilds and polishes the walls of war.
Missing houses grow like second teeth
until the smile is full enough to greet parading presidents
   (the waving torsos of Carter and Schmidt
   on car-roof pedestal passing—
   one of unsuspecting life-like suppliant rubber,
   the other of tempered granite depicting friendly patience
   but fending off the assassin's bullet).
Only in the inner courtyards,
where the echoes of machine guns still rebound,
where landlords are too stingy/lazy,
the bullet scars and naked bricks still show
(those who live here still, still know).

4
Pimp Bismarck, alive and well behind all German desks,
(having successfully denied his bastard progeny)
busily organizes orgies in Madame Berlin's boudoirs.
The thoroughness that killed her now daily resuscitates:
As patron of the arts and crafts he drowns
Theater and Film and Business in over-generous indulgences.
Convulsive festivals, conventions lure the hungry outside eye:
"Wanna buy?
Wanna buy Madame Berlin?"
He displays her in a bell jar—
a naked heart dancing on tubes,
held with seducing firmness, felt and flagellated
by soldiers of four armies,
sprawling, drawn and quartered,
(divided she stands, united she falls)
ecstatic in surrender,
she thrives on her torture.
To free the fantasy of the beholder,
Pimp Bismarck veils her in borrowed arts of the world;
but beneath the finely-spun cultural flair
she frantically fumbles in folds of fat
to find her own natural form.
It is not there.
   But never underestimate an aging whore:
   this glory of Germany has beaten with passion before.
   Excellence pride ambition perfection completion
   were all that she found, became her absolute ends.
   She destroyed her true lover to love such foul friends:
   The passion of Beethoven without music.

Between orgies Mr. Bismarck and Madame Berlin peacefully stroll
through international affairs with modest elegance.
But in the guise of a gesture of gallantry and conscience
(altruistic arms sales),
in the semblance of helpless mediocrity
(so as not to frighten all mediocre governments),
he hears the dream growing in her heart.

5
The green and terrified policeman
afraid to frisk
holds his pistol at my eyes
holds my passport in his motorcycle hand
waits for the radio's hiss
to confirm that I am deadly.
When he says he is protecting me
whether guest or citizen
from terroristic anarchy
I laugh
he shoots
almost.

6
I bought my Berlin Barbara bedsheets
red white striped with pillowcase in starred blue
(for her heavenly head to be home in).
Our two ("anti-fascist leftist," mind you) apartment-mates
found this the height of treason
against the ideal state.
The one (now in the fourth semester of the first volume of Marx)
said he would never lie beneath the German colors
(even though Germany is only a "baby imperialist"),
so how could Barbara lay her body
beneath the symbol of the most evil imperialist aggressor
in the (dialectical) history of man- (and even animal-) kind.
The other (who never did his share of the dishes
because over-stressed in his Engels seminar)
said I was a perverse subverter and should not
live there any more.
So Barbara (with whom both men were in fact infatuated)
and I
left.

7
"Einstein's exile should have been a warning to us,"
says the Geman president extremely retrospectively.
Why Einstein? Why not any one of the millions?
A Jew lived in this room.
A Jewish family lived next door.
sometimes I imagine hearing hurried packing
or screams at the sound of boots;
would I have stopped the soldiers on the stairs?
I would probably have also locked my door quietly
and listened
with that tinge of thankfulness
as they left
left one room emptier
left one apartment emptier
left one building emptier
left one neighborhood emptier
left this unhappy hunted ground emptier.

But no matter—the neighborhoods are teeming once again:
Turks and Pakistanis climb from their shipwrecked cultures
onto this island of plenty,
gather up the crushed hopes of the civilized,
scrub the Mercedes of the merciful,
propagate in utter and dire thankfulness.
Dark children crowd the corners of bomb-torn blocks,
wait in subway ghettos,
lose their souls in the slots of the peep-show,
finally fuck for the needle.
This is their only home,
which they can only leave
to join the Jews who have been invited
to sit cross-legged with the Chumash Indians,
to dine on acorn mush under live oaks
on fields of clouds.

8
Widows, wings still linked in post-war chatter
(ceaseless since you met in bucket brigades to clear the rubble)
permanently dyed and curled for one another's eyes alone
beneath the headwear which signalled reprosperity
(curled phoenix frozen in awakening),
peck at the news, swirl at the bus-stop with the pigeons.
One says to me, "You look just like my fallen husband."

Then or now? You, who flock towards the end of life alone,
Widows, why did you let them go?
Your hats still look like helmets.

9
Berliners ask why I,
whose feet cannot forget the Channel sand,
who has Camino Cielo in his eyes,
remain upon this island in a crimson sea.
My various answers, depending on the weather:
    —the unemployment office has a heated waiting room
    full of friendly Turks and other new Jews; we keep
    each other company in empty honesty, agreeing that
    work is an insult to human dignity.
    –I want to keep the Neo-Nazis down.
    —despite creepy crawly communistic war games which
    rumble all around the Wall, it's safer here than
    too near Vandenberg Air Force Base, thanks.
    —McDonald's has just opened four restaurants here (better
    late than never.)
    —I came here to forgive the Germans: it's taking longer
    than I thought.
    —I guess I'm here because of wife and family.
    —the Wall restrains unbridled circumstance, the flood
    beyond the politician's thumb. Carter may have been
    officially depressed by its sight (although just for him
    they had painted it white in the night),
    but I am officially comforted by such substantial being,
    for most walls are more imposing in invisibility.
    —Berlin doesn't have earthquakes and is the convenient size
    of the blast of one neutron bomb. Not with a whimper,
        please!
    —Oh, Santa B.
    —The U.F.O.'s don't seem interested in Berlin.

III INTERIORS

Tillye Boesche-Zacharow
How should I write the resumé of a half-century on the narrow shoulders of a woman? What for? The artist retreats behind his work. God too retreats into or behind his creation. Read what I write: novels, books about religion and emancipation, children's

TILLYE

It was Your Coldness

that made of me
an iceberg
on which you
shipwrecked.

It was your hardness
that honed me
to become the knife
with which I
want to kill you.

Change of Life

Cold stabs your skin
and you know it's far below zero.
But inside all Hell is burning,
burning youth to ashes.
Changing—you shed your skin like a snake
and ask—how long
can this go on?
Making love: no more fears
like those that for twenty years,
like voyeurs, inhibited your orgasm.
Now the snow melts at last
in the fiery carnage of organs.
Your pumping blood sings in your ears:
Taste at last Desire and Deception
and forget the truth:
you are old!

books; read my poetry, grown of my own pain, joy, and experience. Read my magazine *Silhouette*, where I let others as well as myself express themselves. Who cares who or what I am? A mortal with the hope that her "works" will live a little longer.

BOESCHE-ZACHAROW

Deine Kälte war es,

die aus mir
einen Eisblock machte,
an dem du
Schiffbruch erlittest.

Deine Härte war es,
die mich schliff,
daß ich zum Messer ward,
mit dem ich
dich töten möchte.

Wechseljahre

Man spürt auf der Haut die Kälte stechen
und weiß, es sind viel Grade unter Null.
Doch tief drinnen heizt ein Höllenfeuer,
indem die Jugend Asche wird.
Man wechselt—häutet sich wie eine Schlange
und fragt—wie lange
soll der Zustand gehn?
Beim Lieben spürt man keine Ängste
wie die, die zwanzig Jahre lang
als Voyeure den Orgasmus hemmten.
Erst jetzt zerschmilzt der Schnee
im feuerigen Gemetzel der Organe.
Der Blutkreislauf summt in den Ohren:
Genieße endlich Lust und Lüge
und vergiß die Wahrheit:
du bist alt!

Karl Mickel was born in 1935. He has lived in Dresden, and now in East Berlin. He is a devotee of cigars, red wine, music, bicycles, and reading. He has been guest lecturer in University courses on the German literary inheritance.

In addition to publications in periodicals, some of Karl Mickel's important works include:

KARL MICKEL

Summer in Petzow

Fence under hesitant steps, lathework dried to kindling,
Toneless it crumbles, sole squeaks on wood.
Here was the chain, now rust. Glowing sand! and the wind lays
Free the enameled sign: Beware of the dog!
Branchwork stretched in wind, fruit-catapulting bows.
Under the burst tree the mouth, reclining, grasps
Cherries; cherry-flesh stained, my girl's blouse flutters
Above us, mold of the air, banner, trophy of victory.
Voices blown in from afar. Slurping steps; a farmer
Mutters between pipe and teeth: steal all you can.

Linden Forum

Yellow foliage, on twigs not caught
In highest closeness suspended on bough and branch
So saturated is the air with rain
The air so still that the linden's bodies
Quiet word's breath, thought's breathing
Undresses. I dare not think

Vita Nova Mea 1966, Aufbau, poems.
Einstein—Nausikaa, Die Schrecken des Humanismus in Drei Stücke (Einstein—Nausikaa, The Horrors of Humanism in Three Plays) 1974, Rotbuch Verlag.
Eisenzeit (Iron Age) 1976, Rotbuch, poems.
Gelehrtenrepublik (Republic of Scholars) 1976, Mitteldeutscher Verlag, essays.
Odysseus in Ithaka, 1976, Reclam, poems.

Petzower Sommer

Latten, zu Zunder gedörrt, Zaun unter zögernden Schritten:
Lautlos zerfällt er, es knirscht zwischen Sohle und Holz.
Hier war die Kette, jetzt Rost. Glühender Sand! und es legt der
Wind das Emailleschild frei: Vorsicht! Bissiger Hund.
Astwerk im Winde gespannt, früchteschleudernde Bögen.
Unter geborstenem Baum greift im Liegen der Mund
Kirschen, von Kirschfleisch gefleckt flattert die Bluse der Freundin
Über uns, Hohlform der Luft, Fahne, Trophäe des Siegs.
Stimmen von weit her geweht. Schlurfende Schritte, ein Bauer
Knurrt zwischen Pfeife und Zahn: Stehlt soviel ihr nur könnt.

Lindenforum

Gelbes Laub, den Zweigen nicht verhaftet
In höchster Nähe schwebt an Ast und Ästlein
So gesättigt ist die Luft mit Regen
Die Luft so stille, daß der Linden Leiber
Leisen Wortes Hauch, Gedankens Atem
Entkleidete. Ich wage nicht zu denken

Orderly Hair

I take a long time before taking the bait
Especially with you. Is it because of your hair, that's so
Damned orderly, not an independent strand,
So that I suspect you sleep motionlessly?

And your friendliness gives me the creeps now
That can't work out in the long run, I think
And increase for my part the compliments so much
That insincerity reigns and routine begins

And that's wrong. For if it's because of your hair
That you routinely keep in order, then it requires
The coarse grip, that suddenly spontaneously grasps
Not for the hair—that loosens up by itself then.

So much for the plan. To calculate calculatedness:
I don't like to think about it, but too often do.

Korrektes Haar

Ich brauche immer lange, eh ich anbeiß
Bei dir besonders. Liegts am Haar, das so
Verflucht korrekt ist, keine Strähne selbständig
Das ich vermut, du schläfst bewegungslos?

Auch wird mir deine Freundlichkeit jetzt unheimlich
Das kann nicht gutgehn auf die Dauer, denk ich
Und steigre meinerseits die Komplimente derart
Daß Unernst vorherrscht und Routine aufkommt

Und das ist falsch. Denn wenns an deinem Haar liegt
Das du dir ordnest mit Routine, brauchts
Den derben Griff, der plötzlich planlos zugreift:
Nicht nach dem Haar, das löst sich dann von selber.

So weit der Plan. Berechnendes berechnen:
Ich denk nicht gern dran, aber leider oft.

Beer: for Leising

Neither talkative, nor much for letter writing are you, Richard,
I like to support two elbows on the table
And think it's four. What's come between
Us? Beer. Helga! two more tall ones

White flowers on tawny stalks.
What do I do? You say, I hint
At, I say. The truly wise
When they say something, they say: well maybe.

I know a woman, by hearsay
But sworn to: thirty, nine years on the assembly line
Wherever she goes or lies her arms jerk
She runs to the psychiatrist, for she wishes

To quit. The wish, she complains, is sickly.
He who has ears to see will taste.

Bier. Für Leising

Maulfaul, schreibfaul bist du, Richard, gern
Stemm ich aufn Tisch zwei Ellenbogen
Und denke, es sind viere. Was steht zwischen
Uns? Bier. Helga! noch zwei große

Weiße Blumen auf dem gelben Stiel.
Was tue ich? sagst du, ich deute
An, sag ich. Die Wirklichweisen
Wenn die was sagen, sagen die: Naja

Ich kenne eine Frau, vom Hörensagen
Aber verbürgt: dreißig, neun Jahre am Fließband
Der zucken, wo sie geht und liegt, die Arme
Die läuft zum Psychiater, denn sie wünscht

Zu kündigen. Der Wunsch, klagt sie, sei krankhaft.
Wer Ohren hat zu sehen der wird schmecken.

The Modern Quarter

My hat it has four corners, four-
Cornered is the area here
Every house eight edges and four corners
No one can hide
I saw a woman with an angular behind
She came from an angular nursery school with angular kids
Because the surroundings form the people
Everything is normed
In the usual sizes
Four-cornered pussies
The men draw their consequences too
Exemplary spouses with square cocks
Parallel movements
The right angle as the standard of impulse

German Woman '46

Where's the fun if it's no fun!
Said my Otto, there was a wild fellow.
When we were in the woods, he spoke to the trees:
I'll hack you all to cribs!
For he was a carpenter, unemployed, communist
And lived in the kitchen with his parents.
If you get knocked up, then out you go!
Said my worthy mother, when Otto came to pick me up.
Then Hitler. Otto said: that one'll make war.
Then it was no child again, for the butcher's counter
I wanted none; he wanted a daughter.
Then came war, Otto in the penal battalion
Captured by the Russians, anti-fascism school
Now he comes home, with me it's too late.

Neubauviertel

Mein Hut der hat vier Ecken, vier-
Eckig ist die Gegend hier
Jedes Haus acht Kanten und vier Ecken
Keiner kann sich verstecken
Ich sah eine Frau mit eckigem Hintern
Die kam aus der eckigen Krippe mit eckigen Kindern
Weil die Umwelt den Menschen formt
Ist alles genormt
In den üblichen Größen
Viereckige Mösen
Die Männer ziehn auch ihre Konsequenzen
Mustergatten mit eckigen Schwänzen
Parallele Bewegungen
Der rechte Winkel das Eichmaß der Regungen

Deutsche Frau 46

Spaß muß es machen, sonst machts keinen Spaß!
Sagte mein Otto, 's war ein toller Bursche.
Wenn wir im Wald warn, sprach er zu den Bäumen:
Euch hack ich alle klein zu Kinderbetten!
Denn er war Tischler, arbeitslos, Kommune
Und wohnte in der Küche bei den Eltern.
Wenn du 'n Bauch kriegst, gehst du!
Sagte die Gnädige, als Otto mich abholte.
Dann Hitler. Otto sagte: der macht Krieg.
Da wars wieder kein Kind, für die Fleischbank
Wollte ich keins, er wollte eine Tochter.
Dann war der Krieg, Otto im Strafbataillon
Gefangen bei den Russen, Antifaschule
Jetzt kommt er heim, bei mir hat's aufgehört.

Dresden Houses

Strange incline! the houses stand as if
Nothing had happened here, as if the masonry
Were attacked by wind and rain, as if
Only hail had smashed in windows.
The beautifully-cut rooms! there decay
Stems, it seems, from uninhibited
Growth of wild cherries in the first floor
Slowly, it seems, the residents
Restricted themselves, until at last only one room
Remained with a view to the river.
So there is such a thing!
                         I want to say: darling
This house is peaceful, if I had it I'd have peace
I need peace, thus I must have it.
I'll do what brings money.
                       They who lived here
Amid great industry, noble
Nature, the city at their feet, set in motion
Death's assembly line: pale urchins,
Investment counsellors, bloodthirsty with age, whores
Missing teeth at twenty-five, hunchbacks
In secure bunkers, gone westward, before
Stone and flesh in horrible ranges
Burned together toward the city.

The new life doesn't blossom out of the ruins
There blossom weeds. Weeds
Must go, before the new can come: no tree
Is taller than a man, where late hurry
Put living space, barren houses, without charm
One as the other, in bright colors, with thin
Walls, low ceilings, bathroom
Untiled, good that they're there
And appropriate to the budget, after all
Because the arguments with the landladies are thus
Nonviolently hindered. Because I love peace
I say to this building-style: Yes. The New

Is there such a thing? Peace in this place? Darling, we,
Busy on the upholstery
Feel something like peace between two
Heartbeats, yet the heartbeat of
Two bodies must be the same, that is seldom
And when it is, one knows, it doesn't last.

Dresdner Häuser

Seltsamer Hang! die Häuser stehn, als sei
Hier nichts geschehn, als sei das Mauerwerk
Von Wind und Regen angegriffen, als
Hab nur Hagel Fenster eingeschlagen.
Die schöngeschnittnen Räume! ihr Verfall
Rührt, scheint es, vom ungehemmten
Wachstum wilder Kirschen im Parterre
Langsam, scheint es, haben die Bewohner
Sich eingeschränkt, um endlich nur ein Zimmer
Noch einzunehmen mit dem Blick zum Fluß.
Das also gibt es!
           Sagen will ich: Freundin
Dies Haus ist ruhig, hätt ichs hätt ich Ruhe
Ruhe brauch ich, also muß ichs haben
Ich mach was Geld bringt.
                       Die hier wohnten
Inmitten großer Industrie, erhabener
Natur, die Stadt zu Füßen, setzten in Gang
Des Todes Fließband: welke Lausejungen
Kommerzienräte, mordgeil vor Alter, Nutten
Zahnarm mit fünfundzwanzig, Buckelköpfe
In sichern Bunkern, westwärts weg, bevor
Gestein und Fleisch zu schrecklichen Gebirgen
Zusammenglühten stadtwärts.

Das Neue Leben blüht nicht aus Ruinen
Da blüht Unkraut. Unkraut
Muß weg, eh Neues hin kann: kein Baum
Ist mehr als mannshoch, wo späte Eile
Wohnraum hinsetzt, kahle Häuser, reizlos
Eins wie's andre, buntgemalt, mit dünnen
Wänden, niedern Zimmern, Bad
Ungekachelt, schön, daß sie da sind
Und angemessen dem Finanzplan, schließlich
Weil sie den Krach mit den Vermieterinnen
Gewaltlos hindern. Weil ich Ruhe liebe
Sag ich zu dieser Bauart: Ja. Das Neue.

Gibts das: Ruhe hierorts? Freundin, wir
Beschäftigt auf den Polstermöbeln emp-
Finden was wie Ruhe zwischen zwei
Herzschlägen, doch muß der Herzschlag
Zweier Leiber gleich sein, das ist selten
Und wenn es ist, weiß man, es bleibt nicht.

Peaceful the pauses between the hasty
Thumping steps when the shift worker
From next door goes through the open entranceway:
A peaceful man: his sons yell
Me awake nights, count 'em two, the wife
Makes a delicate impression, the hands
Red: the diapers. Daily she carries
The shopping net three floors up, drags up
Coal winters.
        That is the peace:
Time between lightning and thunder, unrest has holes
Duty doesn't get through before leisure becomes duty.

Before better times come bad winters
Rubble on the rubble: snow, one smashes
With muscle power to free electric machinery
Frost in the coal, frost must battle frost
Trouble in the power station, the little children heat
The sickrooms with their fever
Like next door.
        Then the ice breaks up:
Breathe free, I think, now the neighbor can
Catch up if he must. He is a correspondence student
Black his lids, I see him sitting
Early at books, sleeplessly blindly leafing
His wife plays around, what else can she do, she says:

"In fields of thistles we got to know each other
And bent backs, our ally
We helped, so that the harvest
Came in that he sells us.
As our bite went through that hard bread
We came through! We'd promised it
Ourselves and everyone, that was a hard bread.
Not to go on our knees! The first at the goal line!
The time came for the kiss, the air was dry
Dust in his mouth, he said:
                the grave won't first
heal our backs, if we live!
I don't give up, how else shall I live?

That death's body isn't ours
Which lies ready for us, through thin walls
Giving cold, onto the marriage bed's (he spoke)
Tomb, the Janus-head of our con-
Temporary future: you saw him yesterday
Eating in public, the wife at the flesh
She bites in what's dead, only, her teeth

Ruhig sind die Pausen in den hastig
Polternden Schritten, wenn der Schichtarbeiter
Von nebenan zur offnen Haustür geht:
Ein ruhiger Mann: seine Söhne brüllen
Mich nächtens wach, zwei an der Zahl, die Frau
Macht einen zarten Eindruck, die Hände
Rot: die Windeln. Täglich trägt sie
Drei Treppen hoch die Einkaufnetze, schleppt
Winters Kohlen.
          Das ist die Ruhe:
Zeit zwischen Blitz und Donner, Unrast hat Löcher
Pflicht geht nicht durch, eh Muße Pflicht wird.

Vor bessern Zeiten kommen schlimme Winter
Abraum auf dem Abraum: Schnee, man schlägt
Mit Muskelkraft Elektrobagger frei
Frost in der Kohle, Frost muß Frost bekämpfen
Im Krafthaus Havarie, die Kindlein heizen
Mit ihrem Fieber ihre Krankenzimmer
Wie nebenan.
              Sodann das Eis bricht auf:
Aufatmen, denk ich, kann der Nachbar jetzt
Aufholen muß er. Er ist Fernstudent
Schwarz seine Lider, ich seh ihn sitzen
Früh an Büchern, schlaflos blicklos blättern
Die Frau geht fremd, was bleibt ihr, sie sagte:

"Auf Disteläckern wir lernten uns kennen
Und krumme Rücken, dem Bündnispartner
Halfen wir, daß er die Ernte
Einbringt, die er uns verkauft.
Wie unser Biß das harte Brot durchdringt
Wir dringen durch! wir hattens versprochen
Uns und allen, da wars hartes Brot.
Nicht in die Knie gehn! Erste sein am Rain!
Daß Zeit ist für den Kuß, die Luft war trocken
Staub im Mund, er sprach:
                      Nicht erst das Grab
Soll, wenn wir leben, Buckel heilen!
Ich geb nicht auf, wie leb ich sonst?

Jenes Todes Leib sei nicht der unsre
Der uns bereitliegt, durch die dünnen Wände
Kälte spendend, auf des Ehbetts (sprach er)
Katafalk, der Januskopf des Zeit-
Genossen Zukunft: Du sahst ihn gestern
Öffentlich essen, die Frau vorm Fleisch
Die beißt in Totes, nur noch, ihre Zähne

Laboriously retained, chewed representatively
That which called itself her husband, unfeeling he sat, and
I saw myself sitting in his place
You at hers, the walls grew
Inward, if I stretched my arm
I bumped into cupboards, upholstered, less
Air was in the room than has place in my lungs
I wanted to scream, it was a rattle, you listened
to it . . ."

That's what he said, she to me, I to you. The eyes
Deaden, occasionally the glance
Reaches the ends of the lashes, stiff spears
Aimed where? The body, as if on cords,
Moves, still, in the breath of air the tree
Produces, into which they are knotted.

Where am I? who? "The Poet's Song be cheerful!"
Spoke the man to wife and correspondence student
"Not such tones, friend! Your voice
Should build up something where nothing was, tear down
Forest, draw up forests of chimneys
In less time than a branch grows

Root thick treework in the cities
On cellars, levelled by a war
With stone and flesh and splinters of iron, and
Spread out street nets where the fisher
Spread fish nets, bridges over swamps
Spanning, and let ears grow twain
Where one grew, irrigate and drain
Subdue nature to us, we'll learn of course
To behave: that's work, of all
Pleasures the first, noblest, of goals
The utmost goal, inexhaustible as love!"

I myself want to be a house, if I die
Stone through and through that, unfeeling, rejects
The frost coals storm, rejects them for you.
Willingly I draw your storms outward
In me a heart will beat like thunder
Razes forestings, a window lies open
With your coals I'll heat the city
As soon as you grow cold, I'll frost the continent.
Who penetrates into me, will break his neck
Before he harms you, on the stairway
The little children change above my roof ridge
Weightless

Mühvoll erhalten, kauten stellvertretend
Was sich Ihr Mann nennt, fühllos saß er, und
Mich sah ich sitzen an seiner Stelle
Dich an der ihren, die Wände wuchsen
Einwärts, streckte ich den Arm
Stieß er an Schränke, stoffgepolstert, weniger
Luft war im Raum, als die Lungen faßten
Brüllen wollt ich, Röcheln war's, du hörtests
An..."

Das sagte er, sie mir, ich dir. Die Augen
Stumpfen ab, gelegentlich erreicht
Der Blick die Wimpern Spitzen, starre Speere
Gezielt wohin? Der Körper wie an Stricken
Bewegt sich, noch, im Lufthauch, den der Baum
Erzeugt, in den sie eingeknotet sind.

Wo bin ich? wer? "Des Dichters Lied sei heiter!"
Sprach der Mann der Frau und Fernstudent
"Nicht diese Töne, Freunde! Eure Stimme
Soll hinbaun was, wo vorher nichts war, Wald
Niederreißen, Schornsteinwälder hochziehn
In kürzern Zeiten als ein Ästlein wächst

Einwurzeln dichtes Baumwerk in den Städten
Auf Kellern, die ein Krieg geebnet hatte
Mit Stein und Fleisch und Eisensplittern, und
Auswerfen Straßennetze, wo der Fischer
Fischnetze auswarf, Brücken übern Sumpf
Verspannen, und zwei Ähren wachsen lassen
Wo eine wuchs, bewässern und entwässern
Natur uns unterwerfen, uns natürlich
Benehmen lernen: das ist Arbeit, aller
Genüsse erster, edelster, der Ziele
Äußerstes Ziel, wie Liebe unerschöpflich!"

Ich selber will ein Haus sein, sterbe ich
Stein durch und durch, der Frost Glut Sturm
Unfühlend abweist, weist sie für euch ab.
Nach außen leit ich eure Stürme willig
In mir ein Herz wird schlagen wie der Donner
Waldungen stürzen, fliegt ein Fenster auf
Mit euren Gluten heize ich die Stadt
Sobald euch friert, den Kontinent vereis ich.
Wer in mich eindringt, bricht sich das Genick
Bevor er euch behelligt, auf der Treppe
Die Kindlein über meinen Dachfirst wandeln
Schwerelos

GERD SPRINGBORN

Our landlord schlepps the pails
Crashes the vases in the rubbish
Raises the spade with his arm
That towers, I see only the hand,
Like one of those roly-poly dolls that pop back up
Again and again above the window sill
Then the steel crashes in shards
Quaking the metal sides
Slams the lid
The echo reverberatesratesrates
Through our courtyard
Then the landlord appears again
Half going on his knees with every step
An older man
He rocks his whole body along
And glances sullenly up into the round of buildings
To the windows of HIS tenants.

Gerd Springborn
Born 1936. Teacher of English in Berlin. Always been writing—always been too shy to publish, always at a loss for time (wife, 3 children)—but not complaining.

Unser Hauswart schleppt die Eimer
Kracht die Vasen in den Müll
Hebt den Spaten mit dem Arm
Der ragt, ich sehe nur die Hand,
Wie ein Stehaufmann immer wieder mal über die Brüstung
Dann kracht der Stahl in Scherben
Scheppert an der Blechwand
Kanallt den Deckel
Reverberiertriertriert das Echo
Durch unseren Hof
Da erscheint der Hauswart wieder
Halb sinkt er in die Knie bei jedem Schritt
Ein älterer Mann
Den ganzen Körper wippt er mit
Und mürrisch blickt er auf ins Rund der Häuser
Zu den Fenstern der Seinen, der Mieter.

Das Gute	The Good
Ich ging einmal spazieren	Once I went for a walk
In einem schönen Wald	In a beautiful forest
Und kam zu einer kleinen,	And came to a little,
Kleinen Hütte bald.	Little cabin soon.
In dieser Hütte wohnte	In this hut dwelt
Ein Jüngling hübsch und fein	A youth handsome and fine
Er saß auf einem Stühle	He sat upon a chair
Und trank den gold'nen Wein.	And drank the golden wine.
Der Wein war nur von Wahrheit	The wine was all of Truth
Den dieser Junker trank	That this squire drank
Denn neb'n ihm saß ein Vogel	For next to him sat a bird
Der nur das Gute sang.	Who sang only of the Good.
Vor ihm lag eine Blume	Before him lay a flower
Sie war so wunderschön	It was so wond'rous fair
So daß ich dacht' ich dachte	So that I thought I thought
Das Wunderbarste jetzt zu seh'n.	The most wond'rous now to see.
Sie war aus Gott geboren	It was born out of God
So rein und wunderbar	So pure and wonderful
Sie war die blaue Blume	It was the blue flower
Die schuld am Glücke war	That was the cause of happiness.

That was 1945. Or was it 1946? It was summer, and we sat in a field of blueberries, in the afternoon-summer sun, at the edge of the woods, under the fir, on a cliff-edge the other side of "Wartberg" at Gräfenreuth "in Bavaria" or "Upper Franconia," Post Guide Number 132. (as it can be read from old envelopes. You circled the Post Guide Number. Bavaria was the Third Reich's Territory, its north: a) its south: b) and an efficient Postal Service had thought up this first Postal Code System in the time of one who called himself Führer. His picture sticks above the addresses, with moustache and fateful brow. A look, so serious and heavy and seemingly knowing, and frightening, full of obstinate resolution, so I say now.)
We sat in a field of blueberries, on a sunny summer Sunday afternoon. We'd brought along the milk can of formed and pressed sheet aluminum and everyone picked berries. But I lay down apart in the fragrant thin branches with pointed oval thin lightly-patterned light green leaves and wrote on a little poem. I believe it was my first.
With other verselets I recorded it as conscientiously and cleanly as I could into a little notebook, blue-lined yellowish paper, made only from wood from German forests, a coarse dark gray packing paper as cover (the inside of this cover a rugged landscape in slanting light:

particles, pieces, fibers. They spotted the first and last sheets of writing paper yellow)—without label, barely fastened together with a single zinc-plated paper clip.

In summer '44, in Bavaria, Upper Franconia, in the village, in a village society that until then had known no strangers, they spoke in a way that we couldn't understand, excepting a little:

"Berliner Big Mouths," called Emil Bergmann to us as he came past the courtyard on the coachman's seat of a horse-wagon, one with rubber tires, the only one in the village (for oxen and cows pulled plows and wagons—the cows for the poor, the oxen for the average farmers).

He cracked his whip. What had he meant. Mother knew. Not us, at bottom.

"Laß das gehn—Let that go," said the farmer-woman, the pale woman who went about quietly, always in a black dress. We stood, gaped. "Laß das gehn?"

She didn't want us rattling the iron parts, gears, pieces of field equipment, blade of a cart-plow, plough-handle, chains, rollers. Next to the wall of the neighbors' tract, in the high weeds, behind the house, always in shade, the implements rusted and were worthless. We obeyed: because we felt what was meant. Thus we learned the dialect. She left. We climbed over the little wall into a narrow, dark passageway between the yards, just a hair wider than our shoulders. Blackish slate plates, flaking sheets, fallen from the roofs, blanketed the passage and the ground. From cracks grew maple plants, broad little leaf-screens. Later we dug at the bent stems, loosened the roots out of the moist black grit and planted little trees on the meadow behind the wood piles, right under the barbed wire. They sprouted until the farmer came with the scythe.

We found old nails under the slate tiles, still square, hand-smithed, and I flattened one, and filed it sharp, till it was a little knife. Iron pieces, old coins, lay in the debris in our passageway.

What we understood: That they threw stones at us in "Lower Village" by the pond, at the edge of the village. What had we done? We were the ones that they didn't know. And if we threw back, if we were strong, then they'd be our friends. We didn't know that yet. We didn't know how to throw far and on target. They threw; a stone hit; so I threw too, and saw with despair how my stone fell to the ground, halfway there, spent. What were they shouting? We shouted "Liram larum Löffelstiel," because we couldn't think of anything better. We covered our retreat with our weak throws and tried not to let ourselves be seen there again. At our place in "Upper Village," behind the house up the hill, and over in the forest, there we met no one.

I went to school, just me, I was old enough. I went to the old schoolhouse, down in "Mid Village," the tumbledown building with

the hiproof, yellowish-red. The color peeled from the facing, leaving a dappled pattern. One classroom on the second floor, just one. We sat, first, second, third, all, up to the eighth grade, on the rough wood benches, grooved with heavy graining and much scrubbing, notched, cracked, stained, the light ochre fir-wood, the ink wells set in the writing slabs.
I sat all the way in the front, second grade, at the mercy of the teacher's eyes. Further back, on the right, by the window, the older girls:
Irmgard Ploss, the big, plump, with heavy black braids, with pout-lips, who always acted pliable. The teacher screamed when she forgot the Umlaut over the "o". " 'Plotzlich!' In the seventh grade you must know that it's 'plötzlich!' "
Back there on the right sat Irma Heinrich too. What a name, Irma, never heard it before. What a girl: ash-blond, so finely curled this hair, like a lovely wreath framing the brow, which looked so pure. The nose, this mouth seemed so sweetly, so tenderly fashioned. She was a noble soul for sure. I revered her. I often looked around stealthily over my shoulder when she spoke, softly and confidently. How did she speak?
I had to hear and see. I listened close and followed the play of her facial expressions. With glances I hoped to signal her: Give a sign; show that you see me, that you maybe like me. I'll get bigger, and the difference will get small.
I spoke with her only one or two times, and the hope that I could finally move her clenched my throat. She spoke softly, very restrained, she laughed, at me too, she laughed yes at me, yes good-naturedly. She never gave the sign. How her forehead wrinkled up when she pondered something!
But the yard where she lived, the farmyard of her father, of that big, silent man, was a mystical complex for me. I never went by it without piercing the high windowless weathered-gray planked wall of this barn-fortress, the little twinkling windows of this gable, this whitewashed wall behind the confused apple trees, with my glance. A look through the gate, and the doors. No, it didn't work. A huge dung heap was in the yard, and a dovecote, the biggest, most beautiful I'd seen, high on a green-painted pole, with many holes for flying in and out. Doves cooed. My dove never cooed, not for me.
The teacher didn't live in the schoolhouse, not even in Germany. Of course at that time it was all part of this "Greater German Reich." He came from over there, over the hill from the "Sudeten District," across the border marked only by mossy stones, deep in the forest. (When gathering mushrooms we played, "I'm a German, you're a Czech.")
Sometimes the teacher passed by me when he rolled mornings

through the gravel and the rain-rills of our village road, downhill already, while I still hurried on foot (even as a schoolboy I was usually in a big hurry mornings, no matter how much Mother urged.)
He came on his dark blue and aquamarine bike, as fine as today a Mercedes, his arms stiffly stretched to the handlebars. He rode on this very particular bike, with flashing spokes, the lamp and rims chrome-plated; the front fork arched like a sickle for springiness. He always eyed disapprovingly down through sharp glasses at me when I saw him. Usually it was five to eight, and I needed five minutes for my way.
I must have come at the right time once in awhile because I can remember: when he entered, we stood up as one man and answered devotedly, united, "Heil Hitler."
For some it was like a solemn vow every morning to call "Heil" to this Hitler, or to themselves, in the name of the death-idol, when the gleaming-eyed principal, looking straight forward, stalwartly rattled the signal. As "To the colors!" or "For Germany" Willi Lauterbach may have understood it, that big blond with the sassy nose and the loose mouth, his similar brother, the sinister-looking Helmut Krauthahn, and the other wild ones, also most of the older girls, who had already taken on something motherly, and something of the subservience that seemed predestined for woman.
Hitler, that distant idol: for me he floated vaguely somewhere. I didn't know him. But this teacher tried to teach us Hitler. He had accustomed himself to this fleshy bugaboo—"Then the Führer tore out a pistol; the Bürgerbräukeller was overfilled; he had to get the attention of the people; there were many speakers. Thrice he shot into the ceiling." I too listened with interest. He continued. "Shot into the ceiling?" I asked. "Yes, what do you think, otherwise no one would have heard him. There were Communists, Socialists, a lot of scum, and they all spoke against each other. Then the people listened in his direction, and then the Führer began to speak."
We learned the "Horst-Wessel-Lied"; we heard how the loyal, blue-eyed one was treacherously shot down: martyr-mythos. We sang, "Es zittern die morschen Knochen"—"The weak bones tremble"—"Es dröhnet der Marsch der Kolonne"—"The march of the column drones." We saw films about the struggle of the brave Frisians against the North Sea. Nordsee—Mordsee. How they won land, how the small island went under—and mountain climbers climbed the vertical rock face with rope and light rubber-soled shoes. Why? Was that possible? I asked father.
The teacher ruled over me too. He held my hand so I couldn't pull it away and lashed three, four times, cracking with the thin stick on the hand and occasionally on the upper side of the fingers. Once he hit me because I didn't have the required steel nib, "Cito fein," in my

pen. But there weren't any. Mother had asked in the city, in many shops. To say that: An affront to him. Lies. "They are too to be had, one must keep asking." For me, a burning injustice, which I never forgot.

To lessen the burden of fear, I arrived at the superstitious notion that a pair of hose helped: If I wore these long woollen light gray ones I was apparently immune.

At recesses, he ceremoniously unpacked his sandwich from its vellum wrapper, ate publicly. We swarmed around the house and the restrooms, the cramped brick masonry under the crannied wood construction of the little gables still in the style of Wilhelm, the former Kaiser. The pissoir stank atrociously of ammonia. Yellow crusts. Almost always I stifled my need. And besides, to stand next to the others and pee? They'd laugh.

Years later there was a crowd of young men, when the half-finished playground of the Gräfenreuth Lawn Sports Association was opened with beer and whoop-ti-do. What was it? They surrounded an older man with silvery hair, with a roundish face, with glasses, who softly but determinedly, defensively answered. He instructed now in the city. He had become a democrat for sure. They liked him. They were so much like him, only younger.

A notebook (yellow wood-paper, dark gray grainy cover):

Our Birds

10X!

The lark trills. The starling whistles. The thrush *floots*. The swallow twitters. The wag-tail flips its tail about. The sparrow eats with the *chichens*. The crow caws. The woodpecker knocks. The wild pigeon coos. The jay screams. The wild duck swims. The *falkon* hunts. The hawk screams. The stork wades . . .

He had corrected everything, earlier dictations too. Date: 28.3.45. The next date is the 14.1.46, and everything that follows is written with mere pencil.

What lay between:

The end of a war. The end of the regime. A beginning.

"Refugees" came as harbingers, also from the next city, on the other side of the denied border, where we had often shopped. (We walked from store to store. Mother carried the 20 pounds of potatoes —potatoes from the city to the village—the bread, the cauliflower, whose taste I can remember, all in the rucksack, through the forest, along the field roads, the mountain. My brother and I alternated carrying the head of cabbage. The cauliflower—when I got tired of carrying it, I just rolled it down the hill.) Out of the "Sudeten District" and out of Silesia they came to us. We ourselves were "Evacuees." They were stuffed in unused rooms, in the attic. If one gave to them, then as to moochers. Family Bartsch with seven fresh, snot-nosed, louse-ridden children ("In Silesya lice ain't no sin") were put in the ground floor of the schoolhouse, the Schmidts in a back room on the second floor, father, mother, two daughters. Irmgard Schmidt, ach, Irmgard: her broad-winged nose ran continuously, yellow and greenish, and she sniffed it up and wiped with her hand. Ratzers from Bohemia, thirteen kids, housed in the classroom and swarmed out like the devil, agile and supple, fighting with all the Silesians. A stovepipe stuck out of the window glass on the second floor—Frau Kranz, with audacious big sons, found a place with the neighbors. "At home we had everything," she asserted when she asked for a fever thermometer.

Then soldiers: Stayed two days. In the yard stood incredibly huge wooden tumbrils with spoked wheels. Through the cracks between the set-in side boards we espied yellow and green dried peas. The crates were filled with them, filled to the brim. We carefully poked a few forth. A pig ran squealing through the yard, stood an instant. Then an officer stretched his arm. A small, very sharp report. There lay the pig. I saw how it was brutally halved at the stall door.

April: We took in the family of the factory director. The little daughter especially liked the "chocolate soup"—rye mush. We roasted the kernels from picked ears (did we have a reserve supply? April?), milled them laboriously in the coffee grinder, "two mills daily," each child. The older daughter, Gerlinde, was my new crush. Black hair, like Snow-White's, the skin white as snow and red as roses.

On a late afternoon eveyone went in the cellar, under the narrow whitewashed rough stone vaults, in candlelight, the smell of moldy potatoes. But I had a last glimpse through living room window, and saw, down below on the spring-gray meadowed slopes, gray-brown clumps moving, khaki of the U.S. Army. They were tanks. I knew it. From the barrels burst white. One heard nothing.

We really heard nothing. I don't know, did we sleep in the cellar? On the next day it was down. Bedsheets hung out of the upper gable windows. Hitler's portraits had disappeared. Jeeps dashed through the village. Next to the cottage of the old village crier they sat on the moist grass, Americans, Amis. They ate bread, so white, so soft, that it was like cake. We looked, we saw, we saw only the bread, and would've liked just to taste a corner of these square pliant slices. They ate out of tins. The metal stayed where it lay. They smoked, one after the other, they puffed "Camels," they sprang in the Jeeps. Antennas swayed on the rears. We tagged along after, threw ourselves on the tinfoil with chewing gum.

Taste of Freedom? No, we smelled Power and hardly conceivable wealth: Oppressed beggar-children—Mother explained to us, we weren't allowed to sing these songs any more. We agreed. But this one? ". . . An old farmer with white hair, his youngest son, hardly fourteen years, they didn't shrink from death for their fatherland, they didn't shrink . . . ." No, in it appeared the struggle "against England's domination." We still sang it for awhile, when no one could hear us. The melodies were catchy, in some dull way.

In the forest we found munitions. I found a very, very heavy shining black pistol and threw it in the thicket fast. In a pond in the forest lay for some days the corpse of a woman. We made an effort not to look at it.

Our parents pulled a handcart 15 km across the countryside to trade jewelry for potatoes, grain, a few eggs, a strip of bacon. Our farmer gave us nothing. We gathered: mushrooms, whole and half potatoes, ears of grain, wood, berries. Occasionally we stole a turnip. We picked knotweed leaves as spinach ersatz, even took orach. From the boundaries of fields we took grass for our rabbit, lay in a store of hay.

In summer a man visited us who had dared his way through the Soviet occupied zone and across the "Green Border." In Berlin he had seen the swelled-up bodies floating along the Landwehr Canal and through the flooded U-Bahn tunnels.

We first heard from our many relatives who had stayed there in September. How was it possible? They had all survived, except one married-in uncle, an SA man, who as late as the beginning of May had fallen in the center of Berlin.

We tasted freedom when we could buy again, years later. A heavy, happy sigh of relief that was. But it was liberation that subjected us to incomprehensible guilt feelings: To hear what Germans had committed. At school they told us the whole truth. At the same time they taught us to recognize The Good.

Encounter   by Wolfgang Gersch   spray technique

Paul Gerhard Hübsch (Hadayatullah)
Paul Gerhard Hübsch, born 1946 in Chemnitz, Saxony. Abitur in Frankfurt. Conscientious Objector. In May 1968 he opened, in Frankfurt, the first head shop on the European mainland, which was shut down by the police in October. Sometime dealer. Lived in various communes, including Kommune 1 in Berlin. Edited the

PAUL GERHARD HÜBSCH (HADAYATULLAH)

i dwell in me

1
i dwell in me, thank God.

i dwelt in red wine bottles,
meetings, easter marches,
in search of anthologies:
jazz in my head, rock in my jeans.

i dwelt in beat-escapades,
hitchhiker-dreams, clubprograms,
in search of the secrets of
SDS-cellars and student lounges.
back then.

then on the street.
dance around the golden mattress camp
of the communes.
in search of the key
to LSD, GI dollars and flipped-out
posters.

i,

i dwelt in mirrors, in jasmine
and concrete in stones,
thrown into the dwellings of judges,
stony the heart of the thrower.

lit mag "Törn" (later called "Törn On"). Travel in Europe & Africa. LSD experiments led to time in mental clinics and in jail. In 1969 converted to Islam, in 1970 accepted into the Ahmadiyya movement and received the name "Hadayatullah"—"led by Allah." Edits the literary magazine "WUDD"—Arabic for "Love." Studies Islamistic in Frankfurt. Translates from English, writes poetry, radio plays, satire. Has worked with RELEASE and other anti-addiction groups and schools.

ich wohne in mir

I
ich wohne in mir, Gott sei dank.

ich wohnte in rotweinflaschen,
tagungen, ostermärschen,
auf der suche nach anthologien:
jazz im kopf, rock in den jeans.

ich wohnte in beat-eskapaden,
hitchhiker-träumen, clubprogrammen,
auf der suche nach den geheimnissen
von SDS-kellern und studentenbuden.
damals.

dann auf der straße.
tanz um die goldenen matratzenlager
der kommunen.
auf der suche nach dem schlüssel
zu LSD, GI-dollars und ausgeflippten
plakaten.

ich,

ich wohnte in spiegeln, in jasmin
und konkret in steinen.
geworfen in wohnungen von richtern,
steinig das herz der werfer.

i dwelt in snow, in fire,
in long hair and police cars,
in prison cells, in the loony bin.

i was beside myself,
to become at home in myself.

i lived in the joint,
i pale in memories:

(do you know the bars
of my crib, the iron
frame of the youth hostels, the
fur upholstered car seats?
do you know the dry berlin
U-Bahn benches, the sleeping bag
under the open heavens: how open
am i really?)

(do you know my room with its
books and all the letters,
talks, prayers, the Qu'ran
on the wall?)

dwellings like sleep in the school desk
dwellings in records, empty
beer bottles, broken TV sets.

(do you know the homey tarzan-souled
antique shops? the handbills in flight
from themselves? do you know
the overwound words of drunken poets?
the match boxes of the dealer & freak
do you know the cold wall despair?
the grace, to be led and the
rain, that livens inner deserts?)

dwellings like confetti.

today at home in me.

2
in me: where am i?
in me: the words of Allah.
the holy Qur'an, prayers, the light
of prophets. in me:
moist earth. in me:
colorful sky and sentences like this:
"O Allah, please cleanse me!"

ich wohnte im schnee, im feuer,
in langen haaren und polizeifahrzeugen,
in gefängniszellen, im irrenhaus.

ich war außer mir,
um in mir heimisch zu werden.

ich hauste im joint,
ich, bleich in erinnerungen:

(kennt ihr die gitterstäbe
meines kinderbettchens, die eisen-
gestelle der jugendherbergen, die
fellbezogenen autositze?
kennt ihr die trockenen berliner
U-bahn-bänke, den schlafsack
unter freiem himmel: wie frei
bin ich wirklich?)

(kennt ihr mein zimmer mit seinen
büchern und all den briefen,
gesprächen, gebeten, den Qur'ân
an der wand?)

wohnungen wie schlaf auf der schulbank.
wohnungen in schallplatten, leeren
bierflaschen, kaputten fernsehapparaten.

(kennt ihr die heimeligen, tarzanbeseelten
antiquariate? flugblätter auf der flucht
vor sich selbst? kennt ihr
die überdrehten worte betrunkener dichter?
die streichholzschachteln der dealer & freaks?
kennt ihr die kahlen wände verzweiflung?
die gnade, geleitet zu werden und den
regen, der innere wüsten belebt?)

wohnungen wie konfetti.

heute zu hause in mir.

II
in mir: wo bin ich?
in mir: die worte Allahs.
der Heilige Qur'ân, gebete, das licht
des propheten. in mir:
feuchte erde. in mir:
bunter himmel und sätze wie diesen:
"O Allah, bitte reinige mich!"

(back then in the blue tent called, over
morocco's hot road, naked, destroyed,
in despair, in search of God)

there lies the way of tears.
the flight of hearts.
the future of souls.
the message: Islam,
and well-beaten paths walked anew:
the speech.

(but what do you want
to know from me
that the All-Knowing
doesn't know better,
i can't say it)

that is the script in which i write.
that is the single sand kernel
that i am in love with.
that is the hope of milk
the fear of bitter almonds.

o, the great black eyes
in a white face:

the path of the servant of God
the prophesied messiah,
the nuur-mosque.

o Thou,
Allah,
how i am
in you
at home.

(damals in das blaue zelt über marokkos
heißer landstraße gerufen, nackt, zerstört,
verzweifelt, auf der suche nach Gott)

da ist der weg der tränen.
der flug der herzen.
die zukunft der seele.
die botschaft: Islam,
und eingefahrene wege neu gehend:
die sprache.

(was aber willst du
von mir wissen,
was der Allwissende
nicht besser weiß,
ich kann es nicht sagen)

das ist die schrift, in der ich schreibe.
das ist das einzelne sandkorn,
in das ich verliebt bin.
das ist die hoffnung auf milch,
die furcht vor bitteren mandeln.

o, die großen, schwarzen augen,
in weißem gesicht:

der pfad der Gottesdiener,
der verheißene messias,
die nuur-moschee.

o Du,
Allah,
wie bin ich
in Dir
zu hause.

Monica Streit
I was born in 1948, 3 years after the capitulation, which was never to be called liberation. A girl, catholic, in a working and farming family in the country. Statistically seen, pressed from a mold labelled "Stand still." That it was otherwise, that today I am

MONICA STREIT

Processions

The dragging
community unity parades
of early spring.
Red and white processions
on Corpus Christi of my childhood.
Today, here in the concrete arroyos
those of the students' May Day.
The solemn red and white
of the fabric above the heads.
more colorful and disorderly and longer,
the rows.
But the same burning intensity
equal faith in the Might
of songs and slogans.
Tribute to the conscience-shaping fathers.
Sunday mission to the Interior.
Spring processions.

a feminist, a psychotherapist, and a writer, all in Berlin: perhaps it's because of the many books—die Gedanken sind frei—perhaps because of the responsibility for my later-born brothers, perhaps because of my sassy temperament, perhaps because of the sun in Capricorn. In any case, although I was never yet in New York, nor in San Francisco (which I suspect I'd prefer), having some of my work in this book is wunderbar.

Umzüge

Die getragenen
gemeinschaftschaffenden
Umzüge des frühen Frühlings.
Rot und weiße Prozessionszüge
an Fronleichnamen meiner Kindheit.
Heute, hier in den langen Betonschluchten
die des studentischen ersten Mai.
Das feierliche Rot und Weiß
der Stoffe über den Köpfen.
Bunter und ungeordneter und
länger die Reihen.
Gleiche Inbrunst
gleiches Vertrauen in die Macht der
Lieder und Sprechgesänge.
Tribut den gewissenschaffenden Vätern.
Sonntagsmissionen nach Innen.
Frühlingsprozessionen.

Violent Habituation (In *The Movement Runs its Course*) from **Das Kopfdromedar**

Isn't it funny, since more frequently neglecting the women's taverns and women's parties and since the judgments of the mixed-caste literature-coterie-business have, despite my reluctance, become important to me and since I myself am no longer driven from leftist taverns by trembling, I too read the usual newspapers again. From back to front. Like before. I don't even hate the eternally identical TV newscast from Bonn anymore. And I digest the *Spiegel* magazine, when I occasionally pick it up, in a slow sequence on the homeland toilet from back to front. Before, I used to leave out the cultural section. Just it alone.

Learning for myself the hard way to recognize the credibility gap of one caste, admittedly my own, apparently makes the credibility gaps of the other castes easier for me to bear. Yes, almost interesting. In Women's Bookstores, on the other hand, I am overcome with melancholy. And the periodicals with always the same thoughts and worries plunge me for the whole day into restless brooding. Then, against the pressing suspicion that I don't belong anywhere; incapable of assimilating, unassimilable.

But what's really funny: mugged by four woman-loving karate amazons, who want to even up old accounts from our shared apartment, who, in the suit, deny everything and who, so advised by women's-movement professional women, refuse comment (just to be sure) in front of the men-moved D.A., who then preferred not to interfere in the incomprehensible battle of the hetaerae; since then the slogan "together we are strong" has degenerated for me to, primarily, "together-we'll-beat-you-to-a-pulp-and-deny-everything." And over everything the cloak of silence. For the violence inside is understandable or incomprehensible, being unclear or opaque, in any case sweep it under the rug.

It's damaging to the identity.
One way or another.

from Das Kopfdromedar

I love you. In the knowledge of your childhood Sundays with chicken bones and feathers, amulet researcher. In this early time as mama's child. Closest ally of the mother against the mean father, like myself. But yours was strong and big, you could lean on her. And she with strong, speech-withholding glances breaking rebellion. But you, never talking back, never angry, never screaming. Three years old with migraines. You were such a sweet child. I would have despised you for sure. Never would have played with you, redhaired mother's little daughter from the impoverished part of the right side of the tracks. I suspect: unbearably precocious and correcting.
But you surely would've kept your distance from me: loud, with a dirty throat climbing trees and whistling. A know-it-all too and insolent.
Maybe we would have slowly approached each other. Over the years, thoughts of each other, in dreams working out our wanting to know more and the inexplicable attraction. During the day sneering and avoiding each other.
Now I wish sometimes we would have known each other. In my and in your loneliness. Not just Sundays. But then I realize, by now we'd be total enemies. It's simpler this way. In my thoughts of your childhood I love you.

IV RELATIONSHIPS

SABINE TECHEL

of him it's said he
spent the last ten years
on the apron strings of his
personal revolution
nursing on schnapps and cigarettes

but how nights by accident
he lay in wait for the sight of autos
hidden between 2 construction wagons
and spied after their passing made it clear

that he was preparing an all-out attack.
it is said: he bolted the
doors extinguished the lights
ice flowers on the windows

baby it's great to be back home

the last nights are so clear
I soon know the constellations by heart
during the day it is brighter here the beech
loses its foliage and the sun
arches lower

        your head lies in a distant town
now you must sleep   turn stranger
learn the stars over your city then
we do something alike
        I am so long
alone among friends

Sabine Techel
Born 1953 in Berlin. I write since 1967, with
interruptions. At first on impulse, in the
meantime I am unable to stop. It's no fun at
all. I study German and English.

---

von dem hieß es er habe
die letzten zehn jahre an den
schürzenbändern seiner
persönlichen revolution verbracht
schnäpse und zigaretten nuckelnd

wie er aber nachts versehentlich
dem anblick von autos auflauerte zwischen
zwei bauwagen zufällig verborgen
und ihnen hinterhersah wurde klar

daß er einen rundumschlag vorbereitete.
überliefert wird: er verriegelte die
türen löschte die lichter
eisblumen an den fenstern

baby it's great to be back home

die letzten nächte sind so klar
ich kann nun doch bald die sternbilder auswendig
tagsüber ist es heller hier die buche
verliert ihr laub und die sonne
steht tiefer
        dein kopf liegt in einer fernen stadt
schlafen mußt du jetzt   mir fremder werden
lern über deiner stadt die sterne dann
tun wir was gleiches
        ich bin solang
unter freunden allein.

felix coniunctio

springtime again the radio
plays the White Lilacs. Friends
we call are raving a little
over-stimulated, they call that love

they stick devices before their eyes
they seek the images. Even in wet shoes
their eyes are the only sense outwards
at least against summer they pull on

their skin again, one gets a hold of them
better and mating is easier then. On
retired rails they take their
sensuality out for a ride like a

cub and wonder what
squeaks and caws so. Later in summer the
archaeologists with the sore eyes find
traces of red dust. That is the rust.

unsettled, quietly and softly

They spend the weeks discussing, unsettled, quietly and softly, why they are unable to be able and don't want to want. When it storms they joyfully greet the fright. With trembling hands they meet weekly in an overheated bell jar and guzzle the smoke eagerly into their lungs. Beauties with evil eyes, with wild hair, threads in hand, from which are generated works and wovens. They speak about the Unconscious and feel their way several inches past its padding. At certain points, sugar water tears flow through the perforations, are seasoned to taste with cinnamon and curare, are passed around the circle, weighed, and declared beautiful and passionable.
The rain at the outer borders is not yet gone. Behind it falls steeply a curtain of Chrome-steel fibers. I find that, say many, but none finds the other while searching. Outside it thunders in shades of gray. No one weeps.

felix coniunctio

Schon wieder Frühling das Radio
spielt den weißen Flieder. Freunde
die wir anrufen sind toll, ein bißchen
überreizt, das nennen sie Liebe

sie klemmen sich Apparate vor die Augen
sie suchen die Bilder. In nassen Schuhen noch
sind ihnen die Augen einzige Fühlung nach
außen. Gegen Sommer ziehen sie wenigstens

ihre Haut wieder an, da kann man sie besser
fassen, die Paarung fällt ihnen so
auch leichter. Auf stillgelegten Gleisen
fahren sie ihre Sinnlichkeit spazieren

wie ein Junges und wundern sich was so
quietscht und krächzt. Später im Sommer
finden die Archäologen mit den wunden Augen
Spuren roten Staubs. Das ist der Rost.

no poem

it is so simple to write no poem, that is, simply ignore the cat in the crosslight and not think about your raspberry red cowboy boots forget that it's becoming spring after all, that the snow is bogged down, breed no hunger for something and leave all your good resolutions in the cupboard
don't cry about the bells at noon wanting to buy no white gorse blooms nor ban any black eyes onto paper
above all local and now, fresh, active, wrinkle-resistant and easy-to-care-for vegetate avoid pain abstain from gordian knots and swords forget punchlines deny the scissors in your head speak in its favor

family life

Phoenix my father is unkillable
he lives in a faraway land
is always around me

my mother was a circus horse
in her youth she had a dark mane
when she reared the earth trembled

it was a happy marriage say my parents
my brother is an absolute metaphor
i was supposed to become a Pegasus

tiny and fine in disregard of all presuppositions
flying and galloping in my good times
child of my parents   in my badness   to be a free person

and that I'm now a bastard after twenty-four
years and nothing has become of me I'm supposed to explain
i commence to speak say   I

there the faces turn black. I know I hadn't
and should indeed. I'd have to finally. Indeed I
would indeed yet. And I will, too.

no mail today

where otherwise the letters lay
today two garden pears
ditto tomato, unripe
that's the message

family life

Phoenix mein Vater ist nicht totzukriegen
er lebt in einem fernen Land
ist ständig um mich

meine Mutter war ein Zirkuspferd
in ihrer Jugend hatte sie eine dunkle Mähne
wenn sie sich aufbäumte zitterte die Erde

es war eine glückliche Ehe sagen meine Eltern
mein Bruder ist eine absolute Metapher
ich sollte ein Pegasus werden

ein kleiner feiner über alle Voraussetzungen hinweg
fliegen und galoppieren in meinen guten Zeiten
Kind der Eltern   in den bösen freier Mensch sein

und daß ich jetzt ein Bastard bin seit vierundzwanzig
Jahren und nichts aus mir geworden ist soll ich erklären
ich hebe an zu sprechen sage   Ich

da werden die Gesichter schwarz. Ich weiß ich hätte nicht
und sollte doch. Ich müßte endlich. Überhaupt ich
würde schon noch. Und ich werde auch.

no mail today

wo sonst die post liegt
heute zwei gartenbirnen
dito tomate, unreif
thats the message

by Jochen Melzian   photograph

TELEGRAM TO AMERICA
Name: Michel Boiron
Born: 27 Nov. 54, South France
Occupations: Student of French, German, Art history; French teacher; Work-study in the language lab, Freie U., Berlin; Curriculum author in French; Writer

MICHEL BOIRON

The Lonely Road

A little girl walked on a lonely road. Why do such roads always have to be so lonely? Are they really deserted? But there was nobody, really nobody, apart from that little girl and some subterranean animals which nobody had ever seen, because no human being had eyes powerful enough. The little girl walked, indifferent to the solitude. She walked without stopping, without showing any signs of the fatigue which she should long since have felt.
And the road was just a simple road. Someone walked on it. It was hot. The asphalt sweated a little but it wasn't thirsty. It probably knew the night would come one day to refresh it.
It had been hot for a long time on this road where a little girl walked without feeling any fatigue.
There was also a village, and there they often told the story of a young girl who walked on a road.
But nobody was able to confirm that the road led to the village or that it left it. Nobody had ever left the village.
The old people spent their evenings talking about the past and often inventing it because they hadn't enough to talk about. But when they really had nothing left to tell, well, then they took up the story of the young girl who walked on the road. And everybody listened in wonder.
If visitors absolutely insisted on learning more and on seeing the road, the village people finally had to admit that they had never seen the road. The villagers had never even seen the young girl. They knew that she was there on a road and that she walked always in the same direction. In the evening, the villagers closed their blinds and went to bed. The old people closed their eyes and needed a long time before they fell asleep. And when all was turned off, when there was no more light to trouble the night and when the stars themselves seemed to have fled to another universe, a road formed in the middle of the village, it crossed the houses and even the beds of the inhabitants and even their slow and regular breath, and there was a young child walking, much bigger than the houses.

Goals as writer: Let people dream, without forgetting reality. To be read.
Life principles: Creativity, always to develop further, humor, tenderness.
Life goals: Concretize my dreams.
STOP-STOP-STOP-STOP-STOP-STOP

---

little mornings of habit

she feels nauseous
and can't sleep
how we sleep together
she wakes me when she moves
and each time I wake
she's not sleeping
in the morning
like every morning
I ask her kindly
"Did you sleep well?"
it's only afterward that I remember

les petits matins de l'habitude

elle a mal au coeur
et ne peut pas dormir
comme nous dormons ensemble
elle me réveille lorsqu'elle bouge
et chaque fois que je me réveille
elle ne dort pas
le matin
comme tous les matins
d'une nuit commune
je lui demande gentiment
"Tu as bien dormi?"
ce n'est qu'après que je me souviens

*translated by Johanna Bahne
and Mitch Cohen*

Katja Tiel
I worked as a secretary, translator, bookseller, babysitter for the rich (no more), once played a hippy for a TV film. In the late 50s I began to write. Sound poems and concrete poetry in the early

KATJA TIEL

Portrait 1970

i need you but i can't have you around me anymore and as then the beautiful Thalja comes in she doesn't say what she should, what she thinks what she wishes "you have the prettiest coat on, you are even prettier"—she says other things so that Thalja becomes totally insecure. "with your life," "this profession, how can you even begin," "to reconcile it with your life"

she flirts demonstratively with the boy, who obviously, if you judge by the time of day, has spent the night with Thalja, who caresses Thalja's knee and plays in the long blonde hair. they throw intellectual catchwords to each other—this unusualness raises her above Thalja who starts to stutter.

he who the café doesn't please and who sharply pitches into me also because i stroke the hair of her boy, who was once my boy. there is no limit to this mutuality and nothing remains from such attacks on piety—however is that to be reconciled, starting a relationship with an old friend of his girlfriend, "Clarissa would never have been capable of that"—and now her behavior her coquetry has long been a carried-out sleeping-together

passing over me and the other girlfriend of mine. nothing counts, she must have him, she lets them all know at the first opportunity. she engages all her theater gestures, her esprit shines. in the end she flirts with me like a child who smooches his teddy bear. and at the same time innocently fixates the enticer.

60s, with an exhibition in the International Exhibit of Concrete Poetry. 7 years self-published in my "i-press." I'm interested in the psychological processes underlying grammatical forms. My texts are musical. Speech is erotic. I was greatly influenced by the late Hans Zehder. *im li wenn viel la li sing*, 1981, Medusa Verlag.

Portrait 1970

ich brauche dich aber ich kann dich nicht mehr um mich haben und als dann die schöne Thalja hereinkommt sagt sie nicht das was sie sagen mußte, was sie denkt was sie wünscht "du hast den schönsten mantel an, du bist noch schöner"—sie sagt andere dinge so daß Thalja ganz unsicher wird. "bei deinem leben", "wie kannst du überhaupt diesen beruf" "mit deinem leben vereinbaren"

sie flirtet demonstrativ mit dem knaben, der offensichtlich nach der tageszeit zu urteilen, die nacht mit Thalja verbracht hat, der Th's Knie streichelt und in dem langen blonden haar spielt. sie werfen sich intellektuelle stichworte zu—diese außergewöhnlichkeit erhebt sie über Th. die zu stottern anfängt.

der der (das) café nicht gefällt und die auch mich scharf anfährt weil ich ihrem knaben, der einst mein knabe war, über's haar streiche. es gibt keine grenze bei dieser gemeinsamkeit und nichts bleibt zurück von solchen pietätsangriffen—wie das nur zu vereinbaren sei mit 1 alten freund seiner freundin 1 verhältnis anzufangen, niemals wäre Clarissa dazu in der lage"—und nun ist ihr benehmen ihre koketterie schon längst ein ausgetragener bei schlaf

über mich hinweg und die andere freundin von mir. es zählt nichts, sie muß ihn haben, sie läßt es alle wissen bei der nächsten gelegenheit. sie setzt all ihre Theatergesten ein, ihr esprit glänzt. zuletzt flirtet sie mit mir wie 1 kind das seinen teddybär knutscht. und dabei den verführer unschuldig fixiert.

Bodo Morshäuser
born 1953 in Berlin
published in lit-mags, has read on radio and TV
lives in West Berlin

BODO MORSHÄUSER

Flight in the Morning

Light flows through the curtains, there
your suitcase was standing, now it is floating
with you above the clouds. You flew off
the morning before your arrival, as always.
Yearning before and yearning after. You?
Coming and going, dyeing your hair
in the meantime and being all over again the same one.
No reminiscence of whole years, just arrival
or departure, these are the lasting sensations.
Here are the leftovers of our last breakfast—
I shall wash up, put the glasses and mugs
away orderly for the next
one with you, no with you, all the same—confetti,
all the pieces stamped out of one sheet.
That's not enough for a love story,
that's not enough for a murder. There
your jet vanishes in the mist.

translated by Ulrich Danielowski

Alle Tage (Every Day), poems, Rotbuch
1978.

editor, with Jürgen Wellbrock: *Die Ungeduld
auf dem Papier und andere Lebenszeichen*
(Impatience on Paper and Other Signs of
Life), Edition der Zwei, 1978.

Abflug am Morgen

Licht schwimmt durch die Vorhänge, dort
stand die Reisetasche, nun schwebt sie
mit dir über den Wolken. Du bist abgeflogen
am Morgen vor deiner Ankunft, wie immer.
Sehnsucht davor und Sehnsucht danach. Du?
Kamst und gingst, färbtest in der Zwischenzeit
die Haare und warst aufs Neue dieselbe Eine.
Keine Erinnerung an ganze Jahre, nur Ankunft
oder Abschied, das sind die haltbaren Gefühle.
Hier die Reste unseres letzten Frühstücks—
ich werde abwaschen, Gläser und Tassen
in die Reihe stellen für das nächste
mit dir, nein mit dir, egal—Konfetti,
alle Teile gestanzt aus einem Bogen.
Das reicht für keine Liebesgeschichte,
das reicht für keinen Mord. Da
taucht deine Maschine im Nebel weg.

One of Those Letters

The poems didn't turn out at all, he wrote
and pulled the photo album out of the case.
Perhaps one or the other, but what
happened with you after reading them?
Did a light go on, were things put
into light, where they carried on?
Then why put a light on them, he thought
and did not write it.

The photographs in my hand are right, even
if you are on them, although you didn't want to be.
In contrast to poems they are practical,
just print a million and cover the country with 'em.
Photographers eyes roam about, whoever
falls, cuts a good figure, we live
right in the center of the esthetic of the fall
(please excuse me),
he wrote

and knew he didn't want to see her, simply
didn't want to hear these steps but
she had already left the room, as if
she had never been there.
Think it over well, will you be able to stand it, hearing the woman,
the one you want, saying in the evening:
Anything exciting today? Sometimes I think
the razor-blade under the mirror is between
her and me. Get that?

I hate photographs! Believing in them
was never as hard as looking out of
this hotel room, onto another hotel room,
doubting about poems
and living right next to someone . . .
boundless, boundless. Another light?

translated by Ulrich Danielowski

Einer jener Briefe

Die Gedichte sind alle nichts geworden, schrieb er
und zog das Fotoalbum aus dem Koffer.
Vielleicht das eine oder andere, aber was
ist aus dir geworden nach dem Lesen?
Ging ein Licht an, standen die Dinge nun
im Licht, wo sie weitermachten?
Wozu dann ein Licht auf sie?, dachte er
und schrieb es nicht.

Die Fotos in meiner Hand haben Recht, auch
wenn du auf ihnen bist, obwohl du es nicht wolltest.
Im Gegensatz zu Gedichten sind sie praktisch,
druck' ne Million und kleb' das Land voll.
Herum streunen die Augen der Fotografen, wer
fällt, gibt eine gute Figur ab, wir leben
inmitten der Ästhetik des Sturzes (entschuldige
bitte), schrieb er

und wußte, er wollte sie nicht sehen, diese
Schritte einfach nicht hören, aber da war sie schon
aus dem Zimmer, wie gar nicht dagewesen.
Überleg' dir gut, ob du es ertragen wirst, die Frau,
die du willst, am Abend sagen zu hören:
Was Besonderes heute? Manchmal denke ich,
die Rasierklinge unter dem Spiegel ist zwischen
ihr und mir. Verstehst du das?

Ich hasse Fotos! Ihnen zu glauben
war nie so schwer, wie aus diesem Hotelzimmer
zu schauen, auf ein anderes Hotelzimmer,
an Gedichten zu zweifeln
und neben jemandem zu leben . . .
maßlos, maßlos. Noch ein Licht?

INGEBORG MIDDENDORF

Ingeborg Middendorf
I grew up in the upper class, and got to know its good (being spoiled, luxury) and its bad (hypocrisy, intrigues). I studied literature until I almost forgot how to write. I learned a normal profession (teacher) and gave it up. Publications: 1971 in Peter Hammer Verlag's *We Children of Marx and Coca-Cola*; in the Berlin magazine, *Courage*; erotic stories in *Where the Night Embraces the Day*, Gudula Lorez Verlag; in the Munich magazine, *Gasolin 23*; in *Tübinger Texte*; in 1978, a poetry volume *Die Fehlgeburt/Der Abgang* ("The Miscarriage") for which I received the Förderpreis (Patronage Prize) of the Land (province) North Rhein-Westphalia; various publications in KAKTUS Verlag and *City*, both in Münster. Now I'm working on a "family novel," which I'll finish this year. I was formed by stays in southern Italy, though now I'm more interested in the north. I've no interest in America, maybe because everyone's so crazy about it. I was influenced by R.D. Brinkmann, who grew up in the same city as I did. Also important: Rolling Stones, Brigitte Bardot, my mother—the last since, but not until, her death. I would like an "alternative life" alone with my little son. Also important: Franziska von Reventlo. I am afraid that my child will never grow up, because they will use the weapons of annihilation that have been so long prepared and stockpiled. Our generation has it rough. In the face of the total threat, literature must be radical.

The Miscarriage

When the pregnancy test came out positive, I invited my girlfriends for champagne. They too should see the birdsnest on the balcony with the unfledged blackbirds. We went out onto the balcony. The little blackbird panics, hops high, falls out of the nest to the street and is dead. Then I couldn't drink champagne anymore and sent the girls away.

In Munich, my boyfriend H. heard about my pregnancy. He didn't call me up. Because I was uneasy, I called him up. He said he would have to get used to the idea and drove to Cannes for the Film Festival. So, alone, wanting to have the joy, I bought books about pregnancy and birth, visited friends with children, spoke about living communally with other people who have children.

After waking up and feeling the first signs, my breasts getting large and sensitive, I lay my palm on my belly and sang to my developing child—it must have had the size of a thumb by then:

> my little thumbling, my little thumbling,
> my little thumbling, sleep well
> my little thumbling, my little thumbling,
> my little thumbling, grow large.

The doctor, a woman, embraced me when she confirmed my pregnancy. The birth should come in January.

My boyfriend called up from Cannes. He was happy, too. Everything was more concrete now, not so psychological. When I told him the expected delivery date, he said, the child must have been conceived in April and I didn't come back to Berlin from Crete until the middle of April.

Later I picked him up from the airport. It was impossible, he said, that he could be the father.

I should try to remember.

That I tried once to sleep with a guy on Crete, admitted. But I ended the attempt before it took place. H. spoke of the mentality of the southern peoples, of ejaculatio praecox, of possible possibilities. I showed him my basal temperature curve, reckoned my fertile days out loud. Only he could be the father. But the mood was heartrending, for his doubts remained.

With these doubts, which he shared with his best friends and which led me to ever-meaner fantasies, he had already taken our child from me. I had wanted to get pregnant by him, carry him in me, cradle him in my arms, call him by his name. Give him life. How I have longed for this child, I sobbed. The answer: not me. I always wanted a child from you. Not me!

Then I began to hate him. No more talk of joy. I could only flip out any more. This wronging of my person, this insulting of my wishes. This mean refusal of paternity and of the child. My God, the sensitively sensitive life in me, how it was shaken! I cried, screamed, swung at everything. Hated everything. Every thing, every person. Raged even at the air and sun. Did I still want the child—was it then still there? Didn't it feel everything? No more songs!

H. invited friends over. Couldn't he stand to be with me alone? I made scenes in front of all. Just before Pentecost holidays I went with him, more or less unwillingly, to visit an acquaintance of his who had a child, who lived in Lichterfeld in a garden with other women and children. Well-bounded flowerbeds and lawns, sand boxes. The apartments perfect, the faces panicky. The woman flew to H. with flushed face. She didn't notice me till later. H. laid himself, white-jacketed, in the chaise lounge, smoked, praised the wine and the somewhat teensy duck, puffed the cigarette smoke fashionably in the direction of his admirers. Cannes was spoken of. Film and television projects. The ladies are attentive. I grasped for my book: *Destruction of Hearing and Seeing in Our Culture* and tried to read. My appetite was gone. But I couldn't repress my agitation and rage, stood up, advanced upon the Group Portrait With Gentleman and cried out: The nerve, to invite someone and then to treat them like they weren't there—to the ladies—and from him, H., it was an outrage. The whole atmosphere was unbearable. It makes me so sick I could vomit.

Trembling, I stood before the three. H. raised himself, cigarette in one hand, the other loose on his hip. Master of the situation, in white Star jacket. Not a word from him to me. No gesture. Slow crushing out of the cigarette. The ladies watched.

Hate, Rage, Helplessness. I would have liked to beat them all to a pulp. Smashed into their stubborn traps, till the blood squirts. To have thrown a bomb and blown the whole used-up-ness to smithereens, to mow the whole lawn party mustiness down with a machine gun. But what could I do to them. I turned around. Went.

Drove off with the rattling VW. My Starfighter took off across the intersection against the red light. (Cries, curses, screeching tires, threats, police.)

Back in the apartment. What now? Wait. Footsteps in the stairwell. The relief was only temporary. Heart pounding, heart pains, heartache. I call up a girlfriend. Force a date on her. It is evening. We

speak with each other. The talk keeps coming back to H. H. H. H. H. . . . (Is he implanted in my brain? Am I obsessed? Where am I? Where the others? Where the world around me?)
At two in the morning back in the apartment. No one. No sleeping H. No cursing H. No conciliatory H. I get jittery. Telephone. Where shall I sleep. Not in the apartment. There is no one in the apartment. I reach R., who waits for me, half-asleep and in a somewhat sour mood, with his girlfriend in the overfilled apartment of an acquaintance. 3 in the morning. Guilty conscience, to have disturbed them both. They show me a small room. No curtain, desk, couch. Morning is already lighting. The heart races. Abandoned; abandoned! In the next room cuddle together two in love. My body shakes, kill the pain! But how? Tablets could be harmful. For I'm pregnant. (Am I pregnant?)
The couch, next to it a mattress leaning against the wall, it looks fucked out. On the table, accounts, bills, papers. A little pocket change. Should I steal it? Out the window I see a tree. Blue sky. Pictures: H. in the city. Already in the morning, shortly after the performance he has called up a woman. Visited her. Rung the doorbell. Looked around quickly in the hall, went to her room, took off his clothes without a word. The woman, still young, blond, slim, sits on the bed. Her long dress is patterned in a colorful green. He shoves the skirt hem high. You have nothing on underneath. Penetrates her. Pulls his cock out before he comes. Moans with his head back and eyes closed. He goes into the bathroom. Puts on Bob Dylan. Knock, knock, knockin' on heaven's door, knock, knock, knock . . . "tenderly" shoves a foam capsule in. They ball. After the orgasm, he sings. Laughs. Falls asleep. Later they go out to eat.
Excruciating rage. Pain. Such pain. Where can he be? Where is he? With what woman? (Heart thumping!) I would like to be able to see into every apartment in Berlin. Into every damned apartment in the fucking Federal Republic, the DDR, every apartment in Europe, see into every apartment in every continent. See him! Wherever he is! With whomever he is! See! (Speak?) Unbearable heart-racing! The breasts, are they still taut?
Is the child still there—can it hold out through the fever? Leaving early. Leaving a note behind. Couldn't sleep any more, etc. . . .
Back in the apartment, waiting. Aha, so he hasn't come. Took off somewhere again. Or is there a sign after all? The telephone? A note? In the afternoon a friend calls up. Hello honeypot. How are you? Not so well. I believe you. H. is gone, uh huh. He called me up to say he was fed up, he said. Isn't in Berlin any more. No he didn't say where he was going. You better come to terms with it. Now's time to think it through. It doesn't work like that. You made it hell for him.
Look through all addresses. Call all acquaintances. Again and again.

Ruthlessly, whether day or night. I get to hear phrases like: be strong. And: don't let your head hang. We don't really want to live with these crazy guys. You can turn to women too. But we want to, don't you? And can't. Am I right? Endlessly talking, until I hang up, exhausted. No one calls me up of their own accord!

A letter comes. Special Delivery. Monday morning, seven o'clock. (This idiotic heart-pounding) I open the envelope by holding it over steam. For the content is clear. And there it is, typed, clear as can be: can't, won't live with you. And not because of the momentary pregnancy. After all I'm no bureaucracy. I want to devote myself to my work. Create a new existence. First go on a trip. Don't know where. No return address. No closing! I reseal the letter, cross out my address, scribble thickly: *moved*. Write the address of one of his friends on the front and strike through his name on the back many times, angrily. The coward! The coward!

I dial the number of a friend of H.'s. Yes, H. is there, but he doesn't want to speak with you. That happens sometimes that one just *can't* any more. Blocked! I try to describe my condition. Not sleeping, not able to eat, not working. Fever attacks. Beside myself. Just one word. Please! You are stronger than all of us together, says the friend. Whoever suffers so much outwardly, doesn't suffer inwardly, I think his sentence to completion. Gretchen occurs to me: the person, who you have beside you, I hate in my deepest soul. I hang up.

I can't think about a child any more. Feel nothing any more. Everything limp. Let yet another limit of shame fall: a letter to H. Beg him to come. Just during the pregnancy. Just the first 3 months, which are so dangerous. Even explain my flipping out.

That night I bring an earlier boyfriend to bed with me. Even the smell gets on my nerves. Lets my longing for H. increase. Flee to the next room. Try to sleep. No ease, just panic. Nothing matters to me any more. I dial again the number of H.'s friend. 5 o'clock in the morning. Let it ring and ring. No one picks up the receiver. After awhile the busy signal. I'd like to tear myself to pieces.

I've had hardly any sleep in all these days. Sometimes, after hours of shifting around my chaos: a half fixed up, half dismantled dwelling, no trade, no man who stands by me, a few friends who I may not burden, and again and again the worry about the child—how shall it grow up, when I myself am broken by the confusion. Sometimes, after hours of restless undignified choking on this miserable crust of reality that has fallen to me, sometimes for a moment I fall into distracted slumber.

In the morning, for days now, everything limp. Only morning sickness remains and the worsening fear: is the being in me still alive? Has it died of my fever?

Everything talked to death. Felt to death.

I make a try at working. Talk in my diploma seminar of my idea to write a thesis about pregnancies of single women, programs of self-organization, maybe a curriculum model.
On the same day, at the first meeting with the pregnant women, I feel a sign in my abdomen like my period. I go to the toilet. Bleeding. Not badly. But blood. One of the girls takes me to the Westend Clinic. Pulsstraße 4–14. It is midnight. In the clinic, first a low, then a no-longer-measurable pregnancy hormone level is ascertained. And always changing results with echo diagnosis. After a few days there, the bleedings have stopped, I am released with the instructions, absolute bed rest. Whether the pregnancy is still intact will show itself. Hoping and fearing begins. Light bleeding again: taxi—clinic—examination. Maybe it's not so bad. Or is it? My only hope is in the echo sounding. In any case there is doubt.
H. is back again. As long as it looks like I'll have a child he is from skeptical to rejecting. But the more hopeless my struggle and my chances become, the kinder and more considerate he gets around me, consoles, takes care of me, and even makes a few starts at painting a future for us: Try again. With more calm and patience maybe we'll get more relaxed and he even says: I'm sorry!
As H. has to drive for two days to K., it's clear that the child doesn't live any more. Maybe not for a long time already. Have you had any illness? For example fever, I am asked. Ex post facto there is no way to find a cause for the unhappy course. All that is certain is that I have to be scraped out. "Curetage," I shrink just from the word. Refuse. Cry. Am at my end.
I scream at H. that I hate him. That he is the murderer of my child. That in him I can now see only the murderer of my child, whom I'd like to kill. How does he think he can stand up to my hate, I weep. If any one has to, he says, then he has to bear the hate. And he wants to. H. drives away.
Now I want to walk around with the dead child so long that I die of it. That's insanity what you're doing, says a girlfriend. If the child is really dead, it has to get out of your body. The sooner, the better. Be reasonable.
In the medical dictionary I read about *abortio missio* (dead embryo that is not cast out but remains in the womb and rots. The resulting ptomaine can cause clotting problems that lead to mortally dangerous bleeding): the "extraction" of a missed abortion is one of the most dangerous operations because of the dangerous bleeding and because of the morbidity of the cervix wall.
On the evening before the operation I gave it to H. one more time. In the presence of patients, the nurses, and a visitor I cursed him as the murderer of my child and tried to hit him. Tried to run away from the clinic, too. I wanted to die with the corpse in my belly.

The nurse was supportive. I used to let everything eat into me too, she said. I got sick. Now I scream everything out. Everything direct and don't let anybody abuse me. I know what I'm talking about. I have 4 children and I've had three miscarriages . . . And all with one man. Just don't believe it's any different with other people. They just pretend that it's different.

The next day, H. was there at 8 in the morning. It must have been care and thoroughness. I experienced it as surveillance: the man who accompanies the condemned one to the executioner is punctual and friendly too.

With all my power I resisted the anesthetic, the loss of consciousness. H. stood next to the gurney. When the orderlies came to take me to surgery, H. was gone. He'd had to go get cigarettes. At my urgent request, one of the orderlies goes to the waiting room, where H. might be. Of course he isn't.

The last wave of panic. I try to climb down from the gurney. I am easily overpowered. Manipulation of tubes. Unconsciousness.

While I was still in the hospital, H. organized and carried out his moving out. During his visit to the clinic he tells of cleaning the apartment. Now I am alone. The bleeding has still not stopped ten days after the operation.

I can no longer describe my feelings when I see a pregnant woman. Nor the feeling when I walk past a store with baby clothing and toys. If I see a child I look away.

Kreuzberger Prospekt   by Mitch Cohen   graphite

URSULA RÜHLE

Watertight Argument

Everything is to be understood in its historical context.
The historical context is itself
To be understood in its historical context.
At the present time,
not all understand the historical context in the same way.
This is to be understood in the historical context.

This historical context is changeable.
Every perception is time-bound.
What I see is time-bound.
I myself am time-bound.
Every perception that I have is time-bound.
This perception is time-bound.

The Truth that is not yet realized,
Is not yet perceptible.
To really be true, it must first be brought about.
Before that, it is a not-yet-brought-about-Truth,
That originated in the historical context,
And it is because of this historical context
That it is not yet brought about.

If the historical context changes in such a way
That this Truth becomes real,
I will know that I was right,
If I now say that this Truth is not yet made real.

If the historical context has changed,
The perception will have to change again, too.
Will I recognize the Truth
That is true now but
Just not made real yet?

The Past begins now.

Ursula Rühle
was born on October 10, 1945, and grew up
in Frankfurt am Main. She studied Sociology
in Frankfurt and Berlin, and has lived in
Berlin Kreuzberg since 1970.

Geschlossene Argumentation

Alles ist aus seinem historischen Kontext zu verstehen.
Der historische Kontext selbst
ist aus dem historischen Kontext heraus zu verstehen.
Zur Zeit
verstehen nicht alle den historischen Kontext gleich.
Das ist aus dem historischen Kontext heraus zu verstehen.

Der historische Kontext ist veränderlich.
Jede Erkenntnis ist zeitgebunden.
Was ich sehe, ist zeitgebunden.
Ich selbst bin auch zeitgebunden.
Jede Erkenntnis, die ich habe, ist zeitgebunden.
Diese Erkenntnis ist zeitgebunden.

Die Wahrheit, die noch nicht realisiert ist,
ist noch nicht erkennbar.
Damit sie wirklich wahr ist,
muß sie erst verwirklicht werden.
Vorher ist sie eine noch nicht verwirklichte Wahrheit,
die aus dem historischen Kontext entstanden ist,
und am historischen Kontext liegt es,
daß sie nicht verwirklicht ist.

Wenn der historische Kontext sich so verändert,
daß eine solche Wahrheit wirklich wird,
werde ich wissen, daß ich recht hatte,
wenn ich jetzt sage,
daß diese Wahrheit wahr ist
und nur noch nicht verwirklicht ist.

Wenn der historische Kontext sich verändert
wird auch die Erkenntnis sich verändern.
Werde ich sie wiedererkennen,
die Wahrheit, die jetzt wahr ist
und nur noch nicht verwirklicht ist?

Die Vergangenheit beginnt Jetzt.

HOLGER SCHENK

Flourish

She is slim and
always looks healthy;
usually she has
jeans on, and

once in awhile she's
a bit "naive."
The other day she bent
over to put briquets

in the oven. She
was naked, only her
fingers were black
with coaldust, as

outside it started
to snow and you
heard nothing but
snow shovelling.

Holger Schenk
Born 1955 in Bremerhaven; since 1975 in
Berlin. Editor of the magazine "Kühltürme."

Floskel

Sie ist schlank und
sieht immer gesund
aus; meist hat
sie Jeans an und

ab & zu ist sie
ein bißchen "naiv".
Neulich bückte sie
sich, um Briketts in

den Ofen zu legen. Sie
war nackt, nur ihre
Finger waren schwarz
vom Kohlenstaub, als

es draußen anfing
zu schneien und man
hörte nichts als
Schneeschippen.

MARIA-STEFANIE STERN

you

you have a suneye
and a shadowmouth
your face is round
onto your hair   like a festival
fall stars and moon
onto your sex it snows promises
(though it lies under ice)
your movements bypass you on Monday
and fill you up again on Saturday

in your hands you hold the wrong things
you are your own strange guest
at the side of the audience
you shudder at yourself
and your picture

and yet
you have a suneye and a
shadowmouth
accompanying

Maria-Stefanie Stern
was born in Günzberg/Donau on May 7, 1946. In 1974 she finished training as a teacher. 1975 moved to Berlin. Poems and drawings in diverse magazines. 1980: pedagogy and poesy can't be brought together in one traversable path. Living in Berlin.

du

du hast ein sonnenauge
und einen schattenmund.
dein gesicht ist das rund
auf deine haare (die ein fest sein können)
fallen sterne und mond
auf dein geschlecht schneit es verheißungen—
(trotzdem es unter eis liegt)
deine bewegungen sparen dich am montag aus
und füllen dich am samstag wieder auf

in deinen händen hältst du die falschen dinge
du bist dein eigener fremder gast
auf der seite des zuschauers
erschauerst du vor dir
und deinem bild

und doch
du hast ein sonnenauge und einen
schattenmund
zum begleiter

JOSEPHA GUTELIUS

The Idolaters

I paused on the fifth step, weighed down, pursued by no one. An elevator passed me, ascending, some very still figures inside it, a *jugendstil* lion cage, double-padlocked for people of the house, who had the key, who could enter, who did not ever need to use the stairs. I basked in their providence for a minute or two, and then I went on, on and on, hotly pursuing my disappearing legs. Whatever did I reach the top for, or did I at all, I couldn't have just continued running up, I don't remember. It would not be like me to reach something; probably it was a case of my having climbed up inside the wrong house, it wouldn't be for the first time. I was in the wrong place at the wrong time, or rather, originally it may have been the right time, but now it was too late. Think of him rubbing his bald little head against the telephone receiver, waiting, no one answering. He gets up fitfully, with starts and stops and long empty stares, taking in nothing, then going on, or, what is more likely, not going on, going nowhere, that sounds better. No, truthfully I relish the thought of him moving on, a versicolored blur of chameleoned verisimilitude. He did gradually take up speed, whoever he was. His white gloves wrapped around the elevator's little iron gargoyle, the shafts pulling him up . . . a brief clang of metals and then the lights in the hall above me went out. The stained glass windows let in an oily blue twilight. It was not night elsewhere, but here, inside the house, what could you expect. I paused on each floor, inspecting the name plates. Notaries, dentists, designers, art dealers, etc. Which one of those . . . no, I wasn't going to look anymore, I tired of looking, I was aiming for the top, some little door leading to the roof. Roofs in Berlin are generally not bad to look at, but I was hoping in this exceptional case to find nothing worth viewing, no view of the streets, or

Josepha Gutelius
I lived on lake Wannsee for two years with my (now) husband the German sculptor Benno Schmidbaur, in a gatehouse on the former property of the Springers (the scientific publishers, not Axel)—4 acres of weeds and ancestral trees, shared by an abandoned Messel villa that was occasionally rented out to film companies, but mostly our neighbor stood empty (and spooky looking haunted). The rent (80DM a month) enabled me not to have to do much except write occasional articles on Berlin artists and art "trends" surveys; with a lot of open space to ponder the enigma of Berlin.
I'm 26 now. Been back in New York for almost 2 years. I'm writing prose (not "stories") and work as an editor at W.W. Norton, the publishers. I'm also editing the reborn phoenix, Zero Anthology, a collection of international writing—something that promises to offset American jingoism in the arts.

of the back courts ringing with fountains and women beating their carpets, or dogs with their legs up, letting out the sun; nothing for me to enjoy, hopefully, even from a distance,
    or many viewpoints, but all of them being myself in various ways—all loose ends, nothing intact: my various souls' UFOs or disguised persons, my tribe of suckers, my spiritual immigrants. Misfortune is the key, so I fancied it. Without it to drag me forward, despite the boredom of it, why, at least it got me here, tho tardy and mistaken as always; I was flanked by closed doors which for the life of me, I would not enter. But a nudge from my toe and one of these days the door could open. I passed the door then, not daring to go further, returned, and so it happened that on that day I did enter. Behind the door was a long hall, extending to the back. And there, apparently, everything ended. A hall, mauve and insular, what a break for my eyes was my first response. Nothing to see, nothing for the curious there—except for a painting way up on the wall of a young man in a flannel nightgown, Colt in hand, a glossy finish: this buoyed my waning spirit. For all its unfamiliarity, it was familiar. Who could forget that chin, bulbous and binary, a jaw like a abscessed fork of two prongs; and how could I forget that sweet gun that once was pointed so lovingly at me: of a species that is not beast or man, but let us say android to get the description over with. I knew that face.

One painting, the beginning or the end of a poor soul's fetishistic desire, I'll give him credit for that, however it breaks my heart to admit it. For it was a lousy painting, obviously taken directly from a photo of my former lover. The technique of such things is to project the slide directly onto the canvas, the painter just filling in faithfully. If the painting had been smaller I might have considered hocking it, or—just taking it down and rubbing it against my crotch and placing it in its original position again. Rubbing any object of *kitsch* against my crotch is a trick I learned from the very guy pictured there, only maybe it doesn't bring luck. Recall my former lover OD'd a few years ago. I was taken aback by that memory suddenly, and whisked myself out of the hall, slamming the door behind me without mercy for neighboring ears—the consequences of which I don't like to think about, not even to this day.

V WORK

RALF ROTHMANN

Memo

In the corridor the night cramps
    between the spokes of the baby-stroller.
Here I squat, my forehead deep in my
face, and push a ball of air
around in my mouth,
    dead drunk.
I'd just like one good night's sleep
before I kill myself.

Ralf Rothmann
born 1953. Lives in West Berlin.
Bricklayer and construction work.
Published in lit-mags, anthologies, and has
read on the radio.

Notiz

Im Hausflur klemmt die Nacht
    zwischen den Speichen der Kinderwagen.
Da hock ich, die Stirn tief im
Gesicht, und schieb eine Kugel aus Luft
im Mund herum.
    Besoffen bin ich.
Ausschlafen möcht ich nochmal
bevor ich mich umbringe

What a Day

Should I maybe *not* flip out
    not pound with my fist on the
        canteen table *not* yell
that even the coffee automat swallows down the wrong pipe
if this spring the sun
    throws the first shadows
        through the wire-reinforced window glass
onto my security shoes
should i calmly press the buttons
    pull the levers swallow the dusty
        sayings of the foreman and let everything
keep on going like always as if nothing had
happened with me for two and a half decades

        Okay Okay i don't flip out
i push the daily buttons
pull the daily lever
and glance calmly into this seemingly
    eternal machine hall—

through which sometimes
    a secretary meanders

On her skirt i clip a whistle
    she smiles and evenings

we blink in our beer
and talk about the day
    which was nice
as we hear from the waitress

So ein Tag

Soll ich etwa nicht ausrasten
nicht mit der Faust auf den
Kantinentisch haun nicht brüllen
daß selbst der Kaffeeautomat sich verschluckt
wenn in diesem Frühjahr die Sonne
durchs drahtverstärkte Fensterglas
die ersten Schatten wirft
auf meine Sicherheitsschuhe
soll ich da gelassen die Knöpfe drücken
die Hebel ziehn die verstaubten Sprüche
der Vorarbeiter schlucken und alles
so laufen lassen wie immer als wäre nichts
geschehn mit mir seit zweieinhalb Jahrzehnten

Schon gut ich raste nicht aus
ich drücke die täglichen Knöpfe
ziehe die täglichen Hebel
und schaue gelassen in diese scheinbar
ewige Maschinenhalle—

durch die sich manchmal
eine Sekretärin schlängelt

Der hefte ich einen Pfiff an den Rock
sie lächelt und abends

blinzeln wir in unser Bier
und reden über den Tag
der schön war
wie wir von der Kellnerin hören

Sibylle Klefinghaus
was born in 1949 in a small West German city. She worked for 8 years in nursing, then came the women's movement and serious attempts at writing. A student of anthropology, she is currently

SIBYLLE KLEFINGHAUS

The Other Side

Dentist. The usual pounding heart, the usual clammy hands. She was only there because the pain was unbearable, only because the tablets she'd been swallowing for weeks, as unwisely as a child, no longer helped. The gray chair with its silent raising and lowering mechanism, the gentle gliding backwards to proneness. Tapping the teeth, the little round mirror in her mouth. At the back on the gums the busy movements stop abruptly. "What do you have there?" How long has it been there, when did it grow, painful, sensitive to pressure? Great news. Suddenly she's outside again with a referral in her hand, dental clinic, immediately. Coldness on the street, leaden late January noon sky. The bus comes in ten minutes. Wait, stomp feet, breathe into the wrapped-high shawl to get a bit of warmth. He with his specialist's knowledge. All the things so many doctors have seen in my mouth. Twice cherry-pit size, constricted at the base. That he's no battlefield dental plumber. That he can show his best side. To me, to his assistant. A poor excuse for an audience. Now, as the bus comes, she's already half-laughing about it. But she will call up in the clinic, otherwise she can count on his being upset with her.
The clinic is known for its long waiting time. "Cylindroma tumor," she says the next day into the telephone, "suspicion of cylindroma tumor." She may come tomorrow, 8:00 a.m. She hangs the mouthpiece in its fork, suddenly the booth is very quiet. "Carla is stupid" is scribbled on the wall. Like in a bad film, she thinks. They'll see. Of course it's nothing. That would be insane, if it were something. After so many years. The next morning she's there too early. Alights from the subway and doesn't know what to do with the time. Look for a tobacco shop. Godforsaken region here, where there's a subway station there must be a tobacco shop. Ah here. Buy cigarettes, a newspaper. Outside it's cold and still dark, she shivers, the cigarette that she's lit has no effect on that.

writing her doctoral thesis on Ethnopoetics. Publications include: *Fließpunkte* ("Flowpoints") with three other writers in their own press (1979); and *Das Kopfdromedar: Lesbentexte* ("The Dromedary-Head: Lesbian Writings") with two other writers, published 1981 by PiratinnenSender Press.

At five to eight she enters the building. She takes off her coat, there's a coat check woman who gives her a token, just like at the theater. The woman has a cardboard box in her lap with square-cut gauze. Memories of endless afternoons in the operating room, sorting out equipment, oiling equipment, twisting compresses. The used washed compresses that come wet and crumpled up from the laundry—fluff them up and press them smooth on an overturned bowl. Filling twisted compresses into the sterilization drum. Filling sterile compresses with sterile tongs from the large drums into small ones. Now I'm on the other side, she thinks.
Surgical section, enter only when called. Hand over the documents, the sealed envelope, not in the large room with the eight lined-up dental chairs; a small room, a desk, a chair, twenty students. Twenty pairs of eyes at her mouth, twenty times the mirror in her mouth, twenty times opening and closing her mouth. The professor explains the particularities that they should note, they tell each other what they see, unruffled, without raising their voices. Then she is expected to explain "how it came to this." She begins somewhat unsurely, then speaks concisely and to the point. The twenty are suddenly restless. They look at each other, shift from one foot to another, clear their throats. She knows what she's talking about. She's a member of the profession. Embarrassing. Did she understand everything we just said? Now it's too late. . . . as you know . . . diagnostic clarity . . . therapeutic consistency . . . No, she hadn't known. Or rather yes, of course she'd known, but it hadn't seemed to fit her own case. Not her. Tomorrow she should return, with an empty stomach, a tissue smear would be taken. Now just an imprint of her gums, bite into the pink rubber glob, the sweetish smell, nauseating, retching. None look at her as she leaves the room. Outside, the coat check woman again smiles. "Most of them can't get their mouths open," she says.

In the subway, the taste of rubber again, she feels sick, the nausea spreads through her whole body, cold sweat, cold hands. Not until the subway comes out of the tunnel does she feel better. The daylight lies flattened out over the city, the cars drive with fog beams.

The surgery has white tiled walls, two operating tables stand in it. On one lies a patient covered with cloths, mouth spread open with a metal device. He is conscious, communicates with the three wielding doctors by grunting.

Suddenly fear is present. Without speaking, the nurse points a hand toward the second table. Lay down. Her sweaty hands slip off the metal tubes on the side of the table. Her legs, which she can hardly raise, shake heavily, her mouth is completely dry. So that's how it is. No general anesthetic, just local, and then like the man on the next table. I won't be able to take it. What'll they say if I just go now? She turns her head to the other table. That he allows them to do that. "Don't look over there," says the nurse. But I still hear it. They're saying that they're cutting, that they're sewing, that they're staunching and whether he is in pain. He is in pain, groans loudly, moves under the sheets. Is he tied down? Will they tie me down? They can't, I'm quite reasonable, I know what I can do and what I oughtn't. She stares at the roof, then at the clock on the wall. The nurse pulls sterile sheets over her, only her head is still free. She tries to breathe evenly. When she closes her eyes, her lids flutter so strongly that she prefers to open them again. The nurse puts her right wrist in a leather sleeve, pulls it tight, then the left. She can say nothing. She stares at the clock and thinks over and over the same sentence: Now I've been waiting here for twenty minutes. Now I've been waiting here for twenty minutes. In her ears it starts to buzz, she can hardly hear the voices from the next table. Breathe evenly, she thinks, and always watch the clock. She can't control her breath any more, starts to moan, almost coughs, next she'll start to scream, just scream out, and they won't be able to stop her. No, not this time, thank God, thank God, not yet this time. Pull her breath deep into her belly again, stare at the clock, the buzzing subsides.

The doctor hurries in, presses her ice-cold tied-down hand. Two assistants. She sees how the medium for the local anesthetic is sucked up in two syringes, then the doctor throws a blue sterile cloth over her face, leaving only her mouth free. She no longer sees what proceeds, just the blue cloth very close to her eyes, she can brush it with her eyelashes, blue-dark dusk when she opens her eyes. The first shot in the upper gums, the pain goes through her, she wants to raise her hands to her mouth; tied down. Then the second shot, the pain even harder, several stabs throughout her mouth, ten minutes waiting. The anesthetic starts to take, her tongue gets thick and furry, the inner walls seem to swell shut. No one talks with her any longer except when she audibly sucks in air, someone says she should breathe through the nose, always through the nose. She feels the instruments in her mouth, the hooks, probes, mirrors, hears the scraping and grinding, feels an immense pressure against her upper gums, her whole head pressed backward, she has to swallow saliva, somehow it's not possible, the saliva begins to overflow out of her mouth, then a slurping, sucking sound, the vacuum tube. The doctors hardly talk, they throw their instruments clattering on the instrument table, which must stand about as high as her feet. Breathe through the nose. She sweats, her face is moist, her neck, her hair. "Thread, please"—now it can't take much longer. "Compress." She feels how a large compress is pressed against her gums, and another, and another, suddenly she can't get any air, breathing through the nose doesn't help, no air can get in, her whole mouth full of compresses, she starts moaning, turns her head back and forth, moans louder, the doctors bark commands at her, finally she pounds with her feet, kicks over the instrument table, is out for a few seconds, then at last they've noticed, compresses out, the sweet air, breathe through the nose, calm down, calm.

A transparent plastic "gums" is pushed in, clamped tight to her teeth, intended as a sort of pressure plaster. The sheets are pulled away, the one on her head last, it's over, it's all over. The doctors are already gone, the rubber gloves torn off in going and thrown to the floor, the nurses bend after them. "Come back next week." She raises herself, down from the table, tries to walk, though she thinks she'll collapse any second. But her legs function, the next patient waits at the door. One week, She goes to work as always. She wants to be alone. She waits, while the plastic thing on her gums hurts her almost unbearably, waits till the week is past. She gets up mornings and goes to bed evenings, there's nothing unusual in her life, except that this life is in doubt, but she thinks such thoughts with a smirk because of course she knows: not me.

After seven days she goes back to the clinic and hears what can't be true. Malignant.

She rides aimlessly through the city. It snows, she sits in the bus. With thought she tries to grasp reality, her reality. Again and again her imagination glides to the word "malignant." Suddenly she no longer knows what it means. They can't mean it. If that's a mistake. It is no mistake. Maybe I'll die. But that is a sentence she can't understand, like all who live.

WERKKREIS LITERATUR

"Werkkreis Literatur der Arbeitswelt"

"The Writing Circle for Literature of the Working World is a group of workers and employees who work together with journalists and writers in local workshops. Its task is the representation of the situation of dependent workers, primarily through language"—from the 1970 Program. In the beginning it was reports about "normal" work days, about work processes: increasingly we try to depict the reality of workers more comprehensively. Not only the reality of factory and office are subjects for our literature, but also family life, problems off the job and in free time, historical experience, etc.

Our texts continue with a single goal: to contribute to the democratic alteration of societal conditions; above all, co-operation with the unions, the largest organizations of workers. Since the members go to work each day, the writing cuts into precious free time. To use the time better, we work collectively. Texts are discussed in the group and—when necessary—rewritten together. Brochures are put together, readings organized.

In West Germany there are 30 workshop-chapters of the Circle. The workshops co-operate to produce books about various subjects (shift work, strikes, union representation, international solidarity, women's problems, etc.) which are published in a Fischer paperback series . . . we now have about 30 books with a combined printing of 1/2 million copies.

Literary fame or a chance to collect dust on bookshelves is not important. We want to talk with colleagues about problems of the working world and about our texts, we write for our colleagues.

The following two writers, Joachim Steffenhagen and Reinhard Komor, represent the Werkkreis Literatur der Arbeitswelt in this volume.—Ed.

DER ARBEITSWELT

Joachim Steffenhagen
Since 1949 a Berliner. After finishing school, three years in Lonau in the south Harz. After 1969, extended travel through West and East Europe, North Africa, Mexico, the USA, and

JOACHIM STEFFENHAGEN

thoughts about the zehlendorf spinnery

after 45
the bones were kaputt
and the houses
the streets
and the machines

to keep living
because they needed food
because they needed clothes
the bones
rolled up
their sleeves high
and began to build up

meanwhile
the capital sat
in a safe place
        no pain
and rubbed its hands
over the coming profits
and kept its nose out
as long as sacrifices were made
and dust and dirt

only when the smokestacks
smoked again crawled
out of its hiding place
the spirit of the old and

Canada. Winter 1977-78 with wife and daughter on the Antilles.
Since 1976 a member of the West Berlin Workshop of the *Werkkreis Literatur der Arbeitswelt*.
Published in daily newspapers, in publications of the Werkkreis, and in 1977, in the poetry anthology *Stadtansichten*, (views of the city). My first own poetry volume and a play are in the works.

gedanken über die zehlendorfer "spinne"

nach 45
waren die knochen kaputt
und die häuser
die straßen
und die maschinen

um zu leben
weil sie nahrung
weil sie kleidung brauchten
krempelten
die knochen
die ärmel hoch
und fingen an aufzubaun

derweilen
saß das kapital
an sichren orten
            ohne qual
und rieb sich die hände
ob des kommenden gewinns

und hielt sich raus
solang es opfer gab und
staub und dreck

erst als die schlote
wieder rauchten kroch
aus dem versteck
der geist des alten und

conserving
to demand
what once belonged to it
what at others' costs
arose all new

and slowly
with the flow of time
the spirit took
                again
the reins
in hand

let the bones
dance on its strings
                like this
like that
sucked itself full
of their marrow
to the limit
and threw them away
as soon as they whistle
'cuz he can't use
hollow bones

erhaltenden
zu fordern
was ihm einst gehörte
was auf kosten anderer
ganz neu entstand

und langsam
mit dem fluß
der zeiten
nahm der geist
     wieder
die zügel
in die hand

ließ die knochen
an seinen fäden tanzen
     mal so

mal so
saugte sich voll
mit ihrem mark
bis an den rand
und wirft sie weg
sobald sie pfeifen
denn hohle knochen
braucht er nicht

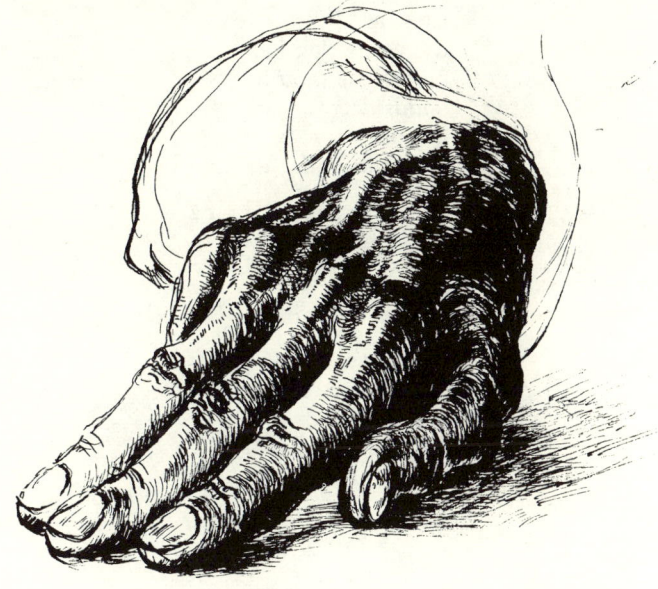

Study of a Hand   by Jürgen Beissert   pen

Mornings

The hammer always sinks at six
between the bells
Just as, in dream,
a new ride has begun
he begins
the burdensome work

The necessity
supported by the understanding
lets habit have its way

And it's even still cold!

Clothes stand by themselves
but pulled a bit
toward here or there
brings the crease
and helps give direction

The way to the subway
isn't far
the white flag hangs
before the mouth
hands deep
in pockets
portfolio under the arm

Down there in the pipe
the faces

the feeling
always the same

the freezer chest
opens its gates
and the goods await
their destination

Morgens

Der Hammer senkt sich jeweils um sechs
zwischen die Glocken
Gerade wenn im Traum
eine neue Fahrt begonnen hat
beginnt er
sein lästiges Werk

Die Notwendigkeit
unterstützt durch den Verstand
läßt der Gewohnheit ihren Lauf

Kalt ist es auch noch!

Die Klamotten steh'n von selber
aber ein bißchen
nach hier und nach da
bringt Falten rein
und trägt zur Richtung bei

Der Weg zur Bahn
ist nicht lang
die weiße Fahne steht
vor dem Mund
die Hände tief
in den Taschen
die Mappe unter dem Arm

Unten im Rohr
die Gesichter

Das Empfinden
immer das Gleiche

Der Tiefkühlschrank
öffnet seine Pforten
und die Ware harrt
ihrer Bestimmung

the basic fact

The basic fact
is of different lengths
and commands accordingly
various amounts of hands

two motors drive it
the one from above
with economic turn
the other from below
by remote control
with a strength
between 3 and 4 kw

the lower has to turn
and control the speed
the upper controls
the brains between the hands and
gives no time
to think

unremitting flows the dark stream
and forces the hands
in its drudgery
just one hour a day
it stands still
in the morning and noon
otherwise the hands fly
just as it wants

every ten seconds
new wounds tear
in the brains of those
who live from the produce of the belt
the motor below
is driven electrically
the engagement of the hands
is dictated
by the upper motor

das eigentliche

das eigentliche
ist von unterschiedlicher länge
und gebietet dementsprechend
über eine unterschiedliche händemenge

zwei motoren treiben es an
der eine von oben
mit ökonomischen dreh
der andere von unten
schützgesteuert
mit einer kraft
zwischen drei und vier kw

der untere muss sich dreh'n
und die geschwindigkeit lenken
der obere bestimmt
und lässt den gehirnen zwischen den händen
keine zeit
zum denken

unermüdlich fliesst der dunkle strom
und zwingt die hände
in seinen fron
nur eine stunde am tag
da bleibt er still
am morgen und mittags
sonst fliegen die hände
so wie er es will

alle zehn sekunden
reissen neue wunden
in die hirne derer
die vom ertrag des bandes leben
der motor unten
ist vom elektrischen strom getrieben
der einsatz der hände
wird vom motor
oben
vorgeschrieben

Reinhard Komor
Name: Reinhard Komor
Occupation: Welder
Born: 1949 in former Hochelheim, now Hüttenberg, Wetzlar District, near Butzbach, West Germany

REINHARD KOMOR

The Release

The assembly work in Brunswick is over. My sweat mixed with oil for six weeks, my blood was sucked away by sawdust and fear sealed contracts with tiredness.
Now it is pounding and quaking again, the engine, held in the track by eroded rails which lead home. An endless, tired trail, on worn-out bearings which have to force the iron wedge into the landscape with tenacious and raping strength always at the same time. On the leeside of this rootless stream of metal, plastic and turned wood I find myself jammed—restless.
Rattling, oozing, stomping and bumping, the movement slows down. Nothing is running smoothly anymore. Corners and edges appear. The power is overpowered. The New wins, the raw hollow mechanism which was told to move. Shouting shrilly the old surrenders. My feelings rub on tempered steel. Iron splinters patter. Glowing iron parts grab my exhausted soul and catapult it, together with my body, out in the open air with a jerk.
On the platform concrete prickles under my feet. I float down the worn-out, but patient, stairs with the stream.
In the smoke-thickened air voices are hanging. Backs together if a newcomer needs room. Roaring elements are speeding up, racing; and the bloated body in the hall starts to suck and vomit again. Ribbons of despair, displeasure, love and reunion tumble softly lit under the roof. They are not the only ones that have got to live here with discharge, urine and excrement.
Not far from here, an elephant will die tonight. Squatted on the green plastic bench, I get carried away. To the left, left, to the right. To the left, right, right. Rocking, hard bumps. Rubber squelches, brushes sweep. The folding door opens to the inside, swings and halts.
With long arms I stand in the hallway. Kick the door into its lock. Seabag down, throw the case away. Breathe! Put the lights on, sit down. Peace, peace. Cool bitter beer plunges down the sooted shaft.

Since 1975 in Berlin. Various employments. Learned goldsmithing. State examination as metal sculptor and designer. Through artistic analysis of the working world, I am today a welder.
Since 1976 a member of the *Werkkreis Literatur der Arbeitswelt*.

My hard mattress welcomes me. Stretched out, I lie on the stony Atlantic coast of northern Spain. Every stone, every rock, it's all familiar. My hand wanders over the big rocks, slips into the water, finds the lamp and turns the light off.
Thousands of visions shoot through my brain, leaving behind bizarre, thin, blackened lines on the damaged screen of my conscience cinema. They vanish like drops out of the broken mercury thermometer. Crawl in the cracks, hiss along the skirting board, disappear in faraway corners.
Grains in a sack of grain. Pressed together, panicking with fear. Measurable, squashable, storable—goods. I, the grain in a sack of grains.
Tormenting tightness, suffocating faintness a second ago, now, suddenly, delicious solitude. Intoxicated by the vast emptiness of space everything trivial falls behind. The love inside me bursts the hard core. My roots, filled with happy fulfillment and peaceful force, tumble down to earth, while in tender sprout the timid bud moves to show favor to the sun.
A hard jerk, I fall down, paralyzing fright overcomes me. Without hesitation the contents of the sack is poured over me.
I land with others in the broad gutter. My only thought: onto my feet, otherwise they will trample me to death. Fearful about my little bit of life I am forced to be brutal. Yelling, I trample on others, hit hard, am only a rag of screaming panic being pushed forward. The stream carries me to the noisy temples of work. The house is locked, my case is packed, finished with, the trip is about to begin. With a warm hole in my body, feet in the gutter, I lie on the bloody road with my nose up in the sky.

I am well. A dove sits next to me in the gutter. Turning its head, the bird looks at me sadly, eye by eye. It's gone.
Above me, Müller laughing, leaning over the roofs on his arms.

Threateningly he bends down and shows his glittering teeth. A few tiles crash down, not very far away. Splinters of clay buzz dangerously near over my head—slowly, like honey-filled bees. He laughs excessively, scornfully with frosty eye sockets. Windows clink. Someone is hastily nailing up his windows with planks at the end of the street. Tar and lead is sticking to me, it drags me down to the mummies. Fear runs once again out of his frosty eyes onto his pestered-to-death slaves. But the gutter sucks them away like young rain and carries them in stinking pipes to the bogs of sunken passion. White, innocently pulverized wheat flour floats down, covers me and the whole district, which sweats out the last orgasm under soft powder.

It is dark. I want to sleep. The landscape stretches underneath me, straightened out like a crumpled table-cloth. Straight and soft. With burning eyes, I look to where the roof stops my imagination. I have got my willpower back again, I am where I want to be.

Strange, my ears get warm, something irritates me, heralds new bindings. My lurking organs are switched to red, they burn. Every noise, even the slightest, which develops and spreads outside, is taken up by my analyzing ears. No matter whether it is a sparrow's fart from the roof opposite or ungainly creeping steam-rollers. They all penetrate into my rented rampart and develop just like japanese paper flowers—they wilt within seconds. Vibrating, but intensively clear, they strive through my brain.

Is it starting again? It does get annoying. Turn over, push the pillow in the right position and everything is gone. I want my peace, need her. I know, I do have the energy to chase the vision.

After all, the fascination is too enormous. Stuck to my sweaty sheet I am incapable of moving. The tiredness crawls back into its corner and gets tired again. My will is strong but indefinite, inexpressible fear comes through the back door. A sensation of fear and a cozy thrill have got hold of me. I can still control myself easily. I reduce the fearful part but it is impossible to get rid of it. I intensify the waiting and the cozy thrill. I want to live it.

The hole next to me is growing. Is it a self-enlarging, portraying, developing picture?

But nothing is growing, on the contrary. The floor, first next to, then beneath my bed, dissolves, gets eaten up. Piece by piece, no noise, no ashes. I am not lying on a picture. Floating on my mattress over the cellar the sheet hangs down like a tablecloth. The cellar with all its junk which nobody wants, hidden from the greedy eyes of tidiness. Shelves, an old TV, stripped loud-speakers. The broken spin-drier with the old copper tub which I could not get out. The doll's-pram is still there. A few rusty screws inside and the screw-driver with the orange-colored handle. To make it lie smooth in my hand I filed the casting seams off. I had been looking for it for weeks, I did not know where I had left it.

I fall, fall into nowhere, no noise, no fear. The cellar stands on a high mountain. There is nothing but the cellar.

Everything in its peculiar, blue-faded light lies naked in unattainable distance. Suddenly, my ear catches a distant, humming noise. It becomes more and more intense, clearer. It's not just a noise. It's a word, changes to a phrase, it's a demand, an inflexible demand.

Far away, fear bursts the asphalt.

I do have difficulties in getting the meaning, in understanding it really. But before the sense of the sentence soaks into my brain, before I am able to decode the sentence, I know that the enforced object is black, very black from the inside.

The speaker is unknown. I don't know what he is called nor how he or it looks.

The light darkens every time his words roll down the blue mountain. The fear reaches the track leading to the abbey.

Now I can decode the words which form a sentence. The sentence behind the pulsating blue painting, constantly being repeated in a low penetrating voice, is: "I will burn, I will burn!"

It forces me to approach the painting. The sentence and I get acquainted. Noticing it, I surrender. The noise intensifies while I approach. It fulfills me. Metal runs through my veins. "I will burn. I will burn!"

The fear is standing before the abbey. Slowly it creeps up from behind. Shivering, I notice it reaching me. Pushes me forward to the blue painting. Then carries me away. I can do nothing, no halt, I am overpowered.

"I will burn, I will burn!"

A terrific ride to hell. Everything is an immense galactic vibration. Not fighting it I will be lost. I open my mouth to rescue myself. But no sound is released. My own will: enclosed. Nothing works. With the speed of light this madness comes nearer. It's got to work. I have to try, otherwise I'll be lost. Sweat freezes on my forehead. I swear that, out of the slick of the tortured corpses, the flower of retaliation will grow. In my deathly fear I shout it out:

"Shit! Shit!"

On this phrasal beam I go on the journey. Not until after a thousand eternities does my willpower hit the image. It goes through like anything. Slight vibration saturates the world. The vision starts to vibrate. Cracks become visible, they move on, cover the whole area. The curtain falls creakingly. Millions of milky splinters sink in a waterglass. Liberated!

      I commence to paint.

translated by Ulrich Danielowski

> Volker Wohlfahrt
> Born: December 18, 1950
> Upbringing: Father not much
> Mother tried
> Then in a Home
> Wife still trying

VOLKER WOHLFAHRT

Hot Coffee

Today I am driven.
A fleeting kiss in front of the plant and out of the car.
I'm still tired. My colleague's "good morning" is too loud. Johannes says, "Volker, you look like you've been drinking." He has red eyes, bags under them, wrinkles. I don't bother answering, ask about coffee, if it's already brewed, and look at the roasting schedule for today.
Colleague Meiner serves me the coffee, "my own roasting," he says. "And take a look at our tons we've run through tonight."
My colleague Winfried, young, slim, chic in the blue baggy Ja-Kopp overalls, comes, noisy and terribly well-slept, into the tasting kitchen. "What's that I hear? Wohlfahrt's shift's #2? Never! We stay Shift #1, the best, you'll see tomorrow, you'll see!" Fine, it's my shift. But just now I want to drink my coffee, smoke a cigarette in peace. I say nothing.
Meiner tells me quickly exactly how much raw coffee remains in the silos. "And now get the hell out of here and give my regards to your wife," I say. He goes. The foreman comes.
Winfried checks the color values of the roasted coffee—they indicate the taste. He has all the work, and I? I get to hear the foreman vaguely trying to explain how much raw coffee remains in the silos.
Listen, tune out, drink coffee, take forms to be signed, and then goodbye. Get the hell out of here so I can finally do my job.
The machines have to be switched to another function.
Testing, checking every roasting for color and water content.
The old beans are together with beans that are too fresh.
Amounts get mixed wrong, have to be mixed all over again.
We work in high gear.

Occupation: Everything and nothing, at the moment, advertising manager with the "Tageszeitung" newspaper. Earlier Shop Steward and Coffee Roaster. Earlier yet, Film Copier, Gravedigger, Lazy Bum, etc.
Salary: 800 marks net.

The second roasting isn't out yet. "Telephone for you. BR* stuff. You're supposed to come into the office."
"Not now. Otherwise we'll have shit coffee." Damn it, if we had just one more roaster, it would be no problem. Then you could immediately devote yourself to any BR matters that arose.
But of course the firm has to save money. Although here in Berlin they cash in 100,000 DM yearly subsidy for every employee, they rationalize. As far as I'm concerned the coffee can get burned. They're insured.
So down into the office. 3 flights of stairs at 13 steps ea. plus 5 steps to the office door. And there they are, the "little" bosses.
"Herr Wohlfahrt," says Voss, the representing plant supervisor, "information has been brought to us that colleague Helga M. has diverted coffee."
My first BR assignment, the chairman has vacation, none of the others are here but me. I've been a member for three days.
How did I get into this. I wasn't satisfied to grouse about the other BRs. I thought I could do it better.
Voss has found someone he can smear again. "She was seen by a co-worker as she packed coffee in her apron and disappeared in the direction of the dressing room. Now we should speak with the woman who saw her." He glances around the whole circle of us. How the employees can take it so for granted to shit on each other.
To report a coffee-swipe is to prove your loyalty to the firm. The employees think well of themselves then, they earn themselves the golden Ja-Kopp Star.
"Frau Kressmann, please come into the office!" is called into the intercom.
Maybe colleague Helga is clever enough to get her coffee out of her locker.

---

*Betriebsrat: production council, business council. An advisory committee made up of employees to represent employee interests in a firm; also, the title of a member of such a committee.

Frau Kressmann has hurried. She is already here, is asked to have a seat, and she begins at once to tell her story. "I've been in the firm for seven years now, I've worked in different departments and worked hard and seen plenty. Once in awhile we have trouble, too, among colleagues. But I've always managed to put it back together again. Some have gone then too. But I've never experienced anything like today. And I won't stand for it."
She takes a deep breath and looks at us challengingly.
And she makes a secure impression. "Well, I saw how Frau M. packed coffee into her apron and left the packing house in the direction of the WC. We were shocked. After all, we can't tolerate something like that. And without wasting much more breath over it, I said: I'm going to the management. Otherwise they might get even nervier. I won't have anything to do with criminals." She looks at us expectantly. Funny. At first none of us react, so that she does get a bit unsure.
Production Master Voss sums up slowly and friendly: "In the work regulations it says that every co-worker has the duty to protect company property. You have done that. We thank you in the company's name. Frau Kressmann, please return now to your work."
She rises, smiles to us in parting and has already left the room. Now Helga M. is sent for. We wait. Why do some people think they have to preserve the order without even being paid for it?
My father, for example, filled up his workshop almost exclusively with tools from his firm. He thought nothing about it. After all, they were pieces of equipment he worked with every day, that he took care of and repaired. And whose worth he knew. He simply took them home then. One day while shopping at a department store he saw someone—and it was someone he knew from work—pocketing something without paying for it. My father didn't only scream "Thief!", he delivered the delinquent immediately to the department manager. He received 20 marks reward and then it started to dawn on him what he'd done. For days no one could speak to him because of it.
I wonder if Frau Kressmann will feel the same?
In the meantime Frau M. has appeared in the office. She is fixed by suspicious glances. She sits down without waiting for a special invitation. Voss looks at her questioningly. "Well?" He doesn't want to bring more than that across his lips. It should be enough for an immediate confession.
Quickly I request to be allowed to speak alone with Frau M. in my capacity as BR. The Business Constitution Law gives me the right to be present at any investigation. As a respectable BR I must try to get to the bottom of the matter. Therefore the talk with her alone. I get it too, even though they aren't required. So we look for another room.

Helga is older than her colleague. A bit round, as if she expected a child. And she's already a lame duck. Serious eyes, thin face, creased skin, well-groomed outwardly. I explain to her what's up. But without naming the other woman. She admits everything without beating around the bush. She's caught. Does it seem to her not to matter? I give her my telephone number and ask that she call me up after work. Frau M. says, before we return to the office, "Well, that's a change of tune, the BR didn't used to worry about such trivialities." Back in the office, the whole meeting moves to the dressing room. Helga has to open her locker. The packages of coffee are taken out and returned to the packing room.

"So Frau M. You can go ahead and empty your locker and go home. You'll be hearing from us." With that, the matter is disposed of for the management, represented by Frau Strupp. Now Frau M. can finally go.

By now I've been a whole hour away from my department. "You asshole, you really left me in the lurch. I can't operate 8 machines at once. Our Chemistry Joe (he means Joe Kühn) will shit a brick when he sees the values."

Winfried was angry. No wonder. On all 8 machines the water values were wrong. After roasting, the beans are cooled with water. They soak water up, too, and thus weigh more. The maximum water-value allowed by law is four percent. Our firm roasts hard on the limit. We've had trouble with our Herr Kühn often enough because the water-values were too low.

"That's how the customers finally get good coffee. Otherwise they have to pour water on it themselves."

"Cut the stupid jokes, Wohlfahrt; Loogie will kick up a storm for sure." We called Kühn "Loogie" for awhile now; as foodstuffs-chemist he had the assignment, like us, to test the taste of the coffee. A taste from the cup and then spit it out. And he always sounded as if he was pulling a green one out from way back there.

"If he fusses just send him to me: I'm the roaster in charge today. If he wants to take me on as roaster and BR then let him rip, I'm steaming already anyway."

"If you say so. The roasting for this hour is already logged." That was nice of him. But then I said, "If we're ever in the same stupid situation, with only one roaster in the department, and it won't be seldom, then we'll just write in the log book that measurements couldn't be made due to lack of personnel. They should hire more people. After all there's enough unemployed." "Isn't that a bit impudent?" objected Winfried.

"Who has to do the work! It's us, isn't it!" "Okay, okay, I take it back." "Forgotten. It's a bad day for me. But next time it gets logged 'lack of personnel,' period."

Winfried is already operating another machine in the back of the shop. Maybe he didn't even listen to me.

We ran from machine to machine and altered the heat of the flames and the amounts of water to get the right relation. After every alteration we had to check the coffee's water and color value: if it was wrong, alter again and check again. Through the confusion Winfried asked me quickly what had happened earlier. I answered that I didn't feel like talking about it while we ran around among the machines. We worked wordlessly further that way.

The time passed quite swiftly. We had even sacrificed our break. That was fine with me. The talk of the day was the theft story anyway and I hadn't the nerve to have to listen to it. I didn't really know what I could've said, especially in regard to Frau Kressmann.

The shifts change. The 3 men from the following shift had already heard what had happened today and wanted to hear the details. But we didn't get to that.

My colleagues from the BR came to us in the lab and took me along to our office. They slapped me on the shoulder. I had no idea what was up. Of course. It was about Frau M. and about the enterprise which "had to be protected," and about the papers of the colleague: people like that should be blacklisted. "The woman is 43 years old and 4 years with the firm" and "with 43 years one must, after all, know what one does. That's not her first time for sure. She had 14 half-pound packages in her locker. At 200 days in the year that's 11,200 packages, that's 67,000 marks. It's unheard of." I tried to ridicule the matter. Actually it was funny. These guys thought like the management. Thank god they had to work now and I could go.

Change clothes. Punch the card. Get out of the building.

"Halt! Herr Wohlfahrt! Bag check!" That was the doorman, whom I'd passed by deep in thought.

On the Anniversary of the Death of Hans Martin Schleyer*

There has already been so much said and written
I have only one question
If Hans Martin Schleyer had, as usual,
ridden with Heydrich on that day
who would have eulogized him
the same ones?

Zum Jahrestag von Hans Martin Schleyer

Es ist schon so viel gesagt und geschrieben worden.
Ich hab' nur eine Frage.
Wenn H.M.S. wie gewohnt
mit Heydrich gefahren wäre an jenem Tage
Wer würde dann seiner gedenken
Die Gleichen?

---

*Hans Martin Schleyer, President of the Employers Association of West Germany, was kidnapped and murdered by the Red Army Fraktion, a West German based terrorist group in Autumn, 1977. This touched off a wave of hysteria in Germany reminiscent of the McCarthy Era in the U.S. Schleyer's funeral featured speeches from prominent German politicians, businessmen, and even labor leaders, extolling his achievements and good qualities. Unmentioned remained his past as industrial official for the Nazis in occupied Czechoslovakia. Schleyer drove to work each day with Heinrich "Hangman" Heydrich, Nazi governor of Bohemia and Moravia and head administrator and organizer of the Nazi "Final Solution of the Jewish Problem." Heydrich died on May 26, 1942, when a bomb, built by Czech resistance fighters, destroyed his auto in Prague. Schleyer was, by coincidence, not in the car on that day.

JUTTA BARTUS

Jutta Bartus—Bibliographical Notes

I was born in Breslau in 1926. Father, an insurance salesman, was strict and friendly, and endeavored to provide his two children with the schooling that he couldn't have. To that end, he hid his critical stance toward the State until the beginning of the war. My impulsive, cheerful mother raved about classical music and Nietzsche. But a few Heine verses survived the Nazi regime in her memory. The mixed petit-bourgeois idyll stimulated my young girl fantasies. Often shut out of the company of my peers because of a hip disease, I built my own dream world where Karl Mohr and Winnetou* were my brothers.

After finishing school in 1944, came war service, in the end—after leaving Breslau—in a military hospital near Dresden. In April, 1945, came the last letter from my father by military post to the new home in central Germany.

The terrible death of my father in the army of the Hangman-General Schörner was a shock barely covered by the responsibilities for a sick mother and a brother who was almost blinded by a combat injury. A series of different jobs followed: servant girl on the Schweta estate, given an allowance, potatoes, and grain; seamstress of uniforms in Riesa, paid partly in meat, bread, and oil; village schoolteacher, sometimes able to scrounge something nutritious from the farmers.

In the summer of 1946, more by chance than intention, a new chapter of my life began. The district officials noticed my work with the otherwise unoccupied and bored village youth; our chorus and amateur drama group. I was called to the first Central Committee of the FDJ† and to the Schwerin Province radio station to be Program Director for Youth, and, one year later I was given a chance to study at the German Theater Institute in Weimar. Confronted with teachers who—with their "de-Nazification papers" in their pockets—rubbed their students' noses in their fascist upbringing, the thought of my

---

*Karl Mohr is a character in Schiller's "The Robbers," similar to Robin Hood. Winnetou, an Indian, is a character in a series of adventure books, long popular in Germany.

†FDJ, Freie Deutsche Jugend—"Free German Youth"—is a youth organization in the DDR, similar to the Boy Scouts but more omnipresent.

father's death forced me to protest. For this I was thrown out of the Institute in December 1948 and in March 1949 I moved with my mother to our relations from Breslau, who had found accommodation in the Rhineland, in the West.

A short, very "instructive" time followed as cleaner of metal parts in a Velbert lock factory, then, to save money to study journalism in Frankfurt, a job as commercial representative for Soliner Steelware.

In the summer of 1950, a drunk ran over the "travelling saleswoman." The long convalescence in the hospital ended all the plans, only the passion for books and the attempts to write remained, along with a job as distributor of office supplies.

The first publication of poems of mine—analyses of my surroundings and of the crimes of the Nazi regime—won friends, one of whom was later to be my husband, Adolf Endler, of Düsseldorf. When, in 1955, he took up the offer of the Verlag der Nationen (Publishing House of the Nations) in East Berlin, I forgot my experiences in Weimar in the face of the West German Adenauer-State's repression of all memory of the Nazi crimes. The witchhunt against communists and other leftists drove me from Düsseldorf to East Berlin, and the hope for socialistic conditions influenced me too.

In a painful process taking two decades, constantly endeavoring critically to depict the conflicts in society, I wrote many works, primarily for radio and television.

Again and again I gave up my Berlin residence in favor of closer contact with work collectives and studies on location—in the lowlands of Wische, the chemical plants near Halle, the lignite mines in Lausitz. The focus of my work was above all the problems of women, the discrepancy between official equality and the lack of possibilities to use it.

My critical stance led to reprimands and humiliations from representatives of the state, and finally—after the imprisoning of my oldest son for attempted "Flight from the Republic" while in the army—since 1975, to silence. After two dozen publications—some quite respected—no more. The break with the DDR-regime is documented in September 1977 in my Emigration Application, addressed to Professor Hager in the Central Committee of the Socialist Unity Party of Germany, the SED: " . . . In this land the methods swing so strongly between punishments and the distribution of privileges, that I must assume that, through the creation and assumption of new functions, a new type of person has developed beside the working class: the pink philistine, who, savoring the power of his position, persecutes with his petit-bourgeois thirst for revenge everything that is unlike himself. I don't want the rest of my life to be senselessly wasted . . . "

The cause of this sharp criticism was not only my personal experiences or the unjust treatment of colleagues like Sarah Kirsch, Reiner Kunze, (even then) Stefan Heym, and many others, but rather above all the recognition of the constant defrauding of working people—the ostensible ruling class—by the corrupt leadership class.

After a few dramatic months my application was approved, and I returned to Düsseldorf with my two youngest sons. My older son followed in summer 1978 from Brandenburg Prison. The Ruth Novellettes were published as my first work in the Federal Republic. New works—a novel, a volume of short stories—are underway.

Düsseldorf, summer 1979

Frau Mitschuleit's Survey

In 1967 I wrote a radio play with this title, and I always remember its background. After a long stay in the chemical works Leuna in Halle, I was back in Berlin with my family, in the old Prenzlauer Berg quarter, where new contacts with Work Collectives weren't hard to make. These were the people for whom I wrote; logical that I should write about them.

I only had to walk a few minutes to reach a large clothing plant, "Treff-Modelle," and the women in the "Anne Frank" Work Brigade were my main conversation partners. At one time I, too, had sat in a hall of sewing machines, and they trusted me. And if I sometimes corrected a badly sewn-on button or an awry hem to save them a little trouble in the stress of their work, they told me about themselves and their problems.

One day early in 1967 I found the Brigade in a condition like that of a stirred up anthill: the hours were to be changed.

For a more continuous use of the machines, the management set up 2 long shifts, one from 6 AM to 2 PM, the other from 2 PM to 10 PM.

And the women had been recruited to this work a few years earlier with the promise of convenient working hours, so they could care for their families. Now they were indignant. I wrote down the problems that arose, every one of them told me of her difficulties. From this came my radio play, a fiction that lay close to reality, in which—in my place—a woman from the Brigade questions the others:

Time: 1967
Place: Berlin, Prenzlauer Berg, a clothing factory
Fade in: Machine Hall

Trude Sänger: (reads) "... inform the plant management that, because of our families, we cannot work shifts. Either the old hours are kept, or we give notice! Did you write that? And to Director Brossat?

Erika Mitschuleit: It's our only choice. With such a list we have clout. If 20 or 30 quit, they'll think twice before going to shifts. All you have to do is give your signature.

Trude Sänger: Will that help? (hastily) Reinsch is coming!

Department Supervisor Reinsch: What's up, Frau Mitschuleit? On the line we don't have the quiltings and you sit here and chatter.

Erika Mitschuleit: Today I'm working a bit less, Frau Reinsch. I'm writing down who can't work if the new shifts are started. That should interest the management.

Reinsch: I'm interested in seeing that you work fast. The coat department is behind schedule since three days ago. We can't afford more *unnecessary* hitches in the assembly line. Please return to your work. You're giving a poor example to the others.

Mitschuleit: I have always done my work, you know that perfectly well. What do you mean: Poor example!

Reinsch: But we can't all just do as we please!

Mitschuleit: And how is it here in the company? Today they change this, tomorrow that. We don't even get asked. They think we'll always stay quiet. But no longer. We have democracy.

Reinsch: What does the assistant manager say to your democracy? And to the fact that you use it to goldbrick?

Mitschuleit: You'll see what happens if you put the lines together.

Reinsch: (attempting to persuade) Frau Mitschuleit, be sensible. I've explained it to you: by setting all four lines together in two big shifts we can use the new machines more continuously. We can't let such expensive machines sit around idle during the day.

Mitschuleit: Do you have children? No, you have none. But you talk! Wait till you have the resignations. *Then* you'll have holes in your plan! You won't be able to fill them if you work all day and all night. Do you think I'm dependent on this company? I can sew for people again. I can rent out a room. I can scrape up my money, plus the state money for the kids.

Reinsch: Even if I *had* children ...

Mitschuleit: Then your husband would do what you couldn't get to. Mine is gone. Sure, for you it makes no difference. Why shouldn't you be for changing shifts. But we on the line, we have to throw away our whole lives, you don't. One week getting up at four, the next not in bed till after midnight. That only affects us—and our children. When they're neglected and ruined who has the guilty conscience? Not you!

Reinsch: With your qualifications, you don't have to remain on the line. How often must I offer it to you?

Mitschuleit: Sure, as assistant manager I'd go home at 4. And the others? It's not just my problem.
Reinsch: Are you really concerned about the others?
Mitschuleit: You can think what you like of me. The will of the majority must be respected.
Reinsch: What! First you stir up the women on me, and then you dare to speak of the will of the majority? Go to your work now, or . . .
Mitschuleit: Or?
Reinsch: . . . I'll have to give you a warning. And that comes in your permanent file! (energetic footsteps fading out)
Mitschuleit: (calling after her) Go ahead and do it! And don't forget I agitated the others!—Well? What's with all of you? Why didn't you say anything? You figure you've got a dummy who'll pull your coals from the fire?

Fade In: Manager's Office

Reinsch: As Manager, you are responsible for the frictionless production process in your 2 Brigades. That's what you're paid for. The plan hasn't been filled for days.
Manager: It looks like today we'll only finish 90 coats. Yesterday it was at least still 110.
Reinsch: 90? With a plan quota for 150? I'm amazed at your ease, Colleague Hendrik. I haven't been able to reach you on the telephone all day.
Manager: I thought it better to let you take a look for yourself what's up here. A report wouldn't do it.
Reinsch: Do you mean to tell me, you had me put off on the phone? (uncontrolled) Am I your errand boy?
Manager: I'm sorry, Frau Reinsch, I saw no other way. How often have I warned you: most of the women came to us because they couldn't work shifts. Now they feel deceived. That makes bad blood . . .

In the further course of dialogue, the sociology of a women's Brigade emerges: There is the good Comrade who agitates for the new shift arrangement, who is good enough to change her mind in the end; Trude Sänger stands for the consume-oriented women, for whom refrigerator, TV, car—all the bourgeois comforts—are more important than love and family. This woman's man leaves her. Then, indifferent, she lets everything be done with her; Vera Kuckelmann, wife of a middle level bureaucrat with personal connections to the plant management, provides comic relief with her shirking and absenteeism; Maria Langhans, who reports about her mentally damaged son—"the child"—has our pity. The fates of these and the other Brigade members are found in every city, in every street in every city. But in the context of the political economy and planned economy of the DDR, they shock. Erika Mitschuleit, who, a widow, struggles alone with the problems of her two growing children, speaks out for all and starts an avalanche that no one can stop. She, who has "always done her work," appeals to the conscience of the others with her refusal:

Mitschuleit: . . . just listen to Margitta! For once she works 2 hours through, and immediately a big mouth. Something so work-shy as you can only be afforded by socialism.

Anne Weber (the Comrade): I never thought our progress would be measured by that!

Margitta Hauser: And is shiftwork progress?

Anne Weber: So you don't want to! That was plain to see.

Hauser: Who's talking about me? My husband's happy about it. Now I can't come along for a week, he says.

Weber: Come along where?

Hauser: To the "Rubble Cow."

Trude Sänger: That's about the worst dive in Prenzlauer Berg!

Hauser: What do you know about it? It's a right jolly pub.

Weber: Do you go there often?

Hauser: Pretty often.

Weber: Do you take your children along?

Hauser: Huh? *Them* I put to bed at 6. 7 at the latest.

Weber: And with the new shift arrangement? Will your husband do it? Will he make them supper?

Hauser: The oldest can fetch rolls, the baker is next door.

Maria Langhans: This "oldest" has just turned eight. (light murmur)

Weber: What, do you only work so that you can go to the bar?

Hauser: Not good enough for you? Makes you sick to think of me in such a dump? You sit at home with your husband at the table with a fancy tablecloth, drink wine, and talk about Progress. I drink beer like my husband and hold a hand of cards like him. What's wrong with that?

Langhans: You should be ashamed of yourself! 4 children! The poor worms. They ought to be taken away from you before they degenerate. You call yourself a mother.

Hauser: I am! I've washed diapers for 8 years now. What good does all the blabber about equality do me if I can't get out? Once in awhile a pretty dress, for once not to have to think: Time again, now you have to hunt up a space in a day care center again, or have you managed to slip past the 4 weeks? (cries)

Weber: Well, you won't have to work shift, I'll see to that! 4 children at 26!

Hauser: And whose fault is that? Oh you can kiss my ass! (chair scraping, hurrying steps)

I had many heated discussions about this text with the Party Representative at the plant until finally—with the addition of a few moralistic dialogues—it was approved. Parallel to the discussion of my text ran the discussion about the new shift arrangements in "my" Brigade. The great surprise came after the first broadcast of the radio play. The plant's Party leadership asked the radio station for an auto with loudspeakers so all the women in all the departments would have a chance to hear the play and afterwards to discuss it in the canteen.

Fantastic, I hear some here say. But when I think of the speech with which the leading cadre of the plant closed the discussion—again and again emphasizing how close the ear of leadership was to the workers—this play, its development, and the solution of the shift problem through a shortened shift on a specific production line for the "problem women"—then I'm not so happy. For my play, with which I wanted to show the other, inhumane side of the "Planned Economy," had been converted to a tool for the leaders.

I felt the same, too, recently when I saw an old DDR film again—"Network," by Eberhard Panitz and Rolf Kirsten. It tells the story of people who helped build the Petrochemical Works in Schwedt.

The first time I saw it, in the early 70's, the film seemed surprisingly critical, almost revolutionary. People were shown who work day and night "for the building of the works—looking towards the socialist year 2000," some workers working themselves into breakdowns. The hard life of separated couples is spoken of, also the difficulties of those women who followed their men to the new-built city on the Polish border. They have lost their relationship to their earlier work collective and can find no substitute on the construction site. They are depressed, or they develop the wish—so absurd in the DDR—to concentrate solely on the private parts of their lives—worries about their children and husbands, furniture and decorating their apartments. And what a bourgeois life they decorate, whether in the apartments, in the relations with neighbors, in the bars or in the "Clubhouse of the Working Class."

I was terribly shaken when I saw the film again, because the first time I hadn't noticed the split that goes through it. The people's lives—both private and working—runs in dark, often gloomy pictures; the integration of the landscape—or of its destruction through the construction of the works—underlines rather than mitigates this; which the sensitive film music of Andre Asriel emphasizes further. The picture is complete when one sees the director, framed in his fur coat, in his moment of triumph.

In response to everything come slogans without interruption: about caring for the people, about the socialist society and the public-

spiritedness that should accompany it, the responsibility for each other. A breathtaking contradiction, intentional or not!
With this second viewing came the disturbing suspicion—in relation to my own works written in the DDR, including "Frau Mitschuleit's Survey." Despite all the criticism of the situation, a lie creeps in: the lie of the socialistic best of all possible worlds, where each person stands in the foreground as a responsibility-sharing citizen-worker. With that, the writer in the DDR—except for the few, so well-known exceptions who have taken a hard path—is manipulated into subordination by the system, so much so that he doesn't even notice his distance from the community, from the working class. Either he can't notice it any more because he has learned to see all aspects of society through the glasses of the Party apparatus, or his efforts toward truth are—see above—converted to praise for those belonging to the leadership. And whoever can't swim in either water, is excommunicated.

VI IDEAS

JAN KOPLOWITZ

Jan Koplowitz
Born 1909 in Kudowa (now Poland). Son of a hotel-owning Jewish family. 1925—member of KJVD, the Communist Youth Association of Germany, left home. Worked as a teacher, bookseller, co-worker and editor of the Workers' Press; 1931-32—editor of the Silesian Workers' Newspaper; 1929—joined the German Communist Party and the Bund Proletarische Revolutionäre Schriftsteller (Society of Proletarian Revolutionary Writers), wrote songs, cabaret skits, & political reviews for Agitprop groups in which he also acted, member of the professional troupe "Roter (Red) Revue"; repeatedly persecuted and arrested for his political activities; 1933—arrested and seriously injured by SA Stormtroopers, escaped to Czechoslovakia, illegal border work, sentenced 9 times to prison, 9 times deported and 9 times illegally returned, work in the "Bert Brecht Club"; acquaintanceship with Egon Kisch, Wilhelm Reich, Herbert Marcuse, Ernst Bloch; underground activity in France, Austria, Switzerland, Poland, Sweden, etc.; 1939—when the Nazis marched into Czechoslovakia, helped organize the escape of 800 political refugees to Poland, went himself through Poland and Sweden to England; in England, 8 years as metalworker, technical inspector, shop steward, also documentary reporting, short stories, film ghost writing (as a political emigrant, he was forbidden to publish film writing); trained agents to be parachuted into Axis territory to work for the Allies; 1947—returned to Germany; cultural work in the metallurgical combine in Maxhütte, radio work, chaired the "Commission for Cultural Education in the DDR," artistic director of the "Berlin Concert and Entertainment Agency," travelled throughout East Germany to report about economic, cultural, and political events; now living in Berlin. 1955 and 1958—Literature Prize of the Trade Unions. Laureate of the Heinrich Heine Prize of the DDR.

Work published in the DDR: *Our Mate Max the Giant*—stories, documentary journalism, songs, poems about the daily work and life of steelworkers; *You Can't Live Without Love*—1956; *Good Luck, Piddl*—1961, story of a young miner during the Weimar Republic; *Heart Ward*—1963, love story of a German emigrant student and a Czech girl who work in the underground against the fascists; *The Assembly Line* and *Städte Machen Leute* (Cities Make People / People Make Cities),—1968 and 1969, documentary reporting about the construction of a new city, Halle-Neustadt; *Stories from the Oilpaper*—1971, remembrances over 50 years; *Bohemia, My Destiny*—1979, autobiographical novel about 3 generations of a Jewish family who own a hotel on the German-Czech border. Now working on *Tracing Back*, in which the author revisits the places throughout Europe where he lived and worked during Fascism, discussing past and present, and the present lives of the emigrants and Jews who survived the Third Reich.

My Credo—To Be Useful: which entails criticism and encouragement, swimming against the stream, and forcing a way forward, close relationship with the working class, and fighting bureaucracy and red tape. Class consciousness and love of truth.

Positive Provocation
(from "The Lengthened Assembly Line," in Neue Deutsche Literatur, Nov. '74)

Halle-Neustadt knows no street names, only numbers of districts, blocks, and houses.

It all started when I told the House Association of Block 615, House 2 (who had invited me) of my sad experiences in my Halle-Neustadt home, the highest apartment of Block 621. Probably I wouldn't have unpacked my worries and cares so openly and uninhibitedly, if an interested echo hadn't come from my hosts. So much togetherness, so much happy activity inspired me to a little speech: Your efforts toward political clarity, your many-sided interests, your activities for international solidarity, your friendly relationship with culture, with the arts, your fellowship in the Tenants Collective was all well-known to me before. Now I experience it among you, learn from your annual report how you care for each other's children, that you write neighborhood self-help with capital letters, that you keep up the value of your building through your own superintendence and repair, going as far as to take the renovation of your balconies and windows into your own hands. You keep up the nearby parks and lawns and make sure the flowerbeds aren't trampled upon and the rosebushes aren't stolen.

My listeners were pleased, beamed at me, but the faces got a bit longer and helpless when I continued: Such community awareness and social behavior requires much love and effort and much pleasure in working together. Nevertheless I wonder whether you shouldn't help the 270 residents of the house where I live, right across from you, to learn from your example and to help them become a tenant and citizen family like yours. You could make it a point in your Cultural Contest. Be sponsors to them, you could call it.

As I spoke the last words, I realized how illogical, how nonsensical my demand was. In all seriousness I had asked that 10 families help 270. But I noticed how they all thought it over, how it smoked in their heads.

The doctor of chemistry finally sighed, "If we only had a partner! There is neither a House Association in your house nor a political organization. The National Citizens Association and the huge firm of BUNA both capitulate before this very house. Where's the office, where's the person, with whom we could speak, who could advise us? It looks unpromising to me."

Am I crazy or megalomaniac, drunk from one glass of beer? I hear myself say, no cry out, "I'll try it!" The words stand in the room, can't be taken back any more! Boy have I bitten off a lot!

One has to lure the people out from the anonymity of locked doors, first of all just get a few of them together, in this house of one-room-renters. And so I tack a notice on the board in the corridor, where otherwise like-new baby carriages and undamaged kitchen bars are offered for sale:

the writer Jan Koplowitz
READS—REPORTS—TELLS STORIES
from unpublished work out of his study
for his fellow tenants and fellow citizens of House 621
on Friday, July 7, at 7:00 PM
in Apt. 88, 4th floor.
Guests welcome!
Bring chairs!

Four hours later the notice was gone. Aha, I thought, someone needed a few tacks. I walked across the street, bought some glue in the store, wrote the notice again, and glued it more or less firmly. The next morning the notice was partly torn off. The remainder couldn't be deciphered. The shreds lay scattered in the corridor. Some bored young rascal! I concluded, and wrote the notice a third time. This time I used a stronger glue. It actually held through the whole day, but in the night it was scratched away very purposefully and carefully and not without effort with the help of a razor blade.

Proven: someone was seriously active to prevent that something should be done together in the ten story house. The challenging glove lay in the arena. Who would stick it out longer? Four more notices were written—and removed. I kept night watch. I was so excited I could hardly sleep anyway. It was like a suspenseful detective story, Jan the supersleuth. One night when I, a bit tired from my watch, went for a breath of air and a bit of exercise, the secret foe did his work. I heard the steps to the elevator still and could even note the floor. They weren't the steps of a young person; otherwise, I brooded, I might have more success with a text like this: SIT IN with Jan Koplowitz. HAPPENINGS guaranteed. GO-GO-GIRLS!

But those who fly about that kind of world wouldn't have been the right listeners for me anyway. Giving in is ruled out! Partial success: on July 22, the memo stays day and night.

It would be worth the effort to write a play about the Workshop Evening I had worried over so much: the mutual attempts at contact, the slow getting acquainted, the first controversy, the first laugh at the intended point, the first excited interruption, questions! The debates, the growing courage to speak, and in the end, how we shouted at each other and laughed with each other. Let it be said, my six chairs were not enough. What remains as most essential: the people who came won't be able to pass each other in the elevator, the corridor, the entrance, without a greeting, without a few friendly comments, without a smile. The next evening is agreed upon. The poet Axel Schulze will be my guest. He too dwells at the top, but at the other end of Block 621.

And now begins the application of my experience, my OPEN LETTER and APPEAL to the hundreds of artists, writers, poets, scholars, musicians, painters, sculptors, singers, actors and actresses, recitors, journalists, all people who have something to say and to offer, creative or performing, who are capable of bringing it across understandably and entertainingly.

Citizens of Halle-Neustadt!

Friends! Colleagues! Commit yourself to organize an evening once each quarter year in your House Association (a DDR Broadcast-slogan once said, "That ought to be possible!") without pay, but not for nothing (culture should never be given for nothing), rather for a donation in the spirit of international solidarity.

Here follows a little secret. After so many rooms meant for cultural activities have been appropriated for other purposes, those in Halle-Neustadt who are interested in the arts have converted bicycle cellars and furnace rooms into meeting places for the House community. But no pianist can transport his instrument to that location! Who says you can't use a banquet hall in a "Gastronom" restaurant or in the "Kulturkabinett"? For such solutions there must be some unbureaucratic people who can register and organize such occasions.

Why shouldn't an artist, painter, sculptor, or designer have something to say about reception and appreciation of art, about taste and kitsch, about color, composition, form, about studios, techniques, and methods?

Why shouldn't the special wishes of interested people be fulfillable? My friends and colleagues should remember that their willingness benefits themselves. If hundreds of creative spirits (not exaggerated, I can call two dozen to mind on the spot)—in Halle-Neustadt as I said—once every quarter year (that's the minimum, the maximum is a question of noble competition and good contact) become active in the circle of their closest neighbors, they produce thereby a cultural atmosphere in which their own audience, their hearers, watchers, and buyers, will thrive. And—just between us, which I should probably avoid saying in an OPEN LETTER—it won't hurt any of us to make use of the recognizing, stimulating, critical, skeptical, piercing, thought-out opinions and questions of our chemical plant workers and other workers.

If one dares to think what might come as a result of such initiatives in Halle-Neustadt (starting with an improvised stage), amazing and alluring dreams and vision open up. But at the beginning of the dreaming and of the development of the *real* possibilities in our young socialist state stands, as a positive provocation, the sober phrase: Once every quarter year . . .

The Initials of the Seigneur
(*from* "The Lengthened Assembly Line," in *Neue Deutsche Literatur*, Nov. '74)

Passendorf Manor probably brought its owner more prestige than profit. *That* the genteel family made elsewhere. But owning land in the countryside was the aristocratic code. It didn't matter if the ground, used for grazing animals, was too wet to bring in profitable harvests of turnips, potatoes, and wheat. For the owners hardly noticed these disadvantages, and the hunt was far enough away from the manor house. There the lord of the manor condescendingly tried to impress the affable Arbitrator with his servants, while the feared Inspector, high on horseback, with a riding crop in his fist as a sign of his authority, ruled over the rural proletariat in his position as Judge. The division of labor, Arbitrator/Judge, functioned without friction until the Farm Laborers Association interpreted justice in another way. Strikes sprung up, and sand fell in the well-oiled machinery. The Seigneur hoped for salvation through the brown army and the swastika, to bring the rabble to its senses. He especially hated the striving of the common people for learning. Because education—or what he took to be education—he regarded as *his* domain. The best example was the manor house, familiarly called "our castle." A country manor in Art Nouveau style, well known in the whole neighborhood.

My Berliner listeners asked me when I told them about the little Passendorf Castle, "What are such reminiscences out of modern history to us, Koplowitz old buddy, particularly in a report about Halle-Neustadt."

Patience! I'm here in the present. Halle-Neustadt is on Passendorf ground, and so the socialist community gobbled its way up to the Manor Park and the dilapidated little castle, or what was left of it after the war: in the meantime, fungus and woodworm had celebrated a wedding in the demolished Sleeping Beauty ruins. For lack of coal, the oaken panelling had supplied fuel for the population in the hard frost, and in the dishevelled and weedy park the foresters found a "Bismarck Oak"—not the striped cake-scrumptiousness named for it in my youth, but a real one. A weathered stone plaque belonging to it gave notice that the tree here was in fact planted for the occasion of a round birthday of the "Iron Chancellor." Not even this deterred the big bad communists from taking possession of the rest of the Passendorf Manor including the park and all the grounds, out of which a

People's Estate was created. They put fungus and woodworm to flight, and since they didn't think much of unknowing and untaught farm laborers and because they needed skilled young workers, they set up a trade school and the Apprentices' Boarding House in the little former castle. Later the Community Music School moved into some of the rooms in the upper floors and tested whether the house was friendly to the Muses.

The attempt must have proven successful, for the city fathers and mothers, like Frau Mayor Liane Lang, decided, with the support of many enterprises, to restore the house to its original form, to stabilize the masonry, to repair the facade in keeping with its style. Architects and construction people did thorough work right away. From a remnant of an undamaged corner of stucco on the ceiling they reconstructed the whole drawing of the Italian decoration, and, with the help of experienced restorers, the remarkable work emerged anew, crowning a splendid, high-ceilinged, well-cut hall. In the whole house, above all in the characteristic reception room, they reconstructed the expensive oak paneling and the woodwork with stained struts, also the ostentatious metal scrollwork on the banister of the front steps, in the stairwell and on the fences. The round-swing little hallway, the ornamental leafwork, the gleaming inlaid parquet, everything matched the original of the turn of the century. New furniture was very carefully matched in form and color, to perfect the unity of the genuine.

It occurs to me: when the last living Princess of Waldstein (a descendant of the General named Wallenstein by Friedrich Schiller), cared for by a somewhat rickety but dignified servant, was allowed to take some of the rooms in the restored Valdstejn-Palais in Prague in the early fifties, and saw again the authentic, esthetically restored Residenz of her ancestors, the stone-old Lady exclaimed, impressed: "The Communists must be extremely rich people. What that must've cost!!!??"

I myself got to know the cheerful old granny. Rich for whom? Money for whom? From whom?

The outside of the Passendorf Manor emerged too in fresh colors and old splendor with its little tower in neoromantic style, with gargoyle water spouts, a beautiful pillared veranda: upstairs a middle level remains to be built so that the youth can celebrate Spring and Summer Festivals and Midsummernight.

To commemorate the tenth year since the founding of Halle-Neustadt, the Manor was reopened with speeches, one by the town councillor for cultural affairs, and one by the Frau Mayor, with a concert and a congratulatory reception with many flowers and fragrant drinks. Unfortunately the Manor was given the prosaic name "Halle-Neustadt Culture House South."

Why so jerking, why so lacking in fantasy? Right there there is a youth club called "The White Rose"* which whets interest with its name alone. Or didn't anyone want to aggravate the old Seigneur even more? How he'll spin in his grave when he hears about the ambitious program of the culture house. It meets the needs of the chemical workers just as well as those of the technical intelligentsia, the apprentices, students, the folklore groups, the taste of the young people, those whom the "Lord" wished so deferential, humble, willing, and obedient.

But the program isn't humble: literary evenings, serious and entertaining; sports events; concerts; author's readings; handicraft circles; lectures; and exhibits. Unfortunately the little castle isn't roomy enough. The brigades of the LEUNA plants took that into account, so that all the chemical workers get something out of the "Passendorf Bush," the park, too. On the grounds near the house they built a Café/Garden-Restaurant. The modern dining rooms are generous and roomy. They feed four hundred garden-guests. The Bismarck Plaque, however, wasn't placed by the oak any more. No one's so eager hereabouts for the kind of visitor who misses it. But the Coat-of-Arms, the playful, intricate initials of the Seigneur, so cunningly embedded in the stone adornment of the outer walls, haven't been dislodged by the new owners.

When I asked the director of the culture house, what or whom they referred to, she answered, unabashedly smiling: "I don't know, but they're pretty, aren't they?"

And that would have grieved the paled Seigneur the most of all.

---

*This was the name of the first oppositional students' group against the fascists at the Munich University. Its young leaders the Scholls, brother and sister, were executed.

KÜNSTLERGRUPPE RATGEB

Künstlergruppe Ratgeb

Twenty-two days in the life of Jörg Ratgeb (1480–1526), the painter after whom our group is named, were decisive in the eradication of every trace of him for 350 years. In these twenty-two days during the Peasants' War he was leader of the rebellious group in Stuttgart and fought actively against the despotism of the nobility. His commitment to the cause of the exploited, his condemnation and public execution by being drawn and quartered, the subject matter of his paintings which depicted the prevailing social circumstances in a clearly didactic manner—these factors have caused his life and work to remain largely ignored in established art history.

We find ourselves in a similar situation today: cultural values are determined by a ruling class, and critical or people's art—insofar as it is not marketable—is silenced.

Our group, made up of five painters, is attempting to battle the illiteracy of commercial press and television, the elite standards of the art market. We want to create art for and with those excluded from the official culture business. Not only is our studio open to everyone, we work in the streets where we can speak with people and bring our medium closer to them. Our aim is not to enrich the existing official art scene by spicing it up with a touch of critique, but to help create a new culture which serves all people.

"Als sie einmarschierten, ruhten wir noch wohlig in unseren Betten"
("When they marched in, we were still cozy in our beds")
Offsetlithographie 1978   by Werner Steinbrecher

depicts the occupation of Prague by the German Nazis in 1939. In the realm of the ever-relevant question of how we participate in political events and what our responsibility is, it becomes obvious that: the populace of the occupied land reacts with open despair, whereas these who rule and those who possess ignore and accommodate themselves to the new conditions. The capitalists reveal themselves as opportunists.

Werner Steinbrecher
born in 1946, grew up in Düsseldorf. Studies in architecture until 1971. After attaining degree and working in architectural planning, began studies in painting. In Berlin since 1974. "Many attempts to analyze and deal with the position of the artist in society . . ." Political activity in the university. Freelance since finishing studies in 1978. Participated in many group and solo exhibits since 1973.

WERNER STEINBRECHER

Nil Fricke
born in 1944, is married, has a daughter. Various occupations and fields of studies until 1975, ending with studies in architectural history at the Technical University in Berlin. Painting since 1957, experiments with many media, "out of which constantly arose conflicts and tensions between myself and my surroundings." Lived in Switzerland between 1965 and 1971. In 1966, first exhibit in Switzerland; since then many exhibits in Berlin and West Germany. Since 1977, "great hopes for the Künstlergruppe Ratgeb, because—even in art—one alone is no one."

"Bundschuh" (The tied shoe) from the series "Blätter zur deutschen Geschichte" ("Sheets on German History"), by Nil Fricke
Linoleumcut 1978

"Bundschuh" was a movement before and during the German Peasants' War, with uprisings led by Josz Fritz in 1502, 1513 and 1527. The peasant's shoe is depicted on the rebel flag. Within the same continuum of history in 1977, peasants take a stand against the building of planned atomic reactors.

NIL FRICKE

"Der Rabe Ralph" ("Ralph the Crow")
Linoleumcut 1979

by Nil Fricke

WERNER BRUNNER

Werner Brunner
The artist was born in Munich in 1941. Eight years public school, then apprenticeship as ironsmith. University studies in architecture and city planning. Interested in art history. Has participated in several art exhibits in Berlin and West Germany.

"Scheißspiel" (Shitplay) by Werner Brunner Linoleumcut 1979

VOLKER BRAUN

Volker Braun
Born in 1939 in Dresden. After his Abitur, he worked in a print shop, then laid concrete pipe and worked as a machinist in the Kombinat "Schwarze Pumpe" ("Black Pump"). 1960–64 he studied Philosophy in Leipzig. Writes poetry, plays, short stories, and notes on the arts. Braun thinks politically and affirms, with criticism, the East German State. From the Foreword to *Es genügt nicht die einfache Wahrheit* (The Simple Truth is not Enough), a book of notes and essays:

"These notes contain, of course, not the opinions of the writer but his thoughts. He doesn't insist on words!

Thoughts are not made in order to spread certain views. The sometimes undaunted tone is an index of their preliminary definition.

And of course I contradict, as do others, myself as well; indeed preferably myself.

In these times, opinions are luxuries anyway if they aren't accompanied by actions (of, for example, the head); and the actions supersede, overhaul the opinions.

The lucid moments lie presumably there where action is demanded."

On Brecht, the Truth Unites

With his thinnest voice, so as not
too much to disturb us, he advised in time
We should simply say where it pinches
So we can heal or cut out the organ.

A hefty: that's it, and it'll fall
If we don't—(as with the classics that were simply there)
An admission that gave us legs.
That was his suggestion, glancing at his grave.

Such is still to be had on paper.
We haven't taken him on, just
Particular terms and the haircut.

Now they wear their hair longer again.
The flesh is thicker and the spirit narrower.
Thus he became a classic and is buried.

In addition to works of criticism and publications in periodicals, Braun's more important works include:

Provokationen für mich (Provocations for myself) 1965, Mitteldeutscher Verlag, poems.
Vorläufiges (Provisional) 1966, Suhrkamp, poems.
KriegsErklärung (Declaration of War) 1967, Mitteldeutscher Verlag, poems.
Wir und nicht Sie (We and not You) 1970, Suhrkamp, poems.
Das ungezwungene Leben Kasts (Kast's Unhindered Life) 1972, Aufbau Verlag, 3 reports.
Gegen die Symmetrische Welt (Against the Symmetrical World) 1974, Suhrkamp, poems.
Die Kipper—Hinze und Kunze—Tinka (The Dumptruck—Hinze and Kunze—Tinka) 1975, Heuschel Verlag, 3 plays (written and played earlier).
Es genügt nicht die einfache Wahrheit (The Simple Truth is Not Enough) 1975, Reclam, notes.
Gedichte (Poems) 1977, Verlag Neues Leben.
Unvollendete Geschichte (Unfinished Story) 1977, Suhrkamp, novella.
Im Querschnitt (Cross Section) ed. Holger J. Schubert 1978, Mitteldeutscher Verlag, poems, prose, plays, essays.

Zu Brecht, die Wahrheit einigt

Mit seiner dünnsten Stimme, um uns nicht
Sehr zu verstören, riet er noch beizeiten
Wir sollten einfach sagen wos uns sticht
So das Organ zu heilen oder schneiden.

Ein kräftiges: das ist es, und es kracht
Wenn nicht—(wie bei den Klassikern, die es halt gab)
Ein Eingeständnis, das uns Beine macht.
Das war sein Vorschlag blickend auf sein Grab.

So was ist noch auf dem Papier zu haben.
Wir haben ihn nicht angenommen, nur
Gewisse Termini und die Frisur.

Jetzt trägt man auch die Haare wieder länger.
Das Fleisch ist dicker, und der Geist enger.
So wurde er Klassiker und ist begraben.

On Climbing High Mountains
(after Lenin)

1
Now we've climbed above the timber line
But the forest has increased.
Now we've reached the camp
Under the peak: that no one sees any longer.
Now we hang onto the line awkwardly
So as not to plunge with the next swing.
Now there's no more forward in the eternal snow
Questionnaires/Bucks/Promises/Old Hat
That'll do it right up to our step.
Now we drag the mountain along with us every day.
Now we get mountain sickness
And each sees himself persecuted by all
Right into the beds and balances.
Now we struggle against bugs.
Now the ways apparently surmount us
With their detritus/corner numerals/privileges
Now we climb over the colleagues
Conquer a place on the ladder.
Where the hell do we want to go.
Is that the mountain we honor
Or an egyptian pyramid.
Why are we so tired.
Shouldn't we have long since turned back
And rappeled down from our stations.
And unhitched ourselves from our harnesses
For our goal lies another way.
Feel our way into the Uncertain from which we climbed up.
Friction our only hold.
Work for days to go back an inch
Disappear to persist.
Ascent is descent; that is, cold.
And to see the peak in an again approachable distance.

2
And now hoot the assholes who never dared a step.
What does that matter.

Vom Besteigen hoher Berge
(nach Lenin)

1
Jetzt sind wir höher als die Baumgrenze geklommen
Aber der Wald hat zugenommen.
Jetzt haben wir das Lager errichtet
Unter dem Gipfel: den keiner mehr sichtet.
Jetzt hängen wir am Seil ungelenk
Um nicht abzustürzen beim nächsten Schwenk.
Jetzt geht es nicht mehr vorwärts in dem ewigen Schnee
Formulare / Kies / Versprechungen / kalter Kaffee
Das reicht uns bis an den Schritt.
Jetzt schleppen wir jeden Tag den Berg mit.
Jetzt hat uns die Höhenkrankheit befallen
Und jeder sieht sich verfolgt von allen
Bis in die Betten und Bilanzen.
Jetzt kämpfen wir gegen Wanzen.
Jetzt übersteigen offenbar uns die Wege
Mit ihrem Geröll / Eckziffern / Privilege
Jetzt steigen wir über die Mitarbeiter
Erobernd einen Platz auf der Leiter.
Wo wollen wir eigentlich hin.
Ist das überhaupt der Berg, den wir beehren
Oder eine ägyptische Pyramide.
Warum sind wir so müde.
Müssen wir nicht längst umkehren
Und von unsern Posten herabfahren.
Und uns aus den Sicherungen schnüren
Denn dieser Weg wird nicht zum Ziel führen.
Tappen ins Ungewisse, aus dem wir aufgestiegen waren.
Die Reibung unser einziger Halt.
Tagelang arbeiten, um einen Zoll zurückzugehn
Verschwinden, um zu bestehn.
Aufstieg gleich Abstieg, heiß kalt
Und den Gipfel in wieder erreichbarer Ferne zu sehn.

2
Und nun schrein die Arschlöcher, die nie einen Schritt wagen.
Was hat das zu sagen.

New Purpose of Hadrian's Army

Of Hadrian the Caesar
Since days of old is reported, between the lines,
That he didn't use his army to wage war,
For which the empire was too huge between some
Brittania and Cappadocia or other, but to travel.
Since the troops he couldn't yet
Discharge before the eyes of the Goths or
    Sassanids
He set them to an unaccustomed task
Not to burn down cities but to found cities.
Where his spearmen set foot, they reached for the trowel
And where they withdrew, the earth was inhabitable.
Extinguished Jerusalem he lifted from the rubble
And Athens, rich in palaces, he adorned with palaces.
Before the lands that he held under his boot
He bent to study the mosaics
What he took, was the measurements of the devastated temples.
The cut he took, was golden.*
In the end he commanded stone masons, bricklayers, and smiths.
Presumably he chose his men, reading from their glances
Not fierce intent but artistic
So that they were still soldiers but already workers
Still skilled in arms, now too with their hands
This all between the lines
In a language long dead. But we again
Think so passionately the same, that it becomes a simile for us.
    Namely
That is so long ago that it's almost true.
For can't we use, in the turnabouts that we dare,
As with the army so the whole state,
If it must be,
To his and a different purpose?
Master of men still, now also
To make them masters of themselves, of their mutual intent?
This Unaccustomedness, that repeals
The rules by becoming the rule?
This Caesarish luxury of the masses
That brings the nations to exult
In their living languages?

---

*In German, a wordplay: "Der Goldene Schnitt" is "The Golden Rectangle." "Seinen Schnitt machen" means "to take his cut," in the sense of taking a portion of profits.

Neuer Zweck der Armee Hadrians

Von Hadrianus, dem Cäsar
Wird seit alters zwischen den Zeilen berichtet
Daß er seine Armee nicht brauchte, um Kriege zu führen
Für die das Reich zu riesig war zwischen irgendwelchen
Britannien und Cappadocien, sondern um zu reisen.
Da er die Truppen schon nicht
Abmustern konnte vor den Augen der Goten oder Sassaniden
Setzte er sie ein zu einem unüblichen Zweck
Nicht Städte niederzubrennen, sondern Städte zu gründen.
Wo seine Lanzenträger landeten, griffen sie zur Kelle
Und wo sie abzogen, war die Erde bewohnbar.
Das erloschene Jerusalem hob er aus den Trümmern
Und Athen, das palastreiche, zierte er mit Palästen.
Vor den Ländern, die er unterm Stiefel hielt
Bückte er sich, die Mosaiken zu studieren
Was er nahm, war Maß an den verwüsteten Tempeln
Der Schnitt, den er machte, war der goldene.
Er befehligte schließlich Steinmetze, Maurer und Schmiede.
Er wählte seine Leute vermutlich, aus ihren Blicken
Nicht kriegerischen Sinn lesend sondern Kunstsinn
So daß sie noch Soldaten waren, aber schon Arbeiter
Schlagfertig noch und kunstfertig zugleich.
Dies alles zwischen den Zeilen
In einer längst toten Sprache. Aber wir wieder
Denken so heftig desgleichen, daß es uns zum Gleichnis wird.
    Nämlich
Das ist so lange her, daß es beinahe wahr ist.
Denn können wir nicht, in den Umwälzungen, die wir wagen
Wie die Armee den ganzen Staat
Wenn er schon nötig ist, benutzen
Zu seinem und einem anderen Zweck?
Mächtig über die Menschen noch, aber zugleich
Sie mächtig zu machen ihrer selbst, ihrer gemeinsamen Sinne?
Dies Unübliche, das die Regeln
Außer Kraft setzt, indem es zur Regel wird?
Diesen cäsarischen Luxus der Massen
Der die Völker jubeln macht
In ihren lebendigen Sprachen?

The Myth of the Cave

Cramped in the petrifactions of our famous cave, in which we have stooped for the last 5000 years, we were (after sheer, prospectless, and from most long since given up training of the neck muscles and back bone) since the detonations of the last fabulous wars still flexible enough to twist ourselves around, so that we could look through the entrance into the glaring light. We perceived the light, well-known as the cause of the shadows that till now were the only verification of our minimal movements. But now as we looked into the open, it was not lit. The great light source that was supposed to shine for us, to which, yes, so many again and again prayed since every new Year Zero, was not there. Nor was there an exit; instead, behind us cowered other people, just as others cowered in front of us in the same twilight. Evidently our bodies themselves or the movement of the bodies must have radiated a weak light, which, added together, held us fast, fleeting, shadowy, on the walls. Taken by surprise by this discovery, we wanted to really hold onto the walls—and grasped, bewildered and shaken, into emptiness, or tripped over the mass of stuff that we possessed. So there were no walls! that was all we needed. Here we sit 5000 years in the cave and it has no walls! That was no cave, we were logicians enough to figure that out. Maybe we dwelt so unfortunately grouped that we had reconstructed ourselves with our imaginings and apparatus and each in his corner thought he gazed into an invincible space. A space of facts, of stone faces. Well, now it wasn't as some of us had thought, that we could simply raise ourselves from the premises. At our first attempts to tear ourselves hurriedly and decisively away, we felt ourselves as if bound and pulled back on chains to the slimy debris, especially since most didn't stir on their portions of the earth, and stood sweating and, to soothe the cutting pain, bent in the contact zones, transitional phases, times of shortage, at the calculator-evidenced ascertainment of calculatable commitment. But those of us who didn't shy from pain and would rather butt their heads against the looming rusty conditions and be-quiet-tactics around us than to kneel down again, these stood fully erect and glared brightly for moments, in particular their forebrains like a phosphorescent mass, and our speechless and half-hearted movements were thrown back black and shamefully clear onto the whole inventory, until the bodies of these youths, cut through by ropes and burnt, rolled amongst our nail clippers, indexes, and umbilical cords. Over them new centuries began to pass, full of new debris, planned costs, ersatz art, and standardized spittle. But in this time began a new, harder training of the painful and wonderful upright gait.

Zeitungsgedicht, redigiert

Was auch geschehen mag, ich sage
Was ich ˋ —————
————— nicht schweige.
————— und zeige
Die Fehler ———————
———————————————
———————————————
Der andern ————————
——————————

Newspaper Poem, Edited

Whatever may happen, I say
What I —————————
————— don't keep silent.
————— and point out
The mistakes ———————
———————————————
———————————————
Of the others ————————
——————————

The Pleasure in the Creative

How can I describe this feeling? If I'd written a poem (or what I took to be one), I arose early and the morning was an enjoyment—as if everything else were different, I was different. All doors stood open to the day.
And this feeling was an unbribable judge: only when it was there did I believe the work well done (even when the feeling deceived).
Later I had a similar feeling, mornings going forth from my beloved. Maybe seafarers felt that way when discovering a coast.
But the feeling is strongest when the work is still unfinished, when the coast is still untrod, and many—very many—shall tread it too.

Goethe's Leaseholders

They've made of Goethe's works a workhouse for the delinquent nation. They direct there like governesses. How little love for the present I feel in their airs.
They've leased his legacy, and sit still in it. They've waxed his thresholds—but no longer dare step over. They live with his books as if the books lived. They are so concerned with the books, as if they had no concerns of their own.
While we in the meadows of the public landscape play our games with him. They are new aristocrats—we are his old friends.

Going All the Way
from: Es genügt nicht die einfache Wahrheit

The statement that the poet should go all the way doesn't say that the poem should go all the way: it can leave the conclusion up to the reader, who belongs to the poem as a driver belongs to a vehicle. The desire for unfinished, merely "programmed" poems, which the reader can complete in his skull, perhaps in an individual way, with some elbow-room for the result according to ability and pressing need, this desire I've heard expressed now a few times by youths. (And they didn't mean exclusively poems. They were newspaper readers).

There are a lot of such "unfinished" poems, stories, plays, with which the writer brings the reader to another, more advanced position than the described event.

But one could assume that the discomfort was not in regard to the endings, but to the whole tone of the texts, how they offer themselves, how they have to be swallowed. One could, pulling the chairs out from under us so that we leave our complacency, say: "That is a mickey-mouse, narrow habit, to sell finished pictures that need only be consumed. We can't work that way any more: everything worked out, jelled sentence constructions, stagnating between book covers, so that it's sour before it ever gets to market. What's it for, if it's just for the appreciation of others who are already sensible to its concerns? We should report poetic material to the brain, which can there be variously assembled and optimized: chains of poetic information, no more than that they begin to function and can be steered, like a car. They must be clean, intact, and reliable—and demand much concentration and skill from the purchaser. Art is no street car route with stubborn rails for half-blind passengers. If art should go all the way, why not all the way to the end of hitherto existing art?"

One could say that. But then we would, stiffened and frightened, not even do what's possible.

Uli Becker
Uli Becker is 25 years old and lives in Berlin-Charlottenburg,
around the corner from Burger King, which is nothing but a
stupid coincidence. Known to his friends as "the nihilist who
buckles his safety belt," weighing 80 kilos in his underwear, he
is a big hulk who rips through every safety net like child's
play. In 1977 in Hamburg's "Edition Nautilus" Press he

ULI BECKER

I Want My Money Back!

Life is like shooting B-pictures, it's said,
if you've passed the point of no return,
all a question of consciousness: I enter

the midnight telephone booth, hoping for the best,
for a human voice, close
my eyes and tap at random any

of the scratched-in numbers, dial, there's no one
there. "Are you lonesome tonight," said Elvis,
now he's dead, and I stand under the neon

in this glass cage, everything dark around me.
I am unarmed, naive, a perfect target
for the unmoored rifleman amok, who lies there

in wait in the 5-story building behind a barricaded door:
One of these office clerks, disappointed in the world,
comes to his conclusion and bends his

finger, and again, again, again. When they try
to get him out of there, he turns the barrel around,
his eerie, "You'll never take me, you pigs!"

echoing in the morning a million times in the headline
of a well-known German revolver paper
through the Omnibusses and U-Bahns, and a photo

of the shot-up telephone booth and a body
under a blanket, the senseless victim:
Approx. 25, blond, as of yet unidentified.

published the volume *Meine Fresse* (My Big Mouth) which consists of a dozen long poems. In 1978 he published in the *Verlag der Manufactur* the poem "People! Animals! Sensations!"
In November and December 1978 Uli Becker and Frank Witzel and the "Edition Nautilus" went on literature tour, "Surprise Attack on Germany," where in 40 days and 30 different cities they gave readings of poetry (their own and otherwise) accompanied by rock music. This tour, up to now the only one of its kind and dimensions outside the financially strong publishing houses, represented the successful attempt to drive poetry forward with the help of the internal combustion motor and to meet "the reader" directly: in the pubs and cellars, cafés and communication centers. And yes, there "he" was, too!

Ich Will Mein Geld Zurück!

Leben ist wie schlechte Filme drehen, heißt es,
wenn man den point of no return passiert hat,
alles eine Frage des Bewußtseins: Ich trete auf

gut Glück in die mitternächtliche Telefonzelle
um eine menschliche Stimme zu hören, mache
die Augen zu und tippe wahllos auf irgendeine

der eingeritzten Nummern, wähle, es ist niemand
da. "Are you lonesome tonight?", sang Elvis,
jetzt ist er tot, und ich stehe unter dem Neon

in diesem Glaskäfig, alles finster um mich herum.
Ich bin unbewaffnet, naiv, ein perfektes Ziel
für den ausgeklinkten Amokschützen, der gegenüber

im 4. Stock auf der Lauer liegt, Tür verrammelt:
Ein von der Welt enttäuschter Sachbearbeiter
zieht seine Konsequenzen und macht den Finger

krumm, und nochmal, nochmal, nochmal. Als sie ihn
da rausholen wollen, dreht er die Mündung um,
sein irres "Ihr Schweine, ihr kriegt mich nicht!"

echot am Morgen millionenfach als Schlagzeile
eines bekannten deutschen Revolverblattes
durch die Omnibusse und U-Bahnen, auf dem Foto

die zerschossene Telefonzelle und ein Körper
mit einer Decke drüber, das sinnlose Opfer:
Etwa 25, blond, bisher noch nicht identifiziert.

The Suffering of the Fugitives

Everything always gets worse, and not just here,
down in Argentina too: what are they trying to
prove, when they spray this artificial polish-
crap on their Granny Smith apples,

before they are allowed to face the world?
You can mirror yourself in them and have a monster-
snout, if you get up close enough to it, but I
can only laugh bitterly at such foolery,

are we at the funhouse here or what? In the
meantime it's gone so far that before use
you have to soak them and scrub them with a
scrub brush—do you think that's normal?

And even if they don't shine then any more
like a Christmas ornament from Santa Claus, what
the hell kind of fruit are they anyway? (Brown spots?
Not down here in Argentina! Everything's piccobello!)

Can anyone anywhere even imagine a shrivelled
Granny Smith, one with worms in it or
even a Granny as a spluttering baked apple,
when you come in from sledding? See!

Sure, René Magritte would have licked his
chops, the things are so poisonous green that you'd
traditionally have to get a belly ache from them,
so blemishless, so anonymous, and as spookily empty

as what his Man on the Street carries
south of his Bowler—compared with that, "paint
by numbers" expresses "character"!
But I am not a painter, I'm a poet, and

while I eat this Granny, I polish
a poem in my head that I will write soon,
about how apples taste in reality,
and that there are worlds between the sick

spawn of a Latin American military
dictatorship and that fruit from the Tree of Knowledge
because of which they, back then, had to pack their bags
and make their getaway: It was just a single bite,

but the taste of it, they say, was THE
revelation and somehow worth all the trouble,
that since then doesn't seem to want to stop.

Das Elend der Vertriebenen

Alles wird immer schlimmer, und nicht bloß hier,
auch unten in Argentinien: Was wollen die damit
beweisen, wenn sie diese künstliche Politur-
scheiße auf ihre Granny Smith Äpfel spritzen,

bevor sie die Weltöffentlichkeit sehen darf?
Drin spiegeln kann man sich und hat einen Mords-
zinken, wenn man nah genug rangeht, aber über
solche Späßchen kann ich nur bitter lachen,

sind wir hier auf der Kirmes oder was?! Es ist
mittlerweile soweit, daß man die vor Gebrauch
regelrecht einseifen muß und mit der Spülbürste
abschrubben—findest du sowas etwa normal?

Und selbst wenn die dann nicht mehr so glänzen
wie 'ne Christbaumkugel bei der Bescherung, was
sind das überhaupt für Früchte? ("Braune Stellen?
Nicht bei uns in Argentinien! Alles piccobello!")

Kann sich vielleicht jemand einen verschrumpelten
Granny vorstellen, einen mit Würmern drin oder
gar einen Granny als brutzelnden Bratapfel,
wenn man reinkommt vom Schlittenfahren? Siehste!

Gewiß hätte René Magritte sich die Finger danach
geleckt, so giftgrün die Dinger, daß man davon
traditionellerweise Bauchschmerzen kriegen müßte,
so makellos, so anonym und gespenstisch leer

wie das, was sein Mann von der Straße südlich
vom Bowler trägt—dagegen strahlen Punkt, Punkt,
Komma, Strich schon richtig "Charakter" aus!
Bloß bin ich kein Maler, ich bin Dichter, und

während ich diesen Granny esse, poliere ich im
Kopf ein Gedicht, das ich bald schreiben werde,
von wegen wie Äpfel in Wirklichkeit schmecken
und daß da Welten liegen zwischen der kranken

Ausgeburt einer lateinamerikanischen Militär-
diktatur und jener Frucht vom Baum der Erkenntnis,
wegen der die damals ihre Koffer packen und
abhauen mußten: Es war nur ein einziger Bissen,

doch vom Aroma her, wie es heißt, war das DIE
Offenbarung und irgendwie den ganzen Ärger wert,
der seitdem nie mehr so richtig aufhören will.

Defeatist Depression
(on the 10th anniversary of the death of Comrade Vance A. Ramos)

Man, doesn't that just spookily fit in
with the whole oppressive atmosphere
in this land, that it wasn't any honest
showdown with a fire hose that
did me up like this: wet down to my bones!

Then at least I could've struck back—
But no, they've come a long way:
A cowardly thunderstorm, like a sleazy
shot in the back. And that's what's symptomatic,
just take a glance out the pub door:

Firehoses are as rare today on our streets
as miniskirts, and the direct confrontation
in front of Café Kranzler is long since passé. Now is
the time for what the insurance companies sell
in the small print as Acts of a Higher Power,

and I swear that's the right name for them!
The power of the late 70's is so highly
developed, so diffuse and so ever-present as
God in Heaven used to be—with the best intentions
a cobblestone won't do it any more!

Not even that good feeling in your belly
when you throw it, soaked but laughing . . .
(Not to speak of making love afterwards,
while Jeans and Parka dry on the heater:
"The Revolution will be a party or nothing at all!"

Defaitistische Depressionen
(am zehnten Todestag
des Genossen Vance A. Ramos)

Mensch, paßt das nicht in gespenstischer Weise
zu der ganzen beklemmenden Atmosphäre
in diesem Land, daß es kein ehrlicher
Showdown mit einem Wasserwerfer mehr war,
was mich so zugerichtet hat: naß bis auf die Knochen!

Da hätte ich ja noch zurückschlagen können—
Aber nein, sie sind schon viel weiter:
Ein feiger Wolkenbruch war's, wie ein schäbiger
Schuß in den Rücken. Und das ist das Symptomatische,
denn wirf mal einen Blick vor die Kneipentür:

Wasserwerfer sind heute auf unseren Straßen
rar wie Miniröcke, und die direkte Konfrontation
vor'm Kranzler ist lange passé. Jetzt ist die Zeit
für das, was die Versicherungsgesellschaften
ganz kleingedruckt als Höhere Gewalt verkaufen,

und ich schwöre, die trägt ihren Namen zu Recht!
Die Gewalt der späten 70er Jahre ist so hoch
entwickelt, so diffus und allgegenwärtig wie früher
der Liebe Gott—Da ist beim besten Willen
mit einem Pflasterstein nichts mehr zu machen!

Nicht einmal mehr das gute Gefühl im Bauch,
wenn du ihn schmeißt, klatschnaß aber lachend . . .
(Und ganz zu schweigen von der Liebe Danach,
während Jeans und Parka am Ofen trocknen:
"Die Revolution wird ein Fest sein oder gar nichts!")

BERT GOREK

but primarily

  good you comb yourself with a dust broom
      shave yourself with a dustcloth
      let might go before right
but only if you bite into the root hairs
      do you occasionally have occasion well
      to concern yourself intensively and independently
      with root quality and first ground
      and with that you gain the right, right,
      to build your own tree house
but from other company hide
      where you crawl and into what you bite for
otherwise they'll shovel you over anyway useless
but I don't want to have brought anything
      of common validity to expression
      I mistrust the experiences
      of some poet or other out of many
but so-ark-poets have written for years
      only from and about what makes them want to throw up
      and about a society
      that primarily vomits them out

Bert Gorek
Born 1956 in Reuterstadt Stavenhagen, school in Greifswald. 1972–1975 apprentice as electronics worker, 1975–76 lighting man at the Staatstheater in Schwerin and at the Theater der Freundschaft Berlin (Berlin Friendship Theater). Since 1977 lighting at the Berliner Arbeiter- und Studenten-theater (Berlin Workers' and Students' Theater). Since 1976 Ark Poetry.

forwiegend aber

gut du kaemmst dich mit einem handfeger
    rasierst dich mit einem staubtuch
    laesst gewalt for recht ergehen
aber nur wenn du in wurzelhaare beisst
    hast du gelegentlich gelegenheit gut
    dich mit wurzelbeschaffenheit & ur grund
    eingehend eigenstaendig zu befassen
    & somit erwirbst du das recht
    erst recht ein baumhaus zu bauen
aber for anderer kumpanei ferbirg
    wo du krauchst & worein du beisst denn
sonst schueppen sie ohnehin dich zu ohne sinn
aber ich will nichts gemeingueltiges
    zum ausdrukk gebracht haben
    ich misstraue den erfahrungen
    irgendwelcher dichter fon fielen
aber aberarkdichter schreiben seit jahren
    nur fon & ueber was sie ankotzt
    & ueber eine gesellschaft
    die sie forwiegend auskotzt

alkfowl rapt dripping

to the kohol of my friends I wish good friends
they know him well know his uses certainly
they can be without a doubil tipsy too
bit onto bit let him be a foe too
                                  snort
                     alkobolds

you shielding & wielding

you bullicemen officers to pieces just one thing
everything you say or do has a point
and you comrades of the league of rage just two
first the struggle goes on and second how

ever it may be left our duty
to do more for it than up till now against it
peaceable but not come to terms with peace
as long as it's only a cease-fire

all this is said often enough and often enough
there is no one who is unjustifiably addressed
despite this jointed promise
the world is left only rightful wounds

alkfoegel gluekkseelen triefig

dem kohol meiner freunde goenn ich gute freunde
die kennen ihn gut kennen seinen nutzen gewiss
die koennen auch teufelsohne truhdelduhn sein
stuekk zum stuekk ihn auch feind sein lassen
zumpe
alkobolde

euch hut & wut

euch ballizeisten ordnungshueterichen nur eins
alles was ihr sagt & tut hat hand & fuss
& euch genossen der liga wut nur diese zwei
erstens geht der kampf weiter & zweitens wie

auch immer seis uns zur pflicht gelassen
mehr dafuer zu tun als bisher dagegen
friedfertig nicht fertig mit dem frieden
solange es nur ein waffenstillstand ist

dies fiele sagt man oft genug & oft genug
ist niemand zu unrecht angesprochen
trotz der gelenken fersprechungen
blieben der welt nur gerechte ferwundungen

Adder Earth Let It Be I Picture Me Something

Girl I Invite You To My Place To Die
Land Loft Lust Sense I Have Bought And Cleaned
If I Show You Your Grave Everything Is In Place
Here You Can Cheerfully Take Off And Play Bagpipes

Why Should You Know Why You Take Off
Since You Do Know That You Take Off Here

Until Then There Are Still A Few Decades Of Time
We'll So Use Them As We Understand Each Other
Whatever You Cook For Me I Will Eat
I Will Roll Cigarettes From Our Tobacco

The Till Now Fully Unjustifiably Valid Mother Earth
We'll Revile As Adder Earth And All That On It Creeps
And Swarms Can Fully Unjustifiably Eat Shit

Natter Erde Lass Gut Sein Ich Mal Mir Was Aus

Maedchen Ich Lade Dich Ein Bei Mir Zu Sterben
Land Luft Lust Sinn Hab Ich Gekauft & Gereinigt
Wenn Ich Dir Dein Grab Zeige Ist Alles Im Lot
Hier Kannst Du Guten Mutes Abhauen & Sakkpfeifen

Wozu Solltest Du Wissen Warum Du Abhaust
Wenn Du Doch Weisst Dass Du Hier Abhaust

Bis Dahin Sind Noch Ein Paar Jahrzehnte Zeit
Die Werden Wir So Nutzen Wie Wir Uns Ferstehen
Was Immer Du Fuer Mich Kochst Werde Ich Essen
Ich Werde Cigaretten Drehen Fon Unserem Tabak

Wir Werden Die Bis Jetzt Foellig Zu Unrecht Gueltige
Mutter Erde Eine Natter Schimpfen & Was Drauf Kreucht
& Fleucht Kann Uns Foellig Zu Unrecht Am Arsch Lekken

moocher pays

thank the tank driver 'leventy years retired
that he has the gall to scream at you
back then we gassed your kind
"forwards and not forgotten"

for today he counts as a person
who upholds society, this is a hold up
therefore the more
forwards and not for gluttons

to handle anti-handle make faces because
sidecardriverstagemanagers aren't the only ones
who stammer such a tinny bluster therefore the more

"forwards and not forgotten"
to give him at least one fat lip
with your right hands or
with your fistlip

nassauer bezahlt

ferdenk es dem panzerfahrer seit zig jahren ade
dass er sich rausnimmt dich anzuschreien
solche wie dich haeten wir damals ferbrannt
forwaerts & nicht fergessen

denn heut zaehlt als mensch
wer was da stehlt & was hier stehlt
also umso
forwaerts & nichts ferfressen

zu handeln gegenhandl zu faksen denn
gespannfahrerbuehnenmeister sinds nicht allein
die solches blechern daherbrechen also umso

forwaerts & nicht fergessen
ihm zumindest eins in die schnauze zu geben
mit deinen rechten haenden oder
mit der faustschnauze

Knud Wollenberger
Born 1948. Citizen of Denmark, living in Berlin (East).

KNUD WOLLENBERGER

Design for a Monument

Against each other stand two. One
held by a knife in his hand, the other
by an actually light laugh. Standing
there just like stone, sculpting figures.

Entwurf für Denkmal

Gegeneinander stehen zwei. Einen
hält ein Messer in der Hand, den anderen
ein eigentlich leichtes Lachen. Stehen
da so wie Stein, schneiden die Gesichter.

Thomas Brasch
Born 1945 in Westow, Yorkshire, the son of an exiled German-Jewish antifascist. 1947, return to what would become the DDR. Cadet in the Nationale Volksarmee. 1963 Abitur. Typesetter, fertilizing worker, machinist. 1964–65 studied journalism at the Karl-Marx University in Leipzig, was

THOMAS BRASCH

Oedipus
from **Kargo**

He hobbles to the street car. Behind him, the security guard closes the factory gate. The quota is filled (1200 circuit boards in 540 minutes). On these feet marches the Future, it says on the poster above the department store. On these feet came Laius' fate across the mountains, says Sophocles. Beaten with blindness. He sits in front of the picture tube and hears the narrator's voice, "The tribe that we found here holds sacred the Cargo Cult, which teaches: Men with white skins are the ghosts of dead men who cannot find their end, no longer live, and are not yet dead." The forgotten class sleeps. The walls tremble from the last streetcar driving through Kastanienallee. Behind the wall the neighbor woman moans. "We sign off now," says the announcer, "a last glance at the clock: it is 11:05 PM Middle European Time. Good night." Shut your trap, Cassandra.

percussionist with the "Jackets." Exmatriculated for "Defamation of leading personalities of the DDR" and "Existentialistic Outlook." 1965-67, work as packer, waiter, construction worker. His script for the Vietnam-Program "Seht auf dieses Land" (Look at this Land) was cancelled after the dress rehearsal for "radical leftist tendencies." 1967-68, studied drama production at the Film College in Potsdam/Babelsberg. 1968 again exmatriculated for "staatsfeindliche Hetze" (seditious agitation)—handing out leaflets against the march into Czechoslovakia. Released from arrest on probation. 1969-71, machinist in the transformer works "Karl Liebknecht" in Berlin. 1971-72, work in the Brecht archives. Since then, free lance work—texts for children's records, plays, reworking plays, translations. In Dec. 1976, emigration from the DDR to the BRD; now living in West Berlin.

Plays: Der Papiertiger
      Lovely Rita
      Die Argentinische Nacht
      Rotter
Books: *Poesiealbum 89*, 1975
      Vor den Vätern sterben die Söhne (Before the Fathers
        Die the Sons), 1977
      Kargo, 1979
Film: *Engel aus Eisen* (Angel of Iron), as writer-director.

Rita's Fantasy
from **Kargo**

2. Melodramatic Essay, eyes closed, hand before my mouth, shivering knees (she's not where I am)

When I see us going down Pieckstraße, I see us on the ship "European Culture." Going down: what gets screamed down over the sea from this ship, is screamed down from a ship that is sinking. What gets screamed down from this ship is screamed by people who are merely not completely dead yet. You can hear poems that sound like the prayers of the drowning; you can hear songs that sound like gurgling; you can hear monologues that pierce your ears like the cries of one thirsting to death in the desert. You can see human couples in the cabins between pieces of furniture for which they have long saved and for which they worked 9 hours each day. The ship is well-built

and provisioned and many of the passengers believe it to be unsinkable. Saturdays, one can go to dress balls in all the common rooms: officers' mess, first class club, middle deck, lower deck. The cultural heritage is cultivated: Sophocles, Shakespeare, Bach, Goethe. (Learn from it!)
Between the busts lies smashed metal that looks like pieces broken off from   KleistLenzBüchnerHeymMozartTheMongoloidsFromStation3-ThePiedPiperofHamelinBraschCatullus. ("There's blood smeared on that, eh.")
Between the dancing, between the excited, between the lovingly embracing, a few people go around with strange movements and call out something about "Going under." Some of them are asked to dance and in the swing of it forget what they saw from the railing. Others of them get locked in single cabins and others are promoted to officers' ranks because of their abilities in sharp observation. From those who remain, some are unable to articulate themselves and their voices sound as if they had water in their mouths. (Aspiring artists whose ambition towers over their ability.) The rest: with wet feet and dramatically raised arms on the deck, staring across to the wild dancing on land (Africa and Latin America), trying to read the language of the dark coast dwellers from their lips, barking words that they take to be the language of the New Culture across to the representatives of the New Culture ("O wonderful naiveté of South American literature, O nobly savage talent of Leroi Jones"), but they are understood neither on land nor on the sinking ship, whose language they speak. Lay their hands upon their ears and hear words from land, hear a cry of hate against their ship.

Finally to the point

There he stands, reviling himself with the meanest cuss-word: I, and doesn't understand his own speech and stretches his arm out for the unknown skin in which you live: come in my cabin, in your arms to forget the sea that roars over us, in your arms to forget my arms and my head and my skin and the shore. "Shall we try to swim." "We'll never swim that far, but if we do, we'll starve on our language." Now you look like a coast dweller from the New World. Or the hopelessly naive. Or the married woman. Or. Now I watch television.

Eulenspiegel
from Kargo

August 72
After presentation of his outline to the VEB* Phonograph, B receives the following note from the head dramatic producer: "We accept your concept. However, Eulenspiegel must not be too strongly a revolutionary, otherwise one wonders why he uses only pranks in the struggle against repression." B. receives a check for the outline.

1/6/1974
Eulenspiegel or the further development and correction of a mythos: A, B, and C sit together. A begins to tell the story of Eulenspiegel as one of a peasant from the defeated peasant army. After some hesitation, B and C participate in the amending and expansion of the mythos of the powerless fool who feathers his nest through the stupidity of his countrymen. The conversation intensifies. The three correct, better, and change the stories they tell each other. They try to outdo each other. At first they were simple tales, then syntheses, in the end they each take roles. As time progresses, they must run through the whole gamut of the art of storytelling and arrive at its limit when Eulenspiegel becomes a murderer (one sings the songs of the peasant women, another speaks Eulenspiegel's part, the third the woman who puts her head in the noose). Then comes the dejection and the last attempt to rescue the figure (burial of the preacher). Then they go at each other.

The whole thing is of course a play of three German intellectuals (rich in thought, poor in deeds), which underscores their helplessness, their flight into Art (storytelling), their growing private randiness while they depict their societal impotence. They notice it at that point where the myth and figure of Eulenspiegel are exploded.

Three actors can easily accomplish this, they only have to act out their own situation in the canteen. They must gradually summon up more and more of their acting ability and try to outdo the others, then the effect is achieved.

Thus, three, describing increasingly their own situation, while they describe the techniques and ambitions, the financial and ideological aspects of Eulenspiegel's pranks.

---

*VEB VolksEigeneBetrieb—People's Own Company, the title for state-owned companies in the DDR.

3/30/1977
Conversation with S and M. It occurs to both of them that the comment about the actors' flight into art only shows the worst side of things. After all, simultaneously it's an advance into Form and thus naturally an opportunity for socially relevant behavior. The description of helplessness is the beginning of its overcoming. With that, I become aware of how strongly it is expected of me, after my shift from one German land to the other, to come out of my hermetic art world, and the summons is so formulated, I should act like a columnist. "Your ascetic concept of art may function there, where you come from, perhaps; here is laughable," one who thinks of himself as an engaged critic of the prevailing conditions here tells me, "sooner or later you won't be able to avoid taking a clear position."
The German-German misunderstanding of taking a position, of having an ideology, as a substitute for a backbone. That is Eulenspiegel's dilemma too; he only uses ideology when he needs it for his subsistence. In all other cases it is a luxury. Art was never a means to change the world, but always an attempt to survive it.

Eulenspiegel's Birth
Now the war is over and lost. Now the citizens of Sangerhausen stand as spectators about the marketplace. In the middle thirteen peasants ready for beheading. Now there stands the chopping block, now there lies the axe, now there sits the Duke, George of Saxony, and wants to have his fun at the execution.
Let the show begin! For each a chance to speak his last words. One article of the Peasants' Manifesto and then: don't reach so far says the neck to the head on the stake. What's *your* mouth open for, the head talks down to the neck.
The first peasant lays his head on the block: we want to have the say, who shall be pastor, and we want to vote whether he must leave office.
Here you can give your voice so that no sound will cross your lips again. The head falls to the cobblestones.
Release us from corporal bondage*. You are hereby released. One head falls after the other to the street. Now all 12 Articles have been spoken, now there lies a mountain of heads; the 13th peasant, with chalk-white face.
Hop to it! think of something good.
He stands and ogles the heap of heads, gawks at the axe and, hop to it, there he is on the head-mountain, throws high his arms and dances as if on a pile of eggs. The Duke's mouth falls wide open.

---

*Leibeigenschaft: serfdom. Literally, body possession. The serfs were the property of the nobles.

13th peasant:
Together we have sworn
to bring the lords some pain
from us they're now well-shorn
what will now be my gain.
The Duke smiles, leans back in his chair.
13th peasant:
They'll hack off my head—O
like a stinking rat
and throw it in the meadow
so the potatoes will grow fat.
The citizens stare, the Duke doubles over with laughter.
13th peasant:
But in 500 years will sprout this seed of blood
Then giant heads will grow; the gore will overflood.
My giant head will roll the castles in the scum,
from rich man and lord, tear the bacon from their bum.
From every lord and rich man I'll suck the arteries dry;
then above will roll the yellow sun, far and nigh.
The Duke rolls on the earth with laughter. Eye to eye with the axe, his glance firm on the future: axe away, the man comes along, he's a scream. What's your name? Meyer? Schulz? Geldfresser? The public nears with opened mouths. He keeps on dancing, he's gone crazy, or what? What's his name?
13th peasant:
The public is a-howlin'
it wants to cry for laughter.
For the cowardly folks of Eulen
I'll be the *Spiegel**, hereafter.
Hop to it, down from the head-pile and into the Duke's carriage. Within 3 minutes slipped out of Death's grasp and sprung into the lap of a high lord.
Duke: when there's nothing more to laugh at, you won't be laughing any longer. Understood?
13th peasant: Understood.
Thus was his birth.
He makes his jokes under the axe. He loves his trade as much as his own neck. The Duke knows this too and praises his court jester as the best in the land to the Count of Hesse. But the latter praises his own jester as the 8th generation of a jester family, a man with a feeling for all the fine points of the trade. The two agree to a contest between their subjects. Whoever loses will lose his position.
Pride of Craftsmanship versus Fear of Death.

---

*Spiegel: mirror.

Eulenspiegel and the Count's Fool are called in. The Count's Fool begins in a superior demeanor: How much water is in the sea? Eulenspiegel sweats: Let all the rivers that run to sea stand still, then I'll measure and give you the answer. The Duke applauds his untaught funmaker. Now Eulenspiegel feels more secure. Eulenspiegel: Where is the middle of the world?

The trained Fool knows this one in his sleep: Where you stand, empty-pate. If I'm off by a centimeter, you've won. Now the Count claps. His subject asks: How many days have passed since the first person was born? Answers Eulenspiegel: 7 days. When they're over, the next 7 start. Applause from the lords.

The contest swings back and forth. The other: What falls from one hole into the other, and in between is a big joke? Eulenspiegel: Man. First he falls out of his mother and then into the grave.

With a glance sidewards to the lords, Eulenspiegel asks the fool: Where are the empty-pates more crooked than the crookedest dog? The fool understands and laughs: in Germany, because they look for the Truth with their noses on the ground and the whole time they're lugging it on their backs. Aha, says Eulenspiegel and looks over to the lords.

The other: What's the difference between a lord and an empty-pate? Eulenspiegel laughs back: A lord can be an empty-pate, but an empty-pate can be a lord.

The two lords laughed at the fools and the fools laughed at the laughter of the lords.

But the Count and the Duke get tired of the game and threaten to punish both if no decision comes. So Eulenspiegel walks to the middle of the hall and shits a pile. He divides it into two halves and eats one. He challenges the Count's Fool to eat the other, and then they'll split the Fool's pile. The Fool gives up: he would rather go naked the rest of his life than to eat shit. Eulenspiegel keeps his job and his opponent is thrown into the street.

Two peasants on the path see Eulenspiegel, first peasant, then fighter, then court jester, now on the street again. One asks, are you sitting there thinking how you can make the cow laugh till milk squirts by itself from the udder? The other asks, are you thinking up a method to turn over the earth the way you twist around words, so that you don't have to get your hands dirty if you have to come back to the village?

Your wits aren't sharp enough to stick a pig. Eulenspiegel waves them away. You'll see a sow lay an egg before you'll see me back in the field as a peasant. Wait here, this evening the butcher will come out of the city with meat for the Duke, and you'll see, I'll get enough from him to eat my fill without bending my little finger. The peasants bet their overcoats against Eulenspiegel's shoes. In the evening the butcher comes and Eulenspiegel goes up to him: give me a piece of meat from this cow and I'll tell you a truth worth more than the whole cow. The butcher agrees to the deal and holds up a big haunch of meat toward Eulenspiegel. The peasants stand nearby and wait. Listen, says Eulenspiegel, if someone offers you for your cow this truth that I'm telling you in this moment, now, don't make the deal, because you have a 100% loss, give me the meat. The butcher cries: Fraud! But the peasants are Eulenspiegel's witnesses. Eulenspiegel gets the meat, and the peasants clap him admiringly on the shoulder.

You see, says Eulenspiegel, you too receive a truth: One gets potatoes more easily from peasants than from their fields, now give me your coats, you've lost your bets. The peasants' mouths open wide. Eulenspiegel puts on both coats, one over the other, and makes his way to the city.

In Nienstetten he comes upon three whose eyes were poked out at the order of Duke George of Saxony. They sit on the stone wall and hunger is in their faces. He goes to them and asks where lodgings are to be found. Immediately they are down from the wall and address him as Lord and bow themselves.

This fawning you'll drive out of them, he thinks, and says: I am Duke George of Saxony. You can thank me for unburdening you of your eyes. There is nothing more to see, times are slack, no tests of will for a determined man like back then, when we smote each other to the blood. He scorns further, the blind peasants bow deeper. He pulls out 2 coins from his purse and lets them tinkle in his hand: you were good enemies in the hard but noble times. Eat and drink now to the health of Duke George of Saxony.

He lets the money tinkle and each of the blinded thinks the Duke has given it to his neighbor, they lick his shoes and go into the tavern beside the wall. In 5 minutes they fly out the door onto the pavement with bloody heads. Eulenspiegel leans on the wall and doesn't laugh. I'll teach them to spit on the boots of their lords instead of licking them.

VII CONFRONTATIONS

Jürgen Fuchs
Born 1948 in Reichenbach. Abitur; Apprenticeship with the railroad; Army; studied Social Psychology in Jena; starting in 1974, published in anthologies and magazines; in 1975, a few weeks before graduation, exmatriculation from the University for "Damaging the Public Reputation of the University" by means of

JÜRGEN FUCHS

Feb. 18, '77
from **Vernehmungsprotokolle** (Interrogation Register)

Interrogator: Well, a talk or a monologue, what shall it be, if I may ask?

Fuchs: A few weeks ago another gentleman informed me, the State Security doesn't have talks with me but rather interrogates me. Why should I have anything to do with your small talk? The legally permitted interval for preliminary proceedings is run out. Take me to trial or set me free.

Interrogator: No, no, not so hasty. Your case is complicated, three months isn't enough. A note is enough and the District Attorney will agree to an extension. We have the power, it's simple enough.

Fuchs: Who's "we"?

Interrogator: The State, the Ministry for State Security, the Investigatory Organ, in this case: I.

Fuchs: You are the State.

Interrogator (laughing): "The State—that's us," a slogan from the good old Ulbricht years. The fact is: I sit here not as some discussion partner or other but as a member of a ministry, and to that extent I belong to the "State," let's not warm up that old problem of State and Society. There are plenty of contradictions, sure. "The State" in itself doesn't exist, therefore there have to be some that identify themselves. And since the withering away of the state obviously is in no big hurry, we can look confidently into the future. Of course we have to watch out, especially for people like you.

Fuchs: Do you feel threatened?

Interrogator: "Threatened" is not the right word, but you yourself know that something's started moving. But you still haven't his literary products; thrown out of the FDJ and the Party; from Nov. 1976 until August 1977 in prison; in August 1977, loss of DDR citizenship and emigration, with family, to West Berlin.

Books:
Gedächtnisprotokolle (Memory Register), 1977
Vernehmungsprotokolle (Interrogation Register), 1978
Tagesnotizen (Notes of the Day), 1979

---

made it. In Czechoslovakia it worked in '68. How it ended, you know. Of course tanks aren't arguments, but arguments can't stand up to tanks. We've been warned. We know now, how it starts. And because we know that, you, for example, are sitting here. Whether our measures can hold back political developments, we don't know. But I do know: We won't give up any position voluntarily.

Fuchs: Who is that: "we"?

Interrogator: You asked me that already. You want to make an allusion that the State Security is the State within the State. I could answer you with phrases, could say for example: the Party and so forth, but I really don't feel like playing naive. You assume there are an upper thousand who decide what all the rest need. I don't know, maybe that's true, but it's well known that many regard us as "The Establishment." But what does it matter, words here, words there, you have to start with what's real, and at the moment it looks like this: Either you hang from the lampposts or we do, pictorially expressed.(*He takes apart a ballpoint pen, puts it back together, his face is lightly red.*)

Fuchs: That a lamppost was already planned for me, I hadn't realized.

Interrogator: Don't take it so literally.

Fuchs: I'd like to take it literally for the moment. You think of lampposts, I don't. If I could do as I wanted, I would open up this secret house to public view, everyone could convince themselves that cells and backrooms maybe aren't as good for people as the police and the secret service believe. And I would take you to a production plant, there you could report to the workers' meeting what interesting functions you fulfilled, with which methods, and so forth. And then I would ask the colleagues to explain to you nicely about your new job in a large, clearly arranged work room. There's no place for your "lampposts," not in my vision of the future anyway. Your fear is unfounded, I can reassure you, "we don't believe in pistols," Pannach says in his song, and not in lampposts either.

Interrogator: So, so, well, fine, you haven't lost your sense of humor, you've been here three months now, let's wait and see, you still aren't acquainted with everything, after six months, for example, usually there are interesting psychological changes, you'll see. (*His face has changed to a grimace, the voice betrays an injured weepiness that masquerades as aggressiveness.*)

Fuchs: I thought you wanted to have philosophical discussions with me, maybe it's better if we let it be.

Interrogator: Don't get ironic, you've left the bounds of an impartial discussion. (*Leans back, obviously regrets his own behavior.*) Ah, so! You don't want to go to the West? I know, I know, now comes the big DDR-avowal and maybe even the Biermann-advice, we should go ourselves. But I'm concerned about something else. While serving your sentence you'll have mighty difficulties with your opinions, the other prisoners will break you. They don't much like to see "Zoneys" there, we don't have to do anything at all. The epoch of the illegal communist cells is over.

Fuchs: So you produce anti-communism.

Interrogator (*smiling*): I was waiting for that, it had to come. Maybe you too will vote NPD* after ten years of Bautzen† and successful expulsion, who knows. But however it is: there are problems always. One way or the other.

Fuchs: You prefer right-wingers.

Interrogator: Who says "prefer," but at least there one knows with what one is dealing. When someone attacks us from the right—taking the hypothetical case you imply—he won't come at us from the left, logically. He doesn't compete for our position. You do know where our neuralgic points are . . . you look at me so funny, don't you think that we have our thoughts too? Why should I hide my opinion? I can afford to have my opinion. Besides: What do you know?—everything that I say can be tactics. So what's the point. (*Looks around, satisfied and emphatically bored, he is vain.*)

---

*NPD: "National Partei Deutschlands," German National Party, a right wing or neofascist party in Germany.
†Maximum-security prison in East Germany.

The Turning Point
from Gedächtnisprotokolle (Memory Register)

We've thrown it away, we've burnt it. If you keep it up, you'll ruin us yet, bring us into prison, your father and me, I don't want to see anything like that again.
Thoughts written on a scrap of paper by a schoolboy: Ramsch* always reddens from the throat upward if we ask him questions that he can't answer. Ramsch with the big speeches on the first day of class: I am a strict opponent of phraseology. There we sat perfectly silent in our seats and thought whatever, but what he was, we soon knew.
His name wasn't Ramsch, his name was Rammler: History, Geography, Civics.
And then these black notebooks, entries every evening, no one may know what gets written there, pack it all away when you get up, take it with you when you leave.
And in the army? We will control your locker, nothing remains hidden, we find everything.
Attacks of fear, you write that too, now they come to control you, now it's your turn. In one night I tore up everything and threw it in the toilet, tiny shreds, a whole bucketful, then flushed, but the drain was stopped up and the shreds swam for a long time on the surface, words and letters and your handwriting in the toilet bowl: now they'll come and get you, but they didn't come.
Afterwards I wanted to write everything down finally, but the lines were short and poor. And a maimed truth is no truth. Fear and anger, curt, sparse, and twisted around triply as if the little world you know consisted only of insinuations and inspectors. And if the others come, will they understand what you mean? Before they shrug their shoulders and shake their heads and find a small feeling? That breaks you and throws you back, there you see the toilet bowl and the vigilant publishing houses, what is true becomes a trifle that nobody recognizes, not you and no one else. But now we're fed up with that.

Ramsch: odds and ends, rubbish, etc. Here, the teacher's nickname.

The Child
from **Gedächtnisprotokolle**

Sometimes we didn't feel anything bad, but absolutely nothing. You better watch out for that one, he's a keen one. Sure he looks pretty childlike, no beard growth and such a voice, but he'll grind you down remorselessly. Behind his back he was called "the child." When we had to put on gas masks, he seemed invigorated: C'mon, C'mon, faster, faster, don't pretend to be tired—grated his thin little voice across the grounds. We were always glad when we weren't under his command. The other non-coms smirked at his zeal.
That's torture, we said and had to watch how someone collapsed and fell in the ditch, had to listen how this thin, light blond man cursed him out.
It was on the way back to the barracks, we wore gas masks and ran in full gear toward our quarter. The breath grew short, some fell behind or were carried by others. The non-coms shot off their last "Imitation Materiel," dummy bombs and stink bombs flew at our feet. When we were permitted to take off our masks, this man still threw fireworks around, he lit the fuses and waited especially long before throwing the charges.
His scream could be heard afar, he rolled about on the street, his hands before his face: a dummy bomb had exploded while he still held it and had burned his face. He cried for help and for his mother. I saw that some soldiers laughed. I have heard that some said: Serves him right, he brought it on himself. If I should say today what I felt: nothing. I saw a human being suffering and felt nothing. Others laughed.

from **Tagesnotizen** (Notes of the Day)

THAT IS EXAGGERATED, isn't it, when someone says, in these department stores we shall die, that is exaggerated, isn't it, even if you're from Over There and maybe can't quite keep up with our life here, that is exaggerated. And not nice either, when someone comes over and we take him in. Maybe you ought to consider just once how much money we spend on you when you say something like that. And to speak of our State like that, about KaDeWe department store, that's what you mean isn't it, if I see right. Let me tell you something: If they Over There had something like that, they'd all be happy. And if they could come over here, they'd all come with big shopping nets and be grateful. That's how it was before the Wall. That's facts. No question about it. What do you mean, die?: buy, is what they'd do, buy, and not stand around with a glum face and then write poems like those. No way. And if you don't like it here, you can go somewhere else. All the rest are just longing for a German passport. Here it's just full of foreigners, they come in like locusts here, through East Berlin. Yeah, whoever doesn't like it here should disappear, that's my opinion anyway. And the great mass, millions, they all think like me. And you know what else: there's always nuts who aren't satisfied anywhere.

from **Tagesnotizen**

I DON'T BELIEVE THAT, says a young blond student with beads around his throat and a writing pad, I don't believe that, while I read poems at the university in Bremen, and told about my father too, how he came from work at four-thirty and fell into the armchair. How he drank a bottle of beer and got upset about the loud music on the radio. He couldn't have held any speeches about his leading role in the plant, which he knew nothing about, because he'd worked the whole day and evenings everything got on his nerves: the spat with my mother, the garden, where the weeds grew, and my long hair. Then he ate and often fell asleep in front of the TV, it didn't matter whether the East or the West was putting on its show. I don't believe that, he says and looks at his notes, no representative of the working class could behave so passively and so hopelessly in a socialistic land. That is a false and distorting portrayal, he says, even if it obviously is about your father, which I don't mean to question.

9/1/'78
from **Tagesnotizen**

But I copied out his songs with the typewriter, she says, and when friends came, we heard them again and again, and when I was alone, after work, before a discussion, and in prison, when everything was supposed to be ended, I sang his songs. And then I sit in the Hockey Stadium, she says, among five thousand people, five or six thousand, and see him standing on the stage, hear him singing, and at a booth his records are sold for nineteen marks eighty pfennig. Then I ran away, she says, and blubbered, and didn't even know why.

photograph by Jochen Melzian

from **Tagesnotizen**

ALWAYS I SEE YOU IN
PRISON
In the visitor's room
Speaker
They named it
And sat nearby and wanted to see everything

You had coffee with you
Fruit
Cigarettes
Sometimes flowers
So that you don't forget
What they look like
You said
Fucking
We never said
Now it's all over
Far out
We never said

Always I see your face
When the blond behind the desk said
The time is up
Say goodbye
But maintain your distance as is proper
Always I see you in prison
In meadows
Between baby carriage
And clotheslines
Helpless, without fear
With a blue handbag

from "Tagesnotizen"

IMMER SEHE ICH DICH IM
GEFÄNGNIS
Im Besucherzimmer
Sprecher
Nannten sie es
Und saßen dabei und wollten alles sehen

Kaffee hattest du mit
Obst
Zigaretten
Manchmal Blumen
Damit du nicht vergißt
Wie sie aussehen
Hast du gesagt
Ficken
Haben wir nie gesagt
Jetzt ist es aus
Haben wir nie gesagt
Ganz toll
Haben wir nie gesagt

Immer sehe ich dein Gesicht
Als der Blonde hinter dem Schreibtisch sagte
Die Zeit ist um
Verabschieden Sie sich
Aber halten Sie Abstand wie es sich gehört
Immer sehe ich dich im Gefängnis
Auf Wiesen
Zwischen Kinderwagen
Und Wäscheleinen
Hilflos, ohne Angst
Mit einer blauen Tasche

Siegfried Heinrichs
(From "mein schmerzliches land") Siegfried Heinrichs, born 1941, luckily in the countryside, there childhood, school, grown up in domestic isolation, herding goats, plundering the neighbors' apples and plums. My mother's problem child

SIEGFRIED HEINRICHS

Smoke Signal

in my oven
I burned many
manuscripts.

its smoke carried
my thoughts.

will it now
be destroyed for
endangering the state?

it was a good
oven.
my verse and its fire
helped me over the
winter.

who will
own it now . . . ?

Rauchzeichen

in meinem ofen
verbrannte ich viele
manuskripte.

sein rauch trug
meine gedanken.

wird er nun
zerstört wegen
staatsgefährdung?

er war ein guter
ofen.
mein vers und sein feuer
halfen über die
winter.

wer wird ihn jetzt
besitzen . . . ?

through sickness, difficulties in the upbringing of a precocious disobeyer. Employment as laborer, soldier, bank clerk, case worker. First attempts at writing after severe illness in 1963; in Feb. 1964, denounced by my own brother, arrested for spreading and production of seditious writings against the wall, barbed wire, and the muzzling of dissenters. Eight months imprisonment with the State Security until condemned in Sept. 1964 to three years in prison, served out to the last day in Waldheim Prison. After my release, work again in different occupations, laborer, church employee, salesperson. Through all these years reading, writing, writing. 1970 marriage, birth of a daughter, 1974 divorce, in Aug. 1978 emigration into the Federal Republic of Germany. Working here white collar—in retrospect thanking the State Security of the DDR for the hard apprenticeship in disobedience, so living and thinking and writing, with residence in West Berlin.

Poems and other manuscripts, including a novel, remain as before in the keeping of the State Security of the DDR, there read and judged and damned as the incredible product of sick delusions and peculiar fantasies.

Sketches from a Socialist Prison
The Book

. . . c'mon, c'mon, get up, masturbate nights till the blood comes, and in the morning no strength in your bones. C'mon, c'mon, move it, whoever doesn't fill his norm today will have his next visit cancelled. I've had it up to here with you lazyboneses. Work right today, I don't want to see any of you on the toilet, whoever wants to smoke, report to me, for five minutes . . .

The voice of the brigadier tore me from my sleep.

Well then, the daily process, five o'clock in the morning, take the bucket with last night's necessities, step before the cell with it, upon command deliver up the shit, march. The steps of the prisoners from all the cells drone on the steel gangway. The bucket is artfully grasped by the handle and on the bottom, lifted, tipped, emptied. Whoever does it for the first time can be sure of the laughter of the others, because it takes some practice to not get shit and urine on your hands but rather to pour it into the huge shit-hole. It was no different for me—laughter when I had my hands full of feces, but couldn't drop the bucket because that would have meant trouble with the warden,

so stay calm, quick, put the hand under water, it stank anyway, back into the cell, wash, breakfast on the last of the marmalade and a thin spread of margarine, then step out to work. Roll call.
Stood still.
Herr Warden, Block 2 with 98 prisoners, 2 sick, reporting for work. Get a move on and let's get to work.
C. next to me looked pale. The liverwurst yesterday, he says slowly, not even a dog would eat it, but us they can feed with it. They must've put rancid rat tails in it, last night I puked till I thought my stomach would come out.
But the voice of the warden interrupts . . . H. report to me. So early in the morning, what could he want . . .
Herr Warden, prisoner H. reporting as ordered.
He sat before a few books and leafed through them. Prisoner H., you've been sent some books. My special packet for good work. He looked at the title.
Well, Thomas Mann, approved, but you should read Socialist literature, it would be better for you.
Herr Warden, I read "New Germany," "Sunday," and "New German Literature."
Yeah, yeah, okay.
But here . . . what's that . . . ?
Ma-la-pa-rte . . . he spells with effort . . .
My God if he lets me have that I'll volunteer to brush the piss gutter clean for thirty days . . .
Well, you know, what do you want with that, *that's* peculiar stuff, what he writes there . . .
It's an anti-war novel, Herr Warden . . .
Well go ahead and take it, but I don't want to hear any complaints, clear? otherwise I clean out your whole locker.
Yes, Sir, understood, Herr Warden.
Snatch it up, shake for excitement, dismiss myself, out, go to work, hide the books, go to A., tell him . . .
Ah, yes . . . for that I've struggled for eight weeks . . . done overtime, made my bed every day in Prussian fashion, volunteered to sweep the courtyard, emptied the garbage and the bucket, . . . now I have him—Malaparte . . .
His novel, so essential to me, "The Skin."
The next days, every hour outside of work is just READ, READ, READ, for the others wait, look up from their "New Germany," how far I am, impatient, nervous, after all the accomplishments of Socialist literature.

photograph by Jochen Melzian

PETER-PAUL ZAHL

Peter Paul Zahl
Born in 1944 in Freiburg/Breisgau, Zahl lived until 1953 in East Germany. He was apprenticed and became journeyman small offset printer. Since 1964 a West Berliner. In 1967 he founded a small press and edited, among others, "die zeitschrift für lesbare literatur—Spartacus" (magazine for readable literature) and "zwergschul-ergänzungshefte" (dwarf-school compensation issues). Active in the new left, member of the Dortmund "Gruppe 61" and a member of the writers' branch of the International Printing and Paper Union. Zahl's experiences with the West German Justice System are described in the petition. His new novel, "Die Glücklichen" (The Happy Ones) won the Bremen Literature Prize and afforded him a short time out of jail to accept the prize. The novel, published by Rotbuch Verlag in Berlin, awaits a willing and able translator (into English) and a willing and able press . . . the novel is long and has much slang . . . any takers? Zahl has been transferred from Werl Maximum Security Prison to the prison in Berlin, Tegel.
Other Publications by Zahl:

Schutzimpfung (Inoculation), poems, 1975

Die Barbaren Kommen (The Barbarians Come), poems and prose, 1976

Von einem, der auszog, Geld zu verdienen (Of one who went out to earn money), 1970, reprinted 1976

Waffe der Kritik, (The Weapon of Criticism), articles and criticism, 1976

Eingreifende oder ergriffene Literatur (Moving or Moved Literature), 1976

Alle Türe Offen (All Doors Open), poems, 1978. Some of these poems have been put to music by the rock groups "Oktober" and "Schmetterlinge" (Butterflies).

Freiheitstriebtäter (untranslatable: Freiheitstrieb is the urge to freedom; Triebtäter is someone who commits crimes of desire, i.e. sexual crimes), poems, prose, documents, 1979

Wie im Frieden (As if at Peace), stories, 1976, reprinted 1979

Schreiben ist (k)ein monologisches Medium (Writing is (not) a Monologue), 1979

petition for Peter-Paul Zahl

"Peter-Paul Zahl, born 1944, poet, printer and author, was sentenced to six months imprisonment in 1972 for printing a poster with the inscription 'Freedom for all prisoners' (Freiheit für alle Gefangenen). After a raid by special branch he went underground. In an encounter with the police who had started firing at him, he fired warning shots—still running away—one of which wounded a policeman. Zahl, himself seriously wounded, was arrested and brought to court after two years' solitary confinement.

Accused of attempted murder of the policeman, he was cleared of the offence, but given four years for resisting arrest and injuring a police officer. In view of his two years of solitary confinement he would have been released in 1976.

Instead, he was once more brought to trial on the same charge as before, the court consisting of only two jurors and three judges. He was found guilty of attempted murder and sentenced to 15 years imprisonment for the same charge on which he had been previously acquitted. The judge in passing sentence said he was imposing maximum sentence on Zahl as enemy of the state' and 'because a special deterrent was needed.' Two books of poetry and prose Zahl had written and had published while in jail were also quoted as reasons for imposing maximum sentence.

"We the undersigned wish to protest against this judgment as being contrary to natural justice and urge that, if there is no legal method of overriding this sentence, the prisoner be amnestied. We also urge that in the meantime he should not be prevented from continuing his literary activities."

J. Cottave, 20 Frognal Lane, London NW.3, Great Britain, Prof. Stuart Hood and 29 others.—

Protests, too, came from the PEN-Centers of the Netherlands, Germany and Switzerland, from Sweden, Hungary, Austria, Italy, France, etc. Information about the "case" (documentation "P.P. Zahl e.g."): Initiativgruppe P.P. Zahl, c/o Verlag Neue Kritik, Myliusstr. 58, D-6000 Frankfurt am Main, W. Germany.

Address of jail, now:

Peter-Paul Zahl
Seidelstr. 39
TAI
1000 Berlin 27
West Germany

february sun

put the bunk at an angle
in front of the window

lie on it
face in the sun

turn the head
regularly

otherwise the bars
make a pattern on the face

often the wind strokes
the closed eyes

I imagine it
to be your fingers

softly the wind strokes
and softly

I think your fingers

for if it were stronger
I couldn't

bear it

translated by Stuart Hood

februarsonne

die pritsche schräg
vors fenster stellen

auf ihr liegen
das gesicht in der sonne

den kopf
gleichmäßig drehen

sonst machen die gitter
muster im gesicht

manchmal streicht wind
über die geschlossenen augen

ich stelle mir vor
es wären deine finger

sacht streicht der wind
und sacht

denke ich mir
deine finger

denn stärker
könnte ich das

nicht ertragen

doors
Stereo poem for 1 voice, (to the music of The Doors)

1 the scream of the butterfly

> We shall bring in our pricks
> before the UN General Assembly.
> —Thorwald Proll

on full moon nights with a south wind
we *smell* our sisters:
   1000 butterflies
   settle on 1000 pricks
   and moths tumble
   before a hundred dark sexes
   of our sisters in ossendorf*
   four hundred yards away
on the dark side of the moon
          —steel cables sway
          a lonely heron
          wing and foot
          our sex
          —the sex in our throats—
          belly-talks
          whirling
          ruinous—
the horizon: feathered with clouds
your womb: four hundred yards away
or four thousand days' journey
a narcotic—
        wet dreams
          —where your ribs end
          I am at home
          dream censorship
          deceit
          even in sleep
          my heart
          a captured predator
          behind the bars
          of your ribs—

---

*Ossendorf— concrete jail of Köln (Rhineland), notorious for its solitary confinement

© by Peter-Paul Zahl, 1976
© by Rotbuch Verlag, Potsdamer Str. 98, D-1000 Berlin 30 (Germany)
Translation by: Prof. Stuart Hood, Erich Fried and friends, London, England
Corrections by: P. P. Zahl

doors
stereo-gedicht für eine stimme

1   the scream of the butterfly
    . . . wir werden unsere schwänze
    vor die UN-vollversammlung bringen.
                    Thorwald Proll

in vollmondnächten mit südwind
riechen wir unsere schwestern:
1000 schmetterlinge
setzen sich auf 1000 schwänze
und nachtfalter taumeln
vor hundert dunklen geschlechten
unserer schwestern in ossendorf
vierhundert meter entfernt:
hinter der dunklen seite des mondes
                stahltrossen schwanken
                ein einsamer reiher
                schwinge und fuß
                unser geschlecht
                das in der kehle
                bauchredet
                wirbelnd
                & in zerfall begriffen
der horizont: wolkengefiedert
euer schoß: vierhundert meter entfernt
oder viertausend tagereisen—
ein narkotikum—
                nasse träume
                wo deine rippen enden
                bin ich zuhaus
                traumzensur:
                betrug
                auch noch im schlaf
                mein herz
                ein gefangenes raubtier
                hinter den gittern
                deiner rippen

bombed back
into the stone age
penetrating to be man
the one out of the picture book
from the old war

    —with the one
    the smallest weakest
    finger very slowly
    to feel out
    the curve of the belly
    with bent arms
    and legs
    to conjure up our prehistory:
    self-deceiving
    with a feeling
    of lightness:
    on full moon nights with a south wind

    we *smell*
    your presence
    in absence
    sisters—

bombed back into the stone age
of rustling four colour print
into the stone age
of those who guard us
and grin
and crack their jokes

2 waiting for the sun

    cada día es un viaje de ida y vuelta
    hacia ninguna parte, hacia la noche.
     —Jorge Carrera Andrade

madness drop by drop
in the sweat
of imaginary embrace
the coming nights:
a breast scraped clean

    —pleasure time:
    a cat's iris
    a guitar
    someone put away
    four thousand days ago
    and then forgot:

zurückgebombt
in die steinzeit:
penetrant mann zu sein
der aus dem bilderbuch
vom altern krieg
    mit dem einen
    dem kleinsten schwächsten
    finger ganz langsam
    die rundung des bauchs
    ertasten
    mit angewinkelten armen
    & beinen
    unsere vorzeit beschwören:
    sich betrügen
    beim empfinden
    von leichtigkeit:
    in vollmondnächten mit südwind
    riechen wir
    eure gegenwart
    in der abwesenheit
    schwestern
zurückgebombt in die steinzeit
raschelnden vierfarbdrucks
in die steinzeit jener
die uns bewachen
und grinsen
und ihre witzchen machen

2   *waiting for the sun*
   Cada día es un viaje de ida y vuelta
   hacia ninguna parte, hacia la noche.
      Jorge Carrera Andrade

wahnsinn tropfenweise
im schweiß
imaginärer umarmung
die kommenden nächte:
eine leergekratzte brust
    lust in der zeit:
    eine katzeniris
    eine gitarre
    die einer fortlegte
    vor viertausend tagen
    und dann vergaß:
    eine saite
    . . . in sich schwingt
    der ton unhörbar

                        a string
                        the note vibrates
                        inaudible
                        infernal
hunger that tenses our thighs
hunger that twists our pelvis
hunger that brings the cell roof
            down on us   —a note too and shivering
                         today spring scents
the cell roof sinks   breast and thighs
the cell roof sinks   and then resting
the cell roof sinks   and pain
                         like being in labour
when you're hungry you gulp
the cell roof sinks
            down on us
                         bombed back: bellies
                         bombed back: fluttering nerve ends
                         bombed back: intrauterine pessary
                         bombed back: lilith
your dream moistens
my breast
your hail pierces my cheeks
your rain wets my womb —when you're hungry you gulp—
the intimacy of our bodies
guarantees from the flesh
for our talking
that it may not fade   —yesterday—
who makes us guarantees today?
who rips the dreams apart?
who stills the hunger?
who once more teaches us to eat?
                        —bombed back into the stone age
                        on the verge of fainting
                        into the choking in the throat
                        if you just catch
                        a glimpse of something female—
bombed back into the stone age
of power
bombed back into this cage here
to be the gorilla man
penetrating to be man
                        —bombed back into the stone age
                        we are meant to become like t h e m
                        only poorer and industrious
                        bombed back into the stone age—

                    infernalisch ...
hunger der unsere schenkel spannt
hunger der unsere becken biegt
hunger der die zellendecke
    niedersenkt auf uns:
die zellendecke senkt sich   ein ton auch und zittern:
die zellendecke senkt sich   heute frühling düfte
die zellendecke senkt sich   brust und schenkel
                                und ruhen dann
                                und schmerz
                                der gleicht dem kreißen
wer hungert der schlingt
die zellendecke senkt sich
nieder auf uns
            zurückgebombt: bäuche
            zurückgebombt: nervenfasern
            zurückgebombt: intrauterine pessare
            zurückgebombt: lilith—
dein traum benetzt
meine brust
dein hagel durchschlägt
meine wangen
dein regen näßt
meinen schoß
                wer hungert der schlingt
die intimität unserer körper
garantien aus fleisch
für unser gespräch
daß es nicht verweht   gestern
wer garantiert für uns heute?
wer zerreißt die träume?
wer stillt den hunger?
wer lehrt uns wieder essen?
            zurückgebombt in die steinzeit
            in die halbe ohnmacht
            in das würgen im hals
            wenn du nur weibliches siehst
zurückgebombt in die steinzeit
der macht
zurückgebombt in den käfig hier:
den mann
penetrant mann zu sein
gorilla mann
            zurückgebombt in die steinzeit:
            wir sollen werden wie *die*
            nur ärmer und arbeitsam
            zurückgebombt in die steinzeit

3 light my fire

> *in the street of the sky night*
> *walks scattering poems*
> —Cummings

nothing is left
but to tear t h i s down
burn it down
level it to the ground
stone age to stone age
burn down the jail
with its white murderers
its concrete
and its dirty sheets
into which we dreamt
and rust

                 —a womb bursts open
                 bloody lips
                 the wholesale trade in sex objects
                 plays barbarism
                 on the spinet of our bones
                 on the rotogravured scaffold
                 on the field of our skin
                 there where your thighs
                 marvellously warm and shady
                 unite
                 the l a w pitches its camp
                 and thrusts you through
                 with its weapons:
                 s e c u r i t y & p u b l i c
                              order

rise
in the breath
of an obsession :
breasts tautened by spring
                 —in these damned full moon nights!—
a harsher sound now:
this joy is a spasm and hurts
                 —did we go after bats
                 in this bank vault?
                 did we come looking for life
                 in this concrete tomb?—
and spew ourselves out
confronted with ourselves again
or with our bloody
beaten up shadows:

3 *light my fire*
Auf der Straße des Himmels geht Nacht und
verstreut Gedichte.
E.E. Cummings

da bleibt nichts
als *dies hier* einzureißen
abzubrennen
gleichzumachen dem erdboden:
die steinzeit der steinzeit
verbrennen den knast
mit seinen weißen mördern
seinem beton
und seinen schmutzigen laken
in die wir geträumt
und rost
    ein schoß bricht auf
    blutige lippen
    der großhandel für sexartikel
    spielt barbarei
    auf dem spinett unserer knochen
    auf dem schafott aus kupfertief
    und auf dem felde der haut
    dort wo eure schenkel
    köstlich warm und schattig
    sich vereinen
    schlägt
    auf sein lager das *gesetz*
    und schlägt euch durch
    mit seinen schwertern
    sicherheit und ordnung
steigt
im hauch
einer zwangsvorstellung:
frühlingsgespannte brüste
    in diesen verdammten
    vollmondnächten
ein harter laut jetzt:
dies glück ist ein krampf
und schmerzt
    gingen wir auf fledermausfang
    in dieses schließfach?
    gingen wir leben zu finden
    in diese gruft aus beton?

for there a r e dynamos in the temples   somewhere
and flights of larks over ripe maize   somewhere
and sparrowhawks that tear steel to pieces   somewhere
and breasts that spit milk and fire   somewhere
and tendernesses
that turn your laugh inside out   somewhere
somewhere   but not here
and beginnings of softness and kindness
              —not in bank vaults
              not behind bars
              not in concrete
              not in stone coffins—
lovers on paper
immured in four coloured print:
five twists of tobacco with papers*
              —your back a chorale
              your muscles a blues
              by B.B. King
              your womb a mystery
              of The Doors
in bed
in summer
in jail
      —we were one   we are one
      at night   at night
      we woke up   we wake up
      next to each other: next to each other:
      the other one   a skeleton
      the world   the law—
watch out!
keep your eyes shut!
keep your ears shut
dive in station
      in the dug-out
adjourn yourself:
t h e y will bomb you back
into the stone age
t h e y want you back
with t h e m!

---

*tobacco with papers—monetary unit in jails
lovers on paper immured . . . —pornography

und speien uns aus
wieder mit uns selbst konfrontiert
oder unseren blutig
geprügelten schatten:
denn da *sind* dynamos in schläfen   irgendwo
und lerchenflüge über sattem mais   irgendwo
und sperber die stahl zerfetzen   irgendwo
und brüste die milch und feuer speien   irgendwo
und zärtlichkeiten
die dein lachen nach außen stülpen   irgendwo
irgendwo   aber nicht hier
und anfänge von weichheit und güte
        in schließfächern nicht
        nicht hinter gittern
        nicht in beton
        nicht in steinernen särgen
sich liebende auf papier:
eingemauert in vierfarbdruck
fünf pack tabak mit blättchen
        dein rücken ein choral
        deine muskeln ein blues
        von b. b. king
        dein schoß ein geheimnis
        der doors
im bett
im sommer
im knast
    wir waren eins   wir sind eins:
    nachts   nachts
    wir wachten auf   wir wachen auf
    neben uns: neben uns:
    der andere   ein skelett
    die welt   das gesetz
paß auf
halt dir die augen
halt dir die ohren zu
geh auf tauchstation
    in den unterstand
vertage dich:
die bomben dich zurück
in die steinzeit
die wollen dich
zurück
zu sich

4 riders on the storm

> There are no clean hands, no innocents, no observers . . . Every observer is a coward or a traitor.
>
> —Frantz Fanon

sadistic dreams
bestial dreams
dreams of torture
dreams of ministers
dreams of violation
dreams
in which we assume the faces
of our enemies

                —through the spyhole
                in the cell door
                the judas
                stares a warder's eye
                it is looking at article I
                of the constitution the one
                about the dignity of humanity—

hammer anvil rosepink mussel
                        yesterday
laughing in coils   yesterday
hammer anvil rosepink mussel
silk-hung laughter   yesterday
: your dream
       has grey wings
            and a white breast

we are wary
of those who mean us well
relentlessly mean us well
t h e y lie and prevent us
t h e y abort us
before our birth

                —ten thousand madmen
                tinkle their songs
                on the old piano
                of our spine
                with their underwater voice
                they call back to work
                to prayers in the stock exchange
                toothless rats is
                what they are and malicious

riders on the storm
Es gibt keine reinen Hände, keine Unschuldigen, keine
Zuschauer . . . Jeder Zuschauer ist ein Feigling oder
ein Verräter.
Frantz Fanon

sadistische träume
bestialische träume
folterträume
ministerträume
vergewaltigungsträume
träume
in denen wir das gesicht
unserer feinde annehmen
          durch das guckloch
          in der zellentür
          den spion
          starrt ein beamtenauge
          es schaut sich
          artikel eins des grundgesetzes an:
          den über die würde
          des menschen
hammer amboß rosenmuschel   gestern
lachen in schlingen   gestern
hammer amboß rosenmuschel
gelächter seidenverhangen   gestern
: dein traum
        hat graue flügel
                  und eine weiße brust
wir hüten uns
vor denen die es gut
unnachsichtig gut mit uns meinen
sie lügen und verhüten uns
sie treiben uns ab
vor der geburt
          zehntausend verrückte
          klimpern ihre songs
          auf dem alten klavier
          unserer wirbelsäule
          mit ihrer unterwasserstimme
          rufen sie zur arbeit
          zur anpassung
          zum gebet in der börse zurück:
          ratten sind sie
          zahnlos & tückisch

.. . sadistic dreams
dreams
in which we assume
the face of our enemies
      —no biting at cords of flesh
      no tongue on the side of the neck
      and in all the precious crannies
here the lambs are guilty
here the crickets are mass-murderers
and if you think
too much about me sister
you'll weaken yourself needlessly
      —faced with this night
      rasped by screams
      strapped up
      in the padded cell
      the white quiet chamber
      eye to eye
      with the camera
      that throws your picture
      without pause
      onto the monitors
      of power—
in the brain
the building takes place in advance tomorrow
cooperation work and pleasure tomorrow
and these shockingly
splendid rainbows
between man and woman   tomorrow
      —fingertips
      cast in downy hair
      and clearly
      agonisingly visible:
      a body which bends
      unborn wave of fever
      tongue tip that glides
      from the elbow
        over the hipbone
          to the womb
      soft traces
      etched in the flesh—
rainbows is what we are
rainbows
the linking of unnaturally
parted lives

. . . sadistische träume
träume
in denen wir das gesicht
unserer feinde annehmen
    kein biß in stränge aus fleisch
    keine zune seitlich am hals
    und in all den köstlichen nischen
hier sind die lämmer schuldig
hier sind die grillen massenmörder
und wenn du zuviel
an mich denkst schwester
machst du dich unnötig schwach
    vor dieser nacht
    von schreien gefeilt
    angeschnallt
    in der beruhigungszelle
    der weißen stillen kammer
    auge in auge mit der kamera
    die dein bild wirft
    pausenlos
    auf die monitoren
    der macht
im gehirn vollzieht
sich der aufbau im voraus morgen
kooperation arbeit und lust morgen
und diese entsetzlich
herrlichen regenbogen
von mensch zu mensch morgen
    fingerkuppen
    gegossen in flaum
    und deutlich
    qualvoll sichtbar:
    ein leib der sich biegt
    ungeboren fieberwelle
    zungenspitze die gleitet
    vom ellenbogen
      über hüftknochen
      zum schoß
    in fleisch geätzte
    sanfte spuren
regenbogen sind wir
regenbogen
verbindung widernatürlich
getrennter leben

artificially separated
selves: here woman   there man
   lips opened   —eyelids opened
   to catch stars   to stroke temples
   crystals and snow back of the knee and hips
   moonflowers dew   hollow of collarbone and belly

*if you don't cooperate
we'll give you
dachau*

                        and if you cooperate
                        you get a dose of pox
                        from power

carve castanets
sister   from my bones
after my death
they should keep you happy
when I'm not there anymore

5 before I sink into the big sleep
*The faces stood in the doorway and looked
down on me. Their expression typically prison-
warder, i.e. dumbly goggling, clumsy and un-
shakeably selfconfident.*
                        —*Cummings*

the road to you is long:
each time the huge key screeches
in iron doors
nine times:
the cell door
the block door
the door of the prisonhouse
the door of the long corridor
into the main building
the entrance door
to the visitor's block
the door in the first floor
of the visitor's block
the door to the waiting cell
and waiting
                      —they bomb
                      they bomb you back
                      back into a lump of flesh
                      140 pounds of flesh
                      appendage to a prick—

künstlich in zwei
geteilten ichs: hier frau　　da mann
　　lippen geöffnet　　　　　lider geöffnet
　　um sterne zu fangen　　um schläfen zu streicheln
　　kristalle und schnee　　kniekehlen hüften
　　mondblüten tau　　　　salznäpfchen bauch
wer nicht kooperiert
dem geht es
wie in dachau
　　　　　　　　　　und wer kooperiert
　　　　　　　　　　holt sich syph
　　　　　　　　　　von der macht
schnitz kastagnetten
schwester
aus meinen knochen
nach meinem tod
die sollen dich erfreuen
bin ich nicht mehr da

5　　　　　*before i sink into the big sleep*
　　　　　... die Gesichter standen im Eingang und blickten
　　　　　auf mich nieder. Ihr Ausdruck typisch gefangenen-
　　　　　wärterisch, d. h. blöde glotzend, schwerfällig und
　　　　　unerschütterlich von sich eingenommen.
　　　　　　　　　　　　　　E. E. Cummings

der weg zu dir ist lang:
jedesmal schreit der handlange schlüssel
in eisernen türen
neun mal:
die zellentür
die tür des trakts
die tür des hafthauses
die tür des langen gangs
zum haupthaus hin
die eingangstür
zum besuchertrakt
die tür im ersten stock
des besuchertrakts
die tür zur wartezelle
und warten
　　　　　　die bomben
　　　　　　die bomben dich zurück
　　　　　　die bomben dich zurück
　　　　　　zurück in ein stück
　　　　　　fleisch:

once more the door
of the waiting cell
then the door
to the visiting room:
             and there you stand
             guarded by special branch
and I guarded by screws
shake off nervousness
go up to you
mime smiling—
I'm the frog prince
and I am captive
give me a kiss
I pray
                    and stop trembling
                    you've no call to
                    together
                    we'll manage

and now start
tell me:
is there s u c h a t h i n g
is there o u t t h e r e ?
                    —with me
                    for a week
                    I carry round
                    your picture
                    your voice
                    and your aroma
then it's over

keep strong
I will
too
                    —we shall hear the scream
                    of the butterfly
                    we shall wait for the sun
                    we shall turn on the light
                    we shall ride the storm

                    before we sink
                    into the big sleep
open the doors
open the doors

a l l d o o r s o p e n

translated by Stuart Hood

                130 pfund fleisch
                anhang zum schwanz
erneut die tür der wartezelle
die tür dann zum besucherraum:
                und du stehst da
                bewacht von lka
und ich bewacht von grünen
schüttle befangenheit ab
tret auf dich zu
und mime lächeln:
ich bin der froschkönig
und ich bin gefangen
gib mir einen kuß
ich bitt dich
                und hör auf
                zu zittern
                dazu hast du
                keinen grund
                gemeinsam
                schaffen wirs
und nun fang an
erzähl:
gibt es *das*
gibt es *draußen*?
                mit mir
                eine woche
                trag ich dein bild
                deine stimme
                und dein aroma
dann ist es vorbei
bleib stark
ich bleib
es auch
                wir werden den schrei
                des schmetterlings hören
                wir werden auf die sonne warten
                wir werden das licht anzünden
                wir werden die stürme reiten
                ehe wir fallen
                in den großen schlaf:
offen die türen
offen die türen
alle türen offen!

Thomas Neubauer
Born 1949, grew up in Thuringia in the DDR, occupational and private odyssey: candidate for the clergy, orderly in home for the aged, pastor's assistant, brewery worker, idler, poem-writer, youth worker, hotbed warmer, cemetery employee. Apart from

THOMAS NEUBAUER

The Request

At the table a fat woman holding on nervously to the document file. Now and then she picks her nose bashfully and casts a longing gaze out the window with her bottle green eyes.
The middle aged man behind her holds his mouth open, and his face, red from whatever, is uneasy, trembly, and, if you like, recognize the sign of the Choleric in the capillaries fanning out under his cheeks. His gray, long-uncleaned suit shows light stains about the fly. But the red cravat gleams in the sun, low behind the church spire; on his lapel, the party emblem too is gleaming, you would think it was polished with Brillo. He looks uncommunicative and takes awhile before parting with his desk to come to me. You want to go to the BRD? he asks.
At that word the fat woman exhales heavily and cleans her nose. I play with the matchbox. Smoking is not allowed today, at any rate, not for me; it could be that people who have only come here to complain about insufficient imports of citrus fruit may remain more relaxed.
In the BRD? he asks.
Why?
Why! If I want to be credible, I have to play the disenchanted, innerly-long-since-emigrated villain, to whom nothing matters, who carries the dagger under his coat to run amok with.
But you grew up here didn't you, says the man. Gone to school here. You're for peace too, though your conscientious objector status raises questions of course, but all in all it's still your Fatherland, the DDR, like the singer you so idolize . . .
He interrupts.
Grown up here! The fat one sweats, shifts here and there in her chair, rubs at her bottle green eyes, because they're watering a little. It's hot.

that, politically suspect, conscientious objector, etc.
1975 emigration/immigration to West Berlin. Since then this and that and nothing final. He regards his writing as the interpretation of occurrences in his life and the representation of the inner as well as outer confusion. This story is from *Im Nachlass Kein Gelächter Mehr* (No Laughter in the Inheritance Any More), 1979. Now working on a novel.

Grown up here! I feel feverish. Pictures dance in my head.
Oblak in toddler clothing. Oblak in—Dynamo Moscow Pants—. Oblak on the first day of school with only a bag of sweets because he refused to carry his school satchel and books. Oblak in the Young Pioneers. A blue kerchief around his neck, following the herd, gathering chestnuts and self-critical, like Ernst Thälmann proud and bold. The limb-stretching homeland. Max needs water. Collecting scrap for Industry. His parents amputate television channels. At school, television dials are painted to check up on who watches "West" at home.
Grown up here!
Wilhelm Pieck died. The veteran workers conduct the brass band. The children cried because the sovereign had kindly eyes. Oblak was reprimanded because he threw stones at a police car and that at age eleven.
The other leader of the workers had kindly eyes too, it said in the readers. He was friends with Teddy Thälmann, it said, and in winter he goes skiing with the working class. But the people whispered, that's only bodyguards and secretly named him Pointy Beard and Sandman and he'd only grown a beard because he once was a pimp and there was still a scar on his chin, the people said.
And we?
On official holidays singing songs for the comrades of the National People's Army. Photos were taken. Children lifted onto tanks. It was permitted to spit apple seeds down from there.
Why should I leave, spoke a soldier, just to smoke perfumed cigarettes; he said, eyes on the Werra, the border river.
And what was fun, inconspicuous in the woods, in the restrooms, clowning and groping, the early, secretly relished horniness, young and hairless beneath the mountain oak, inhaling smoke instead of

climbing the rope, the Count of Monte Cristo rather then Kotschubej, the red cavalry general.
Between corridor and cellar, the sad eyes, childhood fantasies, short-pantsed and more friendly than the verses of the poet Bartel, who the authorities intimately called Kuba. But the fear of being pinned up as a caricature on the classroom wall, as the worst, the dunce, was stronger, left me no peace. It was a back and forth, an up and down, an on and off with the chameleon skin. In the school we were to honor the leadership, at home one made fun of them, and in Sunday School an older man recommended that we believe in a certain Jesus Christ, about whom my grandmother had also reported this and that. Grown up here!
I blinked at the fat woman in her coarsely cut skirt. Naturally this is my Fatherland. Here I learned to live, here I was disciplined and caressed, here I tasted love and spit it out again, here I lay down unconscious and trod between the trees to tear them up, here I waved my little May Day flag in front of the grandstand to disappear in the next alley, as was the custom among the working class, here one saw me gathering potatoes, here one heard me cursing the suffering of the Silesian weavers, here I saw the National Prize winner act Thälmann five times and I read the forbidden Mickey Mouse in bed, here I had verses of praise to recite, my cap pistol in my pocket . . .
My grownupness!
What shall I tell them, they who are used to answering every question with a counter-question?
But you're for peace, they say. Well then. Whoever is for peace, must be for our State and participate, each where he is put. So it must be. I want to puke on the throw carpet where the man with the piss-stained pants stands—be that as it may—he says, while the sun is at its highest,—be that as it may, your Request for Emigration to the BRD, and he stretches the word out savoringly like a Wrigley's in his mouth, cannot be fulfilled, unfortunately—he adds, grinning.
Don't come undone, I think. Bite your tongue.
Your gait straight and out. One sentence more, perhaps, as a warning: I'll come back. I'll hang myself from City Hall or something.
Absolutely inexorable I stagger down the stairs, past the clean-smiling Honeckers with gleaming teeth, which hang where the Ulbrichts used to hang.
Silent, I walk through the sweating city. Dust whirls and faces dance past me like Mardi Gras masks. The bar isn't overfull, since usually one betakes himself to drink only after work. At the counter table sits K., the machinery attendant, erect and large before a bottle of wine

and curses the Amis,* the Russians, the Jews. He renders homage solely to the dead German leaders of the Workers Movement, because they'd turn in their graves, as he says. But that's his personal opinion, he adds, and has nothing to do with the fact that he is commander of the reserve guard unit at the factory, and those at his table, whether Stasi† or not, grin into their beerglasses, as if the day were finished and what happens between Beer and Corn were another world.

**Ami* is German slang for American.
†*Stasi* is the nickname for Staatssicherheit (State Security) and its members.

by Jochen Melzian   photograph

JOCHEN MELZIAN

Realistic Curriculum Vitae
Draft of a personal record for an application for a stipend for doctoral studies: Dec. 19, 1971

I, the undersigned Joachim-Friedrich Melzian, was born in 1944. My father, Hans-Joachim Melzian, was a soldier; Paula, my mother, his wife.
My father fell in 1945 in Berlin.
The political development is well-known; meager coal and dried potatoes. We lived in Charlottenburg district, then in Wilmersdorf. In 1950 I was brought to school.
For 17 years I have lived, with short interruptions, in Spandau, which means, today, old buildings: cold water, cold apartment. But since a month ago, a communal TV antenna.
The interruptions: a Christian Home for Unadapted Youth, university study.
I attended the best school in all of Berlin: for ten years, that means one year twice. Since then I treasure Montaigne and Racine especially and Corneille especially little.
The school was founded by a Brandenburgish prince in 1689, one year after his death. That Heinrich von Kleist, the great author, was a pupil here is maintained only by one encyclopedia; that his guardian was a professor of Greek here appears reliable.
The instruction in mathematics, geography, physics, biology, Greek, and Latin was bad, in French very good, also in Sport: you could often go for a walk.
I had good grades in English, because I listened avidly to the hit songs. I still do that. But now I'm more interested in domestic German hits, like those from Manuela, from Freddy, from Ulrich Roski. Bored with school, I photographed a lot.

So after the Abitur I studied law. In my first semester (summer 1964) I had the opportunity to experience two fascinating classes: "Introduction to Legal Science" from Arwed Blomeyer, and "Formal Logic II" from Eva Cassirer, the daughter of old Ernst Cassirer. Then I studied a year in Freiburg. I worked as a taxi driver, and once I drove Martin Heidegger to the library (35 pfennig tip, in 7 5-pfennig coins).
The whole time I wanted a girl friend, but I acted too stupid. In my despair I took dancing lessons, which failed on two counts.
Sometimes a girl, a photographer from Munich, called me up. Even that didn't ring a bell.
I went back to Berlin, earned a big certificate, and ascertained that I hadn't any notion. I regarded myself as unsuitable and saw no professional prospects for me. Langhans formulated the dilemma so: "I started with law because you can become anything with it, and I stopped doing law when I saw that *I* couldn't become anything with it."
In West Germany just before the elections an old fat man scolded the lazy bums. A few months later he was one himself—with honorarium, office, and secretary. I wanted to become a lazy bum too, and, while on the bum, to learn Russian. I studied Slavic. Slavists have, in addition to subjectively, also objectively no prospects of a job.
I made my tenth or eleventh attempt to learn Russian. I drove a few times to Prague and learned Czech.
I was bored, started photographing again, played in the Perpendikel Theater in a play by Pavel Fiala.
Then I became a Student Assistant.
Experimental Fonetik was fun. Where machines have a finger in the game, I am so moved that tears come to my eyes. As a child I once told someone I wanted to become an engineer. I was answered that that was a terrible shame—with such a Purely scientific father! To shift now is too late, I fear.
From my salary I bought my fifth and sixth car, a Leica (a particularly inspiring machine), and stuff like that.
I was promoted to Scientific Under-Assistant.
Then came the occupation of the ČSSR.
Then the girl I proposed to said no.
Then I got fired.
I applied for a stipend in the ČSSR, where I wanted to write my doctoral thesis about Bohemian Polit-Linguistics. The matter was discussed twice with a gentleman from the Czechoslovakian military mission. The food was good, the stipend I didn't get. The Czech exchange student, who was supposed to come in exchange for me, became Consular Assistant at the mission, and since West Berlin has no military mission in Prague, I stayed here. Once I met him in the

tavern and he said, we ought to sit down together sometime and exchange information about contacts between Berlin students and Czechoslovakian students.

Then I decided, at the suggestion of Herr Professor Doctor K.D. Seeman, to write a Master's Thesis about Jazykov.

I didn't want to write any nonsense and therefore started to count. I lost count often. It took time. Until the 16th of November, 1971. Since then, I am a Master.

And now I'm taking my third fascinating course of study: a FORTRAN programming course at the Technical University of Berlin from Peter Cassiers. I want to write a dissertation about the system of lyrical genres in Russian literature in the time of Pushkin with particular emphasis on the place of the elegies of Jazykov in that system. I don't want to write any nonsense and so I want to support myself with facts (numerical data and statistics). But now everyone wants to know if that's possible at all.

And whether I can do it.

To be required to prove the future . . . that's like business by the book, following every instruction so exactly to the letter that everything breaks down. If, before I may touch a pen, I must prove that it will write, and that I can write, then it might as well be forbidden to write.

All I really want any more is peacefully to compile my notes on Jazykov and his elegies—3 binders, 8½ x 11, each 3 inches thick—to dream of computers, sonographs, oscillographs, filters, autos, photographic equipment, of Prague and beautiful girls, to earn my doctorate, and then—no chance for a job—to go home in peace.

The Predilection of the German Thinker

The predilection of the German thinker to endlessly long sentences is possibly less the result of the alleged anal structuring of the German soul, as is lamented by Muir in his essay, "Translating from the German" in the anthology *On Translating*, which appeared in the year 1966 in New York, that it is connected with the fact that the German co- or non-thinker, or at any rate, think(er)-consumer always assumes that a thought is exactly one sentence long and the end of a sentence the appropriate point in time to interrupt the flow of talk of the thinker and to begin to disprove the just-expressed sentence—to such a degree that even a thinker whose thoughts may perhaps be not at all so simply structured is forced to accommodate a whole, in some cases even a very complex and perhaps protracted train of thought into a single sentence, which is after all the first and last one which he will be allowed to speak undisturbed, if he doesn't want either to resort to the expedient of formulating as his first sentence one in which so many unfamiliar or in-their-present-context unusual words that no one understands him and therefore the others not only allow him to reinforce it with the necessary explanation—in further sentences—but almost request him to reinforce it—approximately that path which Wittgenstein in his *Tractatus logico-philosophicus* followed—or on the other hand to the other expedient, which is to begin with the kind of sentence that appears so primitive that nobody feels the necessity to interrupt it so soon as after the first end of a sentence—in that manner, which Fichte, who, as is well-known, let his primary philosophical text begin with the stipulation "I = I" did it—so that it is again possible to push in explanations, whereby it should be noticed that the last-described way appears increasingly hopeless the more reinforcing explanations are necessary, since here, unlike the first two of the above-named possibilities, where the train of thought with its pause, corresponding to the period in the typeface, or else where the complete definition of every single word in the first sentence has its end and this end appears to the listener as verifiable, for the not necessarily intimately-with-the-speaker's-world-of-thought-acquainted listener, a natural end of the train of thought is not immediately recognizable, so that it can even occur that the discoursing thinker is interrupted in the unfolding of his thought in its entirety by a pert disprover, the prevention of which was the whole point of the exercise.

In other countries they're generally more polite. For example in England. They let you speak your piece there. Because of that, one needn't speak in tapeworms. Actually that's useful for all concerned. You can divide a longer thought into many small pieces so that everyone can understand it. Just as any small child can carry many bricks singly. But no one can carry a whole house at one time.

Aktion Widerstand (Project Resistance)*

> *Like a sandstorm
> the heaviest bombardment
> swept over Berlin.
> Even party members
> and devotees of the regime
> now joined
> the camp of resistance.*
>   *Berliner Morgenpost (Newspaper)*
>   *May 5, 1978*

Like a sandstorm the heaviest bombardment swept over Berlin.
Even the worst procrastinators saw that now it was down to the canned goods.
The stolen territories were almost all lost again
Too bad
The defenseless prisoners were now machine-processed to death
Embarrassing
The great Führer got a tremor, wasn't up to par any more.
That explained it to some
Without making the situation any easier.
In a word there was nothing more to win,
But still this and that to lose.
In this moment awoke Germany's conscience suddenly
(which had never rested perfectly well),
Rubbed its eyes and said to itself:
Now it's really high time
To change the team and rescue the
Canned goods, at least the canned goods:
The State Territory,
The State People,
The Power of the Government,
The Army as Bulwark Against Bolshevism.
And then the deed of liberation was done.

---

*On the 20th of July, 1944, a year and a half after the decisive defeat of Hitler's armies at Stalingrad and shortly after the invasion at Normandy, an assassination of Hitler was attempted by Colonel Count von Stauffenberg and General Goerdeler. The planners were executed. After World War Two, the word Widerstand (Resistance) acquired a halo. "Aktion Widerstand" was the name taken by the opponents of Willy Brandt's progressive administration and its new "Ostpolitik," the official recognition of the alteration of borders and consequent territorial loss on Germany's part as a result of the war.

Aktion Widerstand

> *Wie ein Sandsturm fegte*
> *der schwerste Angriff*
> *über Berlin.*
> *Sogar Parteimitglieder*
> *und Anhänger des Regimes*
> *stießen jetzt*
> *zum Lager des Widerstandes.*
>   *Berliner Morgenpost*
>   *5.11.1978*

Wie ein Sandsturm fegte der schwerste Angriff über Berlin.
Auch die argsten Zauderer sahen, daß es jetzt ans Eingemachte
    ging.
Die gestohlenen Gebiete waren fast alle wieder verloren
Schade
Die wehrlosen Gefangenen wurden jetzt maschinell zu Tode
    verarbeitet
Peinlich
Der große Führer hatte den Tatterich bekommen, war nicht mehr
    auf dem Posten
Das erklärte manchem manches
Ohne deshalb die Lage leichter zu machen.
Zu gewinnen gabs, kurz gesagt, nichts mehr,
Zu verlieren aber noch dies und das.
Da erwachte Deutschlands Gewissen
(Das ja nie ganz geruht hatte)
Plötzlich rieb sich die Augen und sagte sich:
Jetzt ist es aber wirklich höchste Zeit
Die Mannschaft zu wechseln und
Das Eingemachte, wenigstens das Eingemachte, zu retten:
Das Staatsgebiet
Das Staatsvolk
Die Regierungsgewalt
Die Armee als Bollwerk gegen den Bolschewismus.
Und da wurde dann
Die Befreiungstat getan.

First a list was written, on it stood
Who, afterwards, would get which posts.
For the hangman it was very useful afterwards, he concluded from it
Who belonged on which post.
Then soldiers were sent around the city
Unfortunately they didn't know what they should do
So after waiting awhile they returned to their barracks.

Then a general went to finish off the Minister of Propaganda
But the latter showed once again his rhetorical superiority
So the general relinquished his drawn pistol
And later his spoon, logo.

Churchill later had very
Acknowledging things to say about these men.

It only remains to mention that instead of the great dictator,
A great table was murdered,
Which may explain why some old hands are so opposed to violence against objects:
How easily it can turn into violence against persons!

Ja, ja, . . . if Hitler hadn't died,
Then he would still live happily ever after.

Erstmal wurde eine Liste geschrieben, darauf stand
Wer hinterher welchen Posten bekommen sollte
Dem Henker war sie hinterher nützlich, er entnahm ihr,
Wer an welchen Pfosten gehörte.
Dann wurden Soldaten in der Stadt rumgeschickt
Die wußten leider nicht, was sie tun sollten
Begaben sich deshalb nach kurzem Zuwarten zurück in die Kasernen.

Dann ging ein General, den Propogandaminister erledigen
Doch der zeigte sich wiedermal rhetorisch überlegen
So gab der General die vorgehaltene Pistole ab
Und später den Löffel, logo.

Churchill hat sich später
Sehr anerkennend über diese Männer geäußert.

Bliebe nur noch zu erwähnen, daß statt des großen Diktators
Ein großer Tisch ermordet wurde,
Was erklären mag, warum gewisse Leute so sehr gegen Gewalt gegen Sachen sind
Wie leicht kann sie in Gewalt gegen Personen umschlagen!

Ja, ja . . . wenn Hitler nicht gestorben wär,
Dann lebte er heute noch.

VIII HISTORIES

ALFONS KOHLER

Cooling Towers

    Honest
there used to be white and yellow water lilies there. Only the mosquitos bothered me, which I chased and swatted.

    Many stories
were told about this lake. A whole village was supposed to have gone under in it, and the treasure of an incredibly rich miller was supposed to lie on its bed; one need only bring it up. The tangle of water plants kept me from searching the bottom.

    In summer, when it
was hot, when everyone stood senselessly in the church plaza, or sat around in one of the three taverns of the village, I made my way to the lake.

    Imagination
strangled and caressed me, often drove me far from the accustomed village straitness (which I left unwillingly at that time), far from the ugly fat women into the lovely thin arms, until the sperm crept warmly across the back of my hand and dripped into the boat.

    "A piece of use-
less land," said the owner, a farmer in a neighboring village, and sold the lake with the adjacent meadow for three thousand marks. Since then, the boredom of the new master was guarded by a German shepherd.

    A shaky pier
led through reeds two or three meters high. An old worm-eaten skiff, through which water seeped, hung on a rotting pole. I bailed the

Alfons Köhler
Born 1949 in Schweinfurt, in Berlin since
1969. Editor of the magazine *Kühltürme*.

---

water out with my shoes and paddled, also with my shoes, past the water lilies to ever changing fantasies.

                    On the water
rocking and thinking only of myself, disturbed by no one, nothing forbidden, no orders to follow, letting my skin breathe free, catching fish that are thrown back in . . .

                    at this lake
I wrote my first poem.

                  Today they are
building an atomic power plant in the immediate vicinity. The lake was for the most part filled in.

                  Only an occas-
ional water lily appears any more. The reeds lay broken off, uprooted among the refuse. Pier and skiff are unusable.

                  A few stories
remain, as long as they continue to be told.

                  Beer cans lie
in the filth, newspapers, an old beat-up couch, a smashed television, mattresses that lie half in the muck, half in the water, a blacktop path that
          leads up
               to the
                  cooling
                       towers.

STEFAN DÖRING

poem about my grandfather

in white bathing clothes
on the baltic sea beach ahlbeck
i see my grandfather in photographs
and in memory
white with dark cigar
he liked to look from the window to the sports fields
with children playing kickball
immovable stood his chair
where his silence was so uncanny for me

in the dark cupboard, instruments
scalpel, shears, emergency bandages
blurring dusk hours
before the call to supper

photo albums that tuck in memory
in rustling tissue
shards from many vessels
deluding and confounding
and no whole no matter how many pieces

on a very warm August day
the bier and the ambulance rattle
from the kitchen window: the carried grandfather
(very vertically downwards)
the apartment door behind me
slams shut
the key inside the empty flat

Stefan Döring
Born 1954. Abitur, Army, Studied
Electronics, working now as Development
Engineer.

gedicht über meinen großvater

im weißen strandanzug
im ostseebad ahlbeck
sehe ich meinen großvater auf photographien
auch in der erinnerung
weiß mit dunkler zigarre
gern sah er vom fenster den turnplatz
mit spielenden kindern (völkerball)
unverrückbar stand sein stuhl
wo mir sein schweigen unheimlich war

im dunklen schrank instrumente
(skalpell schere notverband)
verschwimmende dämmerstunden
vor dem rufen zum abendbrot

photoalben die die erinnerung einschlagen
in raschelndes seidenpapier
scherben von verschiedenen gefäßen
täuschung und verwechslung
und kein ganzes je mehr teile es werden

an einem sehr sonnigen augusttag
röcheln bahre und krankenwagen
vom küchenfenster: der getragene großvater
(sehr senkrecht hinunter)
die wohnungstür hinter mir
schlägt zu
der schlüssel in leerer wohnung

NORBERT TEFELSKI

Old Typewriter

How often did it
write
Heilhitler

How often did it
omit it

Norbert Tefelski
was born in 1950 in Munich. His texts and cartoons have appeared in diverse magazines. He lives in Berlin and is a member of the Berlin staff of the magazine *Der Tod* (Death). He has had readings and performances with the "Gruppe Schauplazz" and is editor and publisher of the experimental lit-mag *KULT uhr*.

Alte Schreibmaschine

Wie oft hat sie
Heilhitler
Geschrieben

Wie oft es
Unterlassen

Nostalgic One

D'ya remember
how
the minister came
swung the toilet brush, consecrated the water
cried APAGE SATANAS
back then—
after the Corpus Christi
Day procession
           ?

Notoriously
neuralgic-neurotic
old complaints
about the too loud
church music
about the organ
—back then
to puberty

and they were all against us!

While we
wiped up they
caught us
were powerless
in the face
of my explanation
my cock hung out at the moment
only because
it had been rubbed sore
from
bicycling

With embarrassed look
at the pluperfect tense
powder was recommended
—back then
in secret past

Today I don't
know you
any more
hardly recognize myself in the mirror
   there are such thick
   panes of milk glass
   between us!

Nostalgiker

Weißte noch
wie
der Pfarrer kam
die Klobürste schwang, das Wasser geweiht
APAGE SATANAS schrie
damals—
nach der Fronleich-
namsprozession
        ?

Notorisch
neuralgisch-neurotische
alte Beschwerden
über die zu laute
Kirchenmusik
übers Orgeln
—damals
zur Pubertät

und alle waren gegen uns!

Beim
Abwischen habense
uns erwischt
waren machtlos
angesichts
meiner Erklärung
es hinge mein Schwanz (momentan)
nur deshalb heraus
weil alles wundgerieben wär
vom
Fahrradfahrn

Mit verlegenem Blick
zum Plusquamperfekt
wurde Puder empfohlen
—damals
in heimlicher Vergangenheit

Heute kenn
ich dich
nicht mehr
erkenne kaum mein Spiegelbild
   da sind so dicke
   Milchglasscheiben
   zwischen!

The Constitution

Whoever doesn't honor it
Isn't worthy of it

It won't apply
to him

He'll be left
out

Just for him
they'll write
a couple of
new laws

Das Grundgesetz

Wer das nicht ehrt
Der ist es nicht wert

Auf den wird es
Gar nicht angewendet

Der wird links
Liegengelassen

Für den
Schreiben sie
Gleich ein paar
Neue Gesetze

Joachim Meyer
I was born in 1951 in a village on the Weser river. I live in Berlin since 1960. Early fascination with the written word, I liked to write as a child and gulped many books. Later, scientific interests, which led me to study medicine. Strong political engagement in school and at the University. I recognized that medicine was the

JOACHIM MEYER

while watching the demolition of an old apartment building

    splinter in the wrecker's eye
    beam in mine

heating-oven chunks spray
in fountains into the gray heavens
and walls fall like cards

    where housing was
    for money-worry talks
    and small beers
    at the supper table
    holes tower into Kreuzberg gray

here and there still enclosed
by last gallant bricks

    one comes across the street
    speeding, crying out
    and slams at our feet
    fallen to earth

from earth are ye taken
to earth shall ye return

    we stand there and watch
    it didn't hit us
    but over our heads
    the wrecker swings the ball

wrong path for me, turned anew to writing, during the phase of leaving medicine, many poems about the hospital. I study English and German literature now. Learning the craft of writing is in the foreground for me, next to my study. Am writing and illustrating a book. Am interested in literature into which hope and movement can flow, without hypocrisy. I subscribe to no dogmas, life is all that counts. My favorite author is Henry Miller, and my favorite book is his "Big Sur."

---

beim zusehen wie ein altes mietshaus eingerissen wird

    splitter im baggerauge
    balken in meinem auge

und kachelofenfetzen spritzen
in fontänen ins himmelsgrau
und wände fallen wie karten

    wo behausung war
    für geldsorgengespräche
    und kleine biere
    am abendbrottisch
    ragen lücken ins Kreuzberger grau

da und dort noch umschlossen
von letzten tapferen mauersteinen

    einer kommt über die straße
    gesaust im aufschrei
    und schlägt vor unseren füßen
    zur erde nieder

von erde bist du genommen
zu erde sollst du wieder werden

    wir stehen da und sehen zu
    uns hat er nicht getroffen
    bloß über unseren köpfen
    schwenkt der bagger die Kugel

Buildings in Snow   by Jan Huber   etching

at the loading ramp

chalkdust drizzles in all your alveoli
sack after sack spews the loadingcannon
a chalkpregnant monster of prehistory
that rolls itself up on rails
to the moustache / who just relieved the other
raging the 50 kilo cement sacks
in his face / against his chest / into his groin
however certain levers and buttons are set
but he gets on with it / gloved the fists
that's how much a thin man weighs
i think / as i heft another sack
and it slips out of my hands again
but he still has to stack it in the truck
so it goes for an hour and a half
one after the other / until the huge loading room
pukes for all the sacks
that still breathe out chalkdust even
if the moustache / or whoever's there just then
has already sprayed them down for the who-knows-how-manyth time
a guy flees for a moment from the line
grips himself a bottle of beer / open
that there on the ramp asphyxiates in the dust
in the loading gullet the hands of the moustache
in the rhythm of the sack cannonade
on his lips death defiance
it's not his battle / but he doesn't desert
later I hear from the supervisor
who alone of them all wears the regulation helmet
that the battlers in this troop
get 8 marks an hour
and that ain't bad / is it?

an der verladerampe

kalkstaub rieselt in alle deine alveolen
sack um sack speit die verladekanone
ein kalkschwangeres monster der vorwelt
das sich auf schienen heranwälzt
dem schnauzbart / der gerade nen anderen ablöst
wütend die 50 kilo-säcke zement
ins gesicht / gegen die brust / in den unterleib
je nach einstellung bestimmter knöpfe und hebel
er aber packt zu / behandschuht die fäuste
soviel wiegt ein dünner mann
fällt mir ein / als ich einen sack anhebe
und er meinen händen wieder entgleitet
der aber muß ihn noch im laster placieren
so geht das anderthalb stunden
hintereinander / bis der riesige laderaum
sich auskotzt vor säcken
die den kalkstaub noch abatmen
wenn der schnauzbart / oder wer gerade dran ist
sie schon zum x-ten mal mit wasser befeuchtet
ein mann flüchtet mal kurz vom band
greift sich ne flasche bier / offen
die dort auf der rampe im staub erstickt
im ladeschlund die hände des schnauzbarts
im rhythmus der sackkanonade
auf seinen lippen todesverachtung
dies ist nicht sein krieg / doch desertiert er nicht
vom meister erfahre ich später
der als einziger vorschriftsmäßig nen helm trägt
daß die kämpfer in diesem scharmützel
acht mark die stunde bekommen
und das wär doch ein guter lohn / oder?

tender bonds
through
off-colors

in my mouth
the taste like grandfather days
milky smoke
colorful exotic projecting
onto the color-withdrawn
everyday soft tissues
of my gums
sumatra borneo and brazil
serious and solemn
and dutiful
like a procurer
about nineteenhundredten
and modestly luxurious
and sometimes spicily familiar
as in distant days of childhood
—distant—because still too close—
the goodnight kiss
on grampa's prickle-cheeks

with brown cylinders of tobacco
in wood boxes or
cases painted with feudal scenes
as is your grasp
i bind your face
so i already know you
hook-nosed and friendly
and sometimes an embarrassed smile
when we puff your
off-colors into our beards
at thirteen cents apiece
then we lack no colors
you drink café au lait / beige
for me mediterranean wine / rosy
you show me photos
of your mother / rheumatic
sitting in the garden / blooming bright
i hand over poems
the last ones i've written
about growing up

zärtliche verbundenheit
durch
fehlfarben

in meinem mund
der nach großvatertagen
schmeckende milchige rauch
bunte exotik projizierend
auf die farbenentwöhnte
alltagsschleimhaut
des gaumens
sumatra borneo und brasil
ernst und feierlich
und pflichtbewußt
wie ein prokurist
um neunzehnhundertundzehn
und bescheiden luxuriös
und manchmal würzig vertraut
wie in fernen kindertagen
—fern—weil noch zu nah—
der gute-nacht-kuß war
auf opas stachelwangen

mit den braunen tabakröhren
in holzkistchen oder
feudalzeitbebilderten schachteln
je nach deinem griff
verbind ich dein gesicht
so kenn ich dich schon
hakennasig und freundlich
und manchmal verlegen lächelnd
wenn wir deine fehlfarben
aus dem guten angebot
zu dreizehn pfennig das stück
uns in die bärte qualmen
dann fehlen uns die farben nicht
du trinkst milchkaffee / beige
ich wein vom mittelmeer / rosigen
du zeigst fotos mir
von deiner mutter / rheumakrank
sitzend im garten / buntgeblüht
ich reiche gedichte rüber dir
die letzten / die ich schrieb
über die erziehung mein

about mother terror / ominous black
about father terror / wrathful red
you tell me about your stress
as trade school instructor
i tell you of my nervewracking night watches

in the paintbox of our talk
your cares fill
the right basin
and mine the left
off-colors here too
they're complementary colors
but no lack of colors

über mutterterror / düsterschwarz
über vaterterror / jähzornrot
du erzählst mir von deinem streß
als berufsschullehrer
ich dir von meinen nervenden nachtwachen

im tuschkasten unseres gesprächs
füllen deine sorgen
die rechten näpfe
und meine die linken
fehlfarben auch hier
        komplementärfarben sinds
            aber keine fehlenden farben

ERNST WICHNER

fragment

but i
travel through the other europe
have socialism
in my big mouth
and have left it standing
    unfinished
        like the construction workers their building
        when the whistle blows
and our words
resound
naked and strange
and are so injuringly
unfree

Ernst Wichner
Born 1952 in Guttenbrunn, Rumania. Since
1975 in West Germany. Studies German
literature and political science.

fragment

ich aber
reise durch's andere europa
führe den sozialismus
großschnäuzig im munde
und hab ihn doch stehen lassen
    unfertig
    wie die bauarbeiter ihren bau
    am feierabend
und unsere worte
klingen nach
nackt und fremdartig
und sind so verletzend
unfrei

sleeping tablets
an autobiography

so when the war was long enough
over
and the collective farms already existed
and it was ready
then I was born
without any of my own doing
in the middle of the cold peace
and was warped
by dedicated teachers
shortly after Stalin's death
in the spring

and in the wrong country
when it was time
I learned no language
but that in the newspapers
and of objective necessity
and believed
that I helped form
the spring

and the new universities
and their advantages
from inside and outside
well observed,
the red holidayflags
treasured and smiled at,
and was on a first-name basis with
the great portraits
(from bad artist's hand)
in passing
through so much spring

and now I've become so old
that I can smile with understanding
in conforming rounds
as in that state
the comrades do it
sit tight
in this free democratic
swallow sleeping tablets endlessly
and get no smarter
nor younger

schlaftabletten
eine autobiographie

als dann der krieg lang genug
aus war
und es die lpg schon gab
und es war soweit
da bin ich geboren worden
ohne eigenes dazutun
mitten im kalten frieden
und verzogen worden
von eifrigen lehrern
kurz nach stalins tod
im frühling

und habe im falschen staate
als es zeit wurde
keine sprache gelernt
als die der zeitungen
und der objectiven notwendigkeit
und geglaubt
daß ich mitgestalte
am frühling

und habe
die neuen universitäten
und ihre vorzüge mir
richtig
von innen und außen besehn
die roten feiertagsfahnen
geschätzt und belächelt
und geduzt
die großen portraits
(von schlechter malerhand)
im vorbeigehen
durch so viel frühling

und bin nun so alt geworden
daß ich verständnisvoll lächeln kann
in konformer runde
wie es in jenem staat
die genossen tun
sitze fest
in dieser freiheitlichdemokratischen
schlucke unablässig schlaftabletten
und werde nicht klüger
noch jünger

no man's land
report of a journey

1
with the fine drizzle
rain on asphalt (not sarah
and richard's kind: country rain)
the first words arrive
slow and awkward
(like soap-bubbles)
they come in for landing
on things
and pop
in mid-sentence

2
after all the nights of europe
the morning haze in timișoara
      temeschburg
      temesvár
three tongues since all eternities
and (write it down!)
blacks from all over africa
      left alone in need of speech
      in suddenly bursting love
      : things happen, I'm telling you
the newest apartment buildings
    sad &
    already past
like our early loss of hope

still,
always recurring
the old toast
: to freedom!

3
the experiences are all upside down here
between forests and history
swelling up stinkingly
yellow and black smoke
up to the sun

niemandsland
ein reisebericht

1
mit dem feinen geriesel
asphaltregen (nicht wie sarah
und richard: landregen)
treffen die ersten worte ein
langsam und unbeholfen
(wie seifenblasen)
setzen sie zur landung
auf die dinge an
und zerplatzen
mitten im ersten satz

2
nach allen nächten europas
der morgennebel in timişoara
    temeschburg
    temesvár
dreisprachig seit allen ewigkeiten
dazugehörig (unbedingt aufschreiben!)
schwarze aus ganz afrika
      alleingelassen in sprachnot
      plötzlich explodierender liebe
      : da gibt's sachen
      sag' ich dir
die neuesten hochhäuser
     traurig &
     schon vergangenheit
wie unser früher hoffnungsverlust

trotzdem
immer wiederkehrend
der alte trinkspruch
: auf die freiheit!

3
hier stehen die erfahrungen kopf
zwischen wäldern und historie
quillt stinkend
gelber und schwarzer rauch
hoch bis zur sonne

evenings
when the whole brew
plunges in floods from heaven
the violated woods lie down to rest

then the boxbuildings
moan and sweat
mutual nightmares
to some next way out

4
still in the last sleep
masses of wall towering
              long angular shadows
              dusty plazas
              & cathedral & fountains
              & plague monument
fragments preformed:
              "if one who
              smashed the songs
              spoke now . . . "
the memory
of a dream:
        a streetcar
        that runs by
        wheels screech
        in the curve
that wakes me up

5
pumped full with sweet hot coffee
high
    otherwise
boredom runs to seed
"above the rooftops
begins the world"
              that's
              how it is here
but aside from that
the storks fly south
& in the gazettes
the world remains intact
              in spring
              if the waters revenge
              what men neglected

abends
da all die brühe
in sintfluten vom himmel stürzt
legt geschändet
der wald sich zur ruhe hin

dann stöhnen und schwitzen
die schachtelbauten
gemeinsame alpträume
einem nächsten ausweg zu

4
in den letzten schlaf noch
ragt das gemäuer
        lange kantige schatten
        staubige plätze
        & dom & springbrunnen
        & pestdenkmal
bruchstücke vorformuliert:
        wenn einer, der
        die Gesänge zerschlug,
        jetzt spräche . . .
die erinnerung
an einen traum:
        eine straßenbahn
        die vorbeifährt
        räder kreischen
        in der kurve
das weckt mich auf

5
vollgepumpt mit süßem heißem kaffee
high
    sonst
schlägt langeweile ins kraut
"über den dächern
beginnt die welt"
        so
        sieht es hier aus
sonst aber
ziehen störche nach süden
& in den gazetten
bleibt die welt heil
        im frühling
        wenn die wasser rächen
        versäumtes

                        & rain for forty days
                        reason blacks
                        out
"if nothing else helps
then" says gerhard
"then" I say
                        & we stare
                        into the rain
                        & slowly get
                        drunk

6
at the parting then
the words begin
to run over each other
they get shrill and loud
step on their own endsyllable
and at the alarm whistle
fall upon each other once and for all

the last ones
no longer spoken
forget themselves
a few hours later

            & regnen vierzig tage
            setzt bewußtsein
            aus
"wenn nichts mehr geht,
dann" sagt gerhard
"dann" sage ich
      & stieren
      in den regen
      & werden langsam
      besoffen

6
beim abschied dann
beginnen die worte
sich zu überschlagen
sie werden schrill und laut
treten sich auf die eigene endsilbe
und fallen beim trillerpfeifenton
endgültig übereinander her

die letzten
nicht mehr ausgesprochen
vergessen sich
einige stunden später
selbst

HELLA JOANNI

Hella Joanni
I was born in 1950, the first of five siblings. The best part of my childhood was the Rudolf Steiner (Waldorf) School, from which I graduated in 1969 with a normal Abitur. I studied German and Russian literature with a highpoint of a four-month stay in

Christmas Outside

My first Christmas outside my parents' home and my last as a teenager was no sadder than the Christmases in the earlier eight years.
Like every other evening I went on Christmas Eve to the Tea Parlor. That was before the hard drugs showed up, but it was still bad enough. Well-raised, I at least wasn't touched by it, because I watched out for myself. I always wanted to know the Christian names, when I found myself in a with-difficulty-begun conversation, because after all Helmut, Bernard, and Daniel are more original than Muratti, Gringo, and Satan. We had a tea parlor princess, underage rowdy, charming back then, today streetwalking—just listening to her was enough to get into a state. She made like: The cops in white rubber coats on motorcycles—and one after the other—bzzzm / flup—crashing—like white mice—buzzzm / flup! bzzzm / flup!
Well, on Christmas Eve I was there too, and despite everything in a joyful and hopeful mood. It takes a long time, before you stop hoping for miracles and recover from your childhood. It seemed to me like all the tea parlor people were different than usual and in raised spirits. The old tea parlor was before the Edeltrödelmode (noble flea market fad). Everything was dirty, hardly anything was eaten. The seating was mismatched, an armchair, two benches along the wall, a few stools, we sat on the low tables too. Usually it was so full you could hardly get through, but you had to get through to determine who was still in the back nook. Here Dralle handled the bar and put on the records. The light was white and not dull green and red like up front, and another disadvantage was that you had no overview of the coming and going. So you had to push your way back to the front room.
In the front room they had hung a Santa Claus on the wall for the holiday occasion. In the back room Dralle made his jokes with the

Leningrad and an interruption of a half-year, which I spent in Israel. After my exams in 1977 I had difficulty finding a job as teacher, so I worked in a kindergarten and taught German as a foreign language. At the moment I'm suffering praxis-shock working at a school, and could write many a satire about it, but I've neither enough time nor literary ambitions.

---

guests, wordlessly holding an empty Coke bottle tilted from his zipper. A girl who always dressed up in black and violet satin curtains and fringed tablecloths presented him with his Christmas gift by snapping a Trojan onto the cable of the hanging lamp, where the thing stayed hanging the whole evening.

I was already up front again, staring at the wall, which was divided into a red, a yellow, and a black wave, and waited for something Special from the evening. Soon one came in, looked more groomed than we did, sat down next to me, smelled like fresh air, and claimed he'd walked directly in from Wannsee, namely because he'd swallowed speed. He only works half-days, he related, because he still wants to get around to life. At that time I didn't understand that—and that as orderly in the Foresthouse Clinic he provided the withdrawal patients with hashish. I disapproved. He introduced himself as Horst, and we went out together. I started crying and received from him a Kleenex and a hand-rolled cigarette. And he stayed that polite all evening. It was the best thing we could have done, to walk around so much. We passed the Ludwig-Kirch-Platz, there was the Mosque, there was the Russian Orthodox Cathedral, at Fehrbelliner Platz the stern government buildings weren't yet estranged by the mod U-Bahn station. At the crematorium Horst pointed out how it smoked out of the smokestack there, round the clock, visible on Christmas Eve too.

In Japan it is part of good taste to tell each other amusing stories, and it is considered very coarse to talk about oneself or problems and especially to discuss them. Horst entertained me with informative explanations about the city and with stories from his own experience. Soon after the crematorium he recalled how he used to work in the hospital. With stillborn babies or babies who die right after birth, the parents usually forego a burial. The small corpses lie there then in plastic sacks until they are picked up to be burned. How stupid, they should mulch the earth with it, was Horst's opinion. Once one of the sacks fell open, and what appeared? a dear little head, so tiny, so moving. He parts it from the little body, puts it in a jar with formaldehyde and the jar on the shelf at home. Afterwards he forgot it. Then a few weeks later his glance falls on it again. Something had changed, the little eyes have opened up in the meantime and look, look right at him, the blue ones!

Abandoned House in Dahlem   by Christine Arweiler   etching

Hans Schumacher
Born 1931. Literature professor at the Freie Universität in Berlin. Would rather make literature than take it apart, a bloody business to which his stomach and his children compel him. Has published literary criticism in a variety of journals.

HANS SCHUMACHER

Slow Motion

In this perhaps arbitrarily chosen moment, the 500 pound bomb is about 40 cm. from the upper rim of the middle dining room window in the second floor of a typical German apartment house built in the 1920's. There it is only one object among many others. Apart from the fact that its presence is, of course, new and unique for the accumulation of air, walls, bricks, roofs, chimneys, branches, and leaves—so even there flying objects have been seen often enough—perhaps a swallow, a stone thrown by a naughty boy, a piece of paper that sails down through the air to the courtyard, basking today in the gorgeous sunshine. The day really is a beautiful one in the year 1944, mild summer wind rustling fragrant lace curtains in the windows, opened to let in light and air. Between the immediate position of the bomb and the place in the cellar where it will detonate is about 30 m. in a straight line. The bomb slants, 1.50 m. long, 35 cm. wide, and has the characteristic appearance of a bomb, which requires no lengthy explanation, one sees it at first glance, one has, so to speak, a feeling for it. At its sight the eyes pop out of the head, the mouth dries up, the brain begins to sear, the limbs are grasped with an irresistible shaking, one stares at it, would like to look away but can't. Its cylindrical form, with the familiar fins at the back end which guarantee that it hits detonator-first, is of that sober functionality which is the imprint cultivated by the objects of the technological era. A certain contrast to this is achieved by the humorous inscription in yellow oil paint: "Good day and good bye to you Nazi bastards, yours sincerely, Henry." Henry's Bird, as he calls his Vickers-Wellington, has, since dropping it, moved 250 m. further and let fall more "eggs" that are now suspended like drops on an invisible thread above the city, whose lay on the river is, even from a height of 2000 m., recognizably "wonderful." Henry thinks: after the war I'll have to take a steamer cruise there sometime. Aunt Evelyn gushed so adoringly about the romantic fortresses. But first I gotta get outta here in

Three years ago Prof. Schumacher founded a circle of writers, the Literarischer Arbeitskreis, which has produced two anthologies, *Erfahrungen* (Experiences) 1 & 2, and which plans now to produce volumes from individual members of the circle.

---

one piece, and he observes uneasily the white shrapnel clouds of the anti-aircraft guns, which fortunately don't reach the altitude of his squadron.

The bomb glistens in the sunlight, its shadow falls on the yellow facing of the wall of the house. Foreshortened, the shadow looks like an oversized beet root. Not far below, near the dining room window stands a freshly set table, whose middle point is occupied by a big-bellied, brightly painted coffeepot. From its spout rises a thin thread of steam that flattens out in the draft. The pot presides over a herd of valuable old utensils taken—for the birthday of the daughter of the house, sweet sixteen, cute, intelligent—from the glass cupboard, where it dozed away with other hundred-year-old things like Sleeping Beauty, next to miniatures of grandparents in little silver frames, coral necklaces, ruby glasses, ivory carvings, silver sugar bowls, and other stuff that had accumulated in the course of family history: a yellowed Bible, a gilded opera glass, great-grandfather's tassled pipe, grandmother Elisabeth's Lorgnon glasses, an inlaid wooden box with the milk teeth of the birthday girl, Vera, and from her brother Rüdiger, two years younger. Cute sentimentalities. By sacrificing great quantities of food-ration cards as well as by bribing the baker with a bottle of Slivovitz that her husband brought back after the Jugoslavia campaign, Frau Messel was able to order two cakes, to whose consumption, however, it has not come. They remain on the gleaming damask table cloth, exquisitely untouched, decorated with the number 16 in ersatz cream, because the sirens have shooed all the party guests into the shelter of the cellar. Waiting for the birthday child is her flower-decorated place, next to which lies, as a gift, Goethe's *Poems*, which Vera read not just because it was in the school curriculum. Recently she had discovered her weakness for classic literature, and Goethe's "Willkommen und Abschied"—"Welcome and Parting"—had gotten under her skin, for she had just gone through her first secret rendezvous. From her seat one looks directly through the wide-opened window, before which the blue-gray bomb with the yellow script hangs disconcertingly.

The table, good German craftsmanship, is actually much too weighty for normal requirements, one could even say, it has never really been put to the test. With its bowed legs it stands there like a living being, inviting, inspiring trust. It appears to say, come what may, I can take it. And crowding around on it is really enough that is beautiful and nourishing. Solid pre-war goods, when craftsmanship was too proud to produce schlock. In the whole room is nothing which can match in any way the technical sobriety of the bomb. Everything is old-fashionedly full of fillips, flourishes, and curlicues, *gemütlich*, plush. That's how Frau Sabine likes it, lace-edging here and there, beflowered pillowcases on the Biedermeyer sofa, anti-macassars wherever oily hair could brush against the edges of armchairs, Persian carpets whose intricate patterns confuse the eye, throw-rugs to cover the few flaws in the wood floor, a dark Art Nouveau mantelpiece crowned with crystal vases and bowls, above which, a picture of great-great-grandfather Friedrich Wilhelm Messel in the uniform of a sharp-shooter, dark-haired and looking with a friendly, dreamy look into an imaginary distance. The good-natured, boring, foothill landscape behind him appears to lay in evening light, red glow above dark green forests. A fat, tiled heating oven takes up the corner. It is fired up from the kitchen. All is gleaming, despite the miserable wartime cleansers and polishes. Everything in the apartment stands there with a peaceful steadfastness and certainty, as if it belonged precisely there and nowhere else.

A hundredth of a second later nothing much has changed, with the exception of the destruction of Ma Messel's good coffeepot. The steelish-gleaming bomb hit it square, unfortunately. The shards of the rosebud-decorated lid, the spout, the splendid handle and the painted-flowerlet belly stand like a swarm of butterflies over the table; the contents, good, black genuine bean coffee (to organize which, Lieutenant Messel had almost risked the military court) is in the process of pouring out over the table cloth, a trousseau piece. A terrible mess, how shall one get it out again?

The bomb has unceremoniously carried out its entrance into the room. Now it is there, and hardly to be ignored. The little defect which it has caused, has, in a strange way, brought it into an almost friendly contact. Things like that happen often with strangers. One is frostily reserved toward them the whole time until, in embarrassment, they pull some clumsiness or other. Among excusings and insistences that it doesn't matter, the first bonds are forged, which then often last until death. Which will, however, not wait much longer, because the touch of the detonator with the rosebud lid has triggered the sensitive mechanism with which, after a short hesitation, the explosive material hidden under the steel shell will be brought to fruition. But outwardly there is not yet anything noteworthy. The presence of the bomb over the breakfast table and in the inside of the pot doesn't excite anyone, because things are as incapable of feeling as of thinking. Frau Messel, who sits 25 m. away in the cellar, hasn't a notion yet of the accident. She'll experience it soon, for the bomb itself is on its way to bring her the news. The question is whether she will be able to muster any sadness and bitterness over the loss of the pot, the rest of the utensils, the baroque table, the table cloth, the glass cupboard, the Goethe in morocco leather, the wine glasses, carafes, etc. Indeed one doesn't dare have hope for the table, however solid it looks. A hundredth of a second later it is smashed to pieces, chewed up, splintered, along with the shredded cloth, the utensils, the squashed cakes, the whirling cream pitcher, the bent silver spoons, cake forks, and cake cutter, which follow the unwelcome guest through a suddenly-grown two-meter-wide hole in the roof of the quarters of the bachelor and Head Justice, Dr. Mansfeld.

The break-in of the bomb in the silken stillness of the tobacco-perfumed twilight reminds one of the mob storming the palace of Versailles. The comet tail of shards, cake-remnants, mortar, splintered mouldings, floorboards, beams, table legs, and carpet shreds that it brings along is most offensive. The marble busts, possessed by the master of the house, show a dignified shock. Their high-born expression seems to mirror the countenance that Dr. Mansfeld cultivates when sentencing. This morning he had again much occasion for that. An invalid caretaker had made a stupid joke about the straightening out of the front in the Ukraine. For Undermining of the Defense Forces he was sentenced to three years in prison. A Polish conscripted laborer didn't get off so easy. He had taken a pair of torn boots from a site full of rubble. And for looting there's the death sentence!

The bomb smashes impartially busts and pedestals, the desk slab on which everything stands, bores its way through bundles of documents with well-founded judgments, which in this instant mix up with the remnants of cake from Vera's birthday table, and now disappears in a hole that it rams in the cellar roof. It apparently wants to land in front of the cellar-bunker's door, barricaded with planks and beams: high time to turn to the inhabitants of the cellar, before it's too late. A hundredth of a second before the disintegration of the body, its forms demand no particular attention. Under the husk of clothes they are not much more noteworthy than other people's, even smaller differences like Negroes (black skin, kinky hair) or Jews (crooked nose, repulsive, decadent intelligence) that they might have had, play no role and produce nothing essential to tell them apart.

Frau Messel is authenticated Aryan and her daughter too, luckily.

The Head Justice was able, with great difficulty, to keep his Jewish grandmother secret, otherwise he would be standing on the Russian front now, and wouldn't have this honorable, state-supporting office, which actually should have brought him around to the idea of justice, particularly in the distribution of foodstuffs. Despite the scarcity, he has preserved for himself a healthy Nordic layer of lard, which contrasts strongly with the delicate undernourishment and pale color of Fräulein Messel. Without wanting to, Vera recites automatically verses from Goethe, yet something hinders her breathing, her hands lie like stones in her lap, it seems to her as if a fire is going through her spine. Yet it will never cross her mind that anyone could have justified doubts as to her further existence. Life is simply in her, even if fear has almost transformed her into the wall that she presses against, while the rumble of a thousand airplanes vibrates it and the ground shakes and trembles with the ever-approaching bomb explosions like a ship in a storm. Her mother sits facing her on a rickety basketwork chair next to the supporting beam and is more distant and stranger than ever in life, she would like to take the three steps over to her and take shelter in her lap, but that's kilometers away, she doesn't dare get up and leave her secure place. But how is it secure? she thinks suddenly alarmed, yet she sticks to the kitchen chair as if nailed on. No, it will never happen! What then? and she confuses her hopes and her fears, and then she wants very much to remember something, but she doesn't know what, and something occurs to her, and she says it very slowly, and what she says carries her away so light and free, like the white flash breaking out of the cellar wall, explaining to her the whole deep meaning: Kennst du das Land, wo die Zitronen blühn . . .

The Head Justice has the very strong feeling that it's all a dream. He calls this out to himself again and again and does quite well that way. He is really satisfied with himself and thinks, on the Somme 1916 he didn't bear up as well, then he notices suddenly that his flesh just doesn't want to. It's like a growing resistance in him, he looks down at himself and feels totally naked. It's not at all embarrassing, for Frau Messel and her half-grown daughter are nothing but broomsticks for him, and indeed everything seems to be made of wood. The glimmering light is of wood too and the plastered wall, everything seems to be only a thin barracks, and he sits there all alone and unprotected like in his sauna-hut in the Hunsrück and he looks down at himself and has so much body, so much flesh, he sits there with cheeks pinched together and waits to forget that he is there and then it was as if the oven of the sauna burst, monstrous heat surrounded him and he said to himself: it is only a dream.

Frau Messel had still remembered in time to leave the windows open so that the panes wouldn't break when the pressure waves come and to turn off the gas. Hopefully nothing will happen to the old utensils, first it would be too bad because it comes from grandmother and second you can't get any new utensils anymore anyway. And you couldn't take anything out of storage, the bigwigs of course had had all the best taken out to the country and their families too. They had champagne brought to them from France, once we too got a bottle on an order of requisition, but what's one bottle, when after all we won the war against France, you'd think they could distribute you more to eat. Just don't let the light go out, in the dark I'm afraid. If only Schmitz, the repulsive block warden, doesn't get wind of where we got the coffee and the cakes for Vera's birthday, she can really use it, to get something on her ribs for once, how she looks so thin and how fat Mansfeld . . .

When the fire brigade has rummaged through the debris, they find under the ruins three dead and four living house inhabitants. One of the dead is a young French girl, who had the bad luck to fall in love with a German occupying soldier, and, threatened with murder by her patriotic countrymen, had fled like a shot to her in-laws in Germany. Dead too are Frau Messel and her hopeful daughter. Little Rüdiger was therefore left behind alone without parents, since his father had already fallen on the Russian front two days earlier, without anybody having known. On the morning in question, Rüdiger had had a strange premonition and, despite the vehement protests of his mother who had wanted him there at the birthday celebration, had driven into the country with the Hitler Youth. Dr. Mansfeld suffered severe burns, a leg had to be amputated, but he survived due to his excellent physical condition. The reduction of his pension through the de-Nazification is more than made up for by the generous war-victim-allowance.

Index of Authors and Artists

Arweiler, Christine, 375
Bartus, Jutta, 234–241
Becker, Uli, 268–273
Beissert, Jürgen, 77, 79, 96, 117, 219
Boesche-Zacharow, Tillye, 134–135
Boiron, Michel, 180–181
Bolster, Peter, 98–105
Böltz, Gerd, 124–125
Brasch, Thomas, 282–289
Braun, Volker, 258–267
Brunner, Werner, 256–257
Cohen, Mitch, 15–22, 195
Döring, Stefan, 344–345
Fauser, Jörg, 70–83
Fricke, Nil, 254–255
Fuchs, Jürgen, 292–301
Gersch, Wolfgang, 159
Gorek, Bert, 274–280
Gutelius, Josepha, 202–204
Hadayatullah, 160–165
Heinrichs, Siegfried, 302–304
Hirschfelder, Uli, 46–58
Huber, Jan, 354–355
Hübsch, Paul Gerhard (Hadayatullah), 160–165
Huston, Tom, endpapers
Joanni, Hella, 372–374
Keller, Stefan, 122–123
Klefinghaus, Sibylle, 210–213
Köhler, Alfons, 342–343
Kolbe, Uwe, 36–45
Komor, Reinhard, 224–227
Koplowitz, Jan, 244–251
"Künstlergruppe Ratgeb," 252–257
Lackner, Peter, 126–131

Lahtela, Silvo, 114–116
Meinicke, Michael, 13–14, 94–97
Melzian, Jochen, 4–5, 35, 59, 110, 178–179, 299, 305, 331–339
Meyer, Joachim, 352–361
Mickel, Karl, 136–149
Middendorf, Ingeborg, 352–361
Miersch, Alfred, 64–69
Morshäuser, Bodo, 184–187
Neubauer, Thomas, 328–331
Rathenow, Lutz, 106–113
Rothmann, Ralf, 206–209
Rühle, Ursula, 196–197
Schenk, Holger, 198–199
Scheurer, Hans J., 60–63
Schmich, Bernd, 84–89
Schumacher, Hans, 376–381
Speier, Michael, 90–92
Springborn, Gerd, 150–158
Steffenhagen, Joachim, 216–223
Steinbrecher, Werner, 253
Stern, Maria-Stefanie, 200–201
Streit, Monica, 166–169
Techel, Sabine, 172–177
Tefelski, Norbert, 346–351
Theobaldy, Jürgen, 24–34
Tiel, Katja, 182–183
"Werkkreis Literatur der Arbeitswelt," 214–215
Wichner, Ernst, 362–371
Witzel, Herbert, 118–120
Wohlfahrt, Volker, 228–233
Wollenberger, Knud, 281
Zabke, Reinhard, cover, 121
Zahl, Peter-Paul, 306–327

Index of Titles

Abandoned House in Dahlem, 375
Abflug am Morgen, 185
Adder Earth Let It Be I Picture Me Something, 278
After Work, 88
Aktion Widerstand, 336–339
alkfoegel gluekkseelen triefig, 277
alkfowl rapt dripping, 276
"Als sie einmarschierten," 253
Alte Schreibmaschine, 347
"Always I see you," 300
An den Haltestellen, 53
an der verladerampe, 357
The Applause, 113
The Attempt Is What Matters, 68
At the Bus Stops, 52
At the Butcher's, 70
at the loading ramp, 356

baby it's great to be back home, 172–173
the basic fact, 222
Beer: for Leising, 140
beim zusehen wie ein altes miets-haus eingerissen wird, 353
Bettina, 117
Bier. Für Leising, 141
Bilder aus Amerika, 33
The Book, 303–304
Buildings in Snow, 354
Bundschuh, 254
"But I copied out," 298
but primarily, 274

Change of Life, 134
Change of Location, 112
The Child, 296
Christmas Outside, 372–374
The Coal-Handler's Warmth, 122
The Constitution, 350
Cooling Towers, 342–343

Defaitistische Depressionen, 273
Defeatist Depression, 272
Deine Kälte war es, 13
Design for a Monument, 281
Deutsche Frau 46, 143
doors, 310–327
Dresdner Häuser, 145–149
Dresden Houses, 144–148
Driving Back in November, 102–104
du, 201

das eigentliche, 223
Eine Art Nächstenliebe, 25
Einer jener Briefe, 187
Ein Paar Minuten März, 57
Eiskeit III, 91
Das Elend der Vertriebenen, 271
Encounter, 159
Entwurf für Denkmal, 281
The Escalator at Pont de Sèvres, 115
Es Kommt auf den Versuch an, 68–69
euch hut & wut, 277
Eulenspiegel, 285–289

Fairly Confused, 98
Fame, 80–82
family life, 176–177
Fantasy, 106
Feb. 18, '77, 292–294
februarsonne, 309
february sun, 308
Feierabend, 89
felix coniunctio, 174–175
A Few Minutes of March, 56
Flight in the Morning, 184
Floskel, 199
Flourish, 198
forwiegend aber, 275
Foreword for those who don't get it afterward, 116
For Thomas, on the Thirteenth, 54
fragment, 362–363
Frau Mitschuleit's Survey, 236–241
Furnished Apartment, 26
Für Thomas, am dreizehnten, 55

gedanken über die zehlendorfer "spinne," 217–219
gedicht über meinen großvater, 345
German Woman '46, 142
Geschlossene Argumentation, 197
Gewitter über einer Kastanie am Nachmittag, 103
Goethe's Leaseholders, 266
Going All the Way, 267
The Good, 152–158
Das Grundgesetz, 351
the guilty, 36
Das Gute, 152

High Noon, 50
Die Hosen Deines Vaters, 61
Hot Coffee, 228–232

Ice Age III, 91
Ich bin erzogen im Namen einer Weltanschauung, 39
Ich Will Mein Geld Zurück!, 269
ich wohne in mir, 161–165

"Ick been ein Brrr leaner" says this Santa Barbarian solemnly, 126–131
The Idolaters, 202–204
"I don't believe that," 298
i dwell in me, 160–164
"I love you," 169
"Immer sehe ich dich," 301
The Initials of the Seigneur, 249–251
It was Your Coldness, 134
I Want My Money Back!, 268
I Was Raised in the Name of a Weltanschauung, 38

Kicks in the Head, 64–66
A Kind of Charity, 24
Korrektes Haar, 139
Kreuzberger Prospekt, 195
"Künstlergruppe Ratgeb," 252–257

landscapes, 124
landschaften, 125
Letter Found in a Bottle, 118–120
Like the Movies, like Life, 46–48
Like This Summer Dress, 34
Lindenforum, 137
Linden Forum, 136
little mornings of habit, 181
The Lonely Road, 180

Malli Kneeling, 77
Malli Sitting, 79
Mauern, 101
Mein junges Leben, 29–31
Melanie, 44–45
Memo, 206
Metamorfosis, 43
Metamorphosis, 42
Metrogeruch, 90
Metzgerei, 71
The Miscarriage, 189–194
Mitch, 96
Mobliertes Zimmer, 27
The Modern Quarter, 143
moocher pays, 280

Morgens, 221
Mornings, 220
The Myth of the Cave, 264
My Young Life, 28–30

nassauer bezahlt, 280
Natter Erde Lass Gut Sein Ich Mal Mir Was Aus, 279
Neubauviertel, 143
Neuer Zweck der Armee Hadrians, 263
1977—aber nicht für die Akten, 85–87
New Purpose of Hadrian's Army, 262
Newspaper Poem, Edited, 265
niemandsland, 367–371
9/1/'78, 298
1977—but not for the files, 84–86
no mail today, 176–177
no man's land, 366–370
no poem, 175
Nostalgic One, 348–350
Nostalgiker, 349–351
Notiz, 207

Oedipus, 282
"of him it's said," 172
Old Typewriter, 346
On Brecht, the Truth Unites, 258
On Climbing High Mountains (after Lenin), 260
One of Those Letters, 186
On the Anniversary of the Death of Hans Martin Schleyer, 233
Orderly Hair, 138
The Other Side, 210–213
"Our landlord schlepps," 150

P., 108–109
People—Fairy Tales, 95–96
"petition," 307
les petits matins de l'habitude, 181
Petzower Sommer, 137
Phantasie, 107

Pictures from America, 32
Places 1, 114
The Pleasure in the Creative, 266
poem about my grandfather, 344
Poesie & Praxis, 59
Poesy & Praxis, 58
Portrait 1970, 182–183
Positive Provocation, 245–248
The Predilection of the German Thinker, 335
Prison, 97
Processions, 166
Prompt, 111

Der Rabe Ralph, 255
Ralph the Crow, 255
Rauchzeichen, 302
Realistic Curriculum Vitae, 332
The Release, 224–227
The Request, 328–331
Requiem for a Goldfish, 72–78
Rita's Fantasy, 283–284
Die Rolltreppe von Pont de Sèvres, 115
Rückfahrt im November, 103–105
Ruhm, 81–83

Sacco & Vanzetti, 36–37
Scheißspiel, 257
schlaftabletten, 365
die schuldigen, 37
Shitplay, 257
Sketches from a Socialist Prison, 303–304
sleeping tablets, 364
Slow Motion, 376–381
Smoke Signal, 302
So ein Tag, 209
Statement, 92
Stellen 1, 114
"Die stillen Zimmer," 89
"The still rooms," 88
Storm over a Chestnut Tree in the Afternoon, 102
Study of a Hand, 219

"subwaysmell," 90
The Suffering of the Fugitives, 270
Summer in Petzow, 136

tender bonds through off-colors, 358–360
"That is exaggerated," 297
thoughts about the zehlendorf spinnery, 216–218
Tritte in den Kopf, 65–67
The Turning Point, 295

Umzüge, 167
"Unser Hauswart schleppt," 151
unsettled, quietly and softly, 174

Violent Habituation, 168
Vom Besteigen hoher Berge (nach Lenin), 261
"von dem Heiß es," 1973

Walls, 100
die wärme, die der kohlenhändler gibt, 123
Was sie aus dir machen, 63
Watertight Argument, 196

Wechseljahre, 135
We Live with Cracks, 40
"Werkkreis Literatur der Arbeitswelt," 214–215
What a Day, 208
what they make of you, 62
"When they marched in," 253
while watching the demolition of an old apartment building, 352
Wie dieses Sommerkleid, 34
Wie im Kino, wie im Leben, 47–49
Wir leben mit Rissen, 41

you, 200
Your Father's Pants, 60
Your Kiss, 94
you shielding & wielding, 276

zärtliche verbundenheit durch fehlfarben, 359–361
Zeitungsgedicht, redigiert, 265
Ziemlich verwirrt, 99
Zu Brecht, die Wahrheit einigt, 259
Zum Jahrestag von Hans Martin Schleyer, 233
12 Uhr mittags, 51

ZEITSCHRIFT FÜR NEUE LITERATUR
Berlin, Heidelberg · Herausgegeben von:
Michael Speier und Jan-Cornelius Schulz

Gedichte von:
Christoph Meckel, Jürgen Theobaldy, Karl Krolow,
Walter Helmut Fritz, Wolfgang Bächler, Harald Hartung,
Rose Ausländer, Bodo Morshäuser u.a.

Übertragungen neuer Lyrik aus:
Mexiko (Sabines, Zaid, Pacheco, Novo) Heft 2
Griechenland (Melissinos, Frangopoulos, Papanastassiou)
  Heft 3
Italien (Sanguineti, Spatola, Costa, Tiziano, Niccolai,
  Immovilli) Heft 4
Schweden (Martinson, Gustafson, Norén, Thoursie,
  Lundkvist) Heft 5
Jugoslawien (Puslojić, Slamnig) Heft 6
Katalonien (Brossa, Salvat-Papasseit, Espriu) Heft 7
Frankreich (Tilman, Biga, Venaille, Delvaille) Heft 8
England (Anne Beresford) Heft 9

Einzelheft: 4,50 DM   *Jahresabonnement: 20 DM*

PARK Verlag M.Speier, D-1000 Berlin 44, Nogatstr. 39
Germany

OHIO UNIVERSITY LIBRARY

Please return this bo...
have finished with it.
...ust be return...

PT 3807 .B4 B38 1983

Berlin, contemporary writing
from East and West Berlin

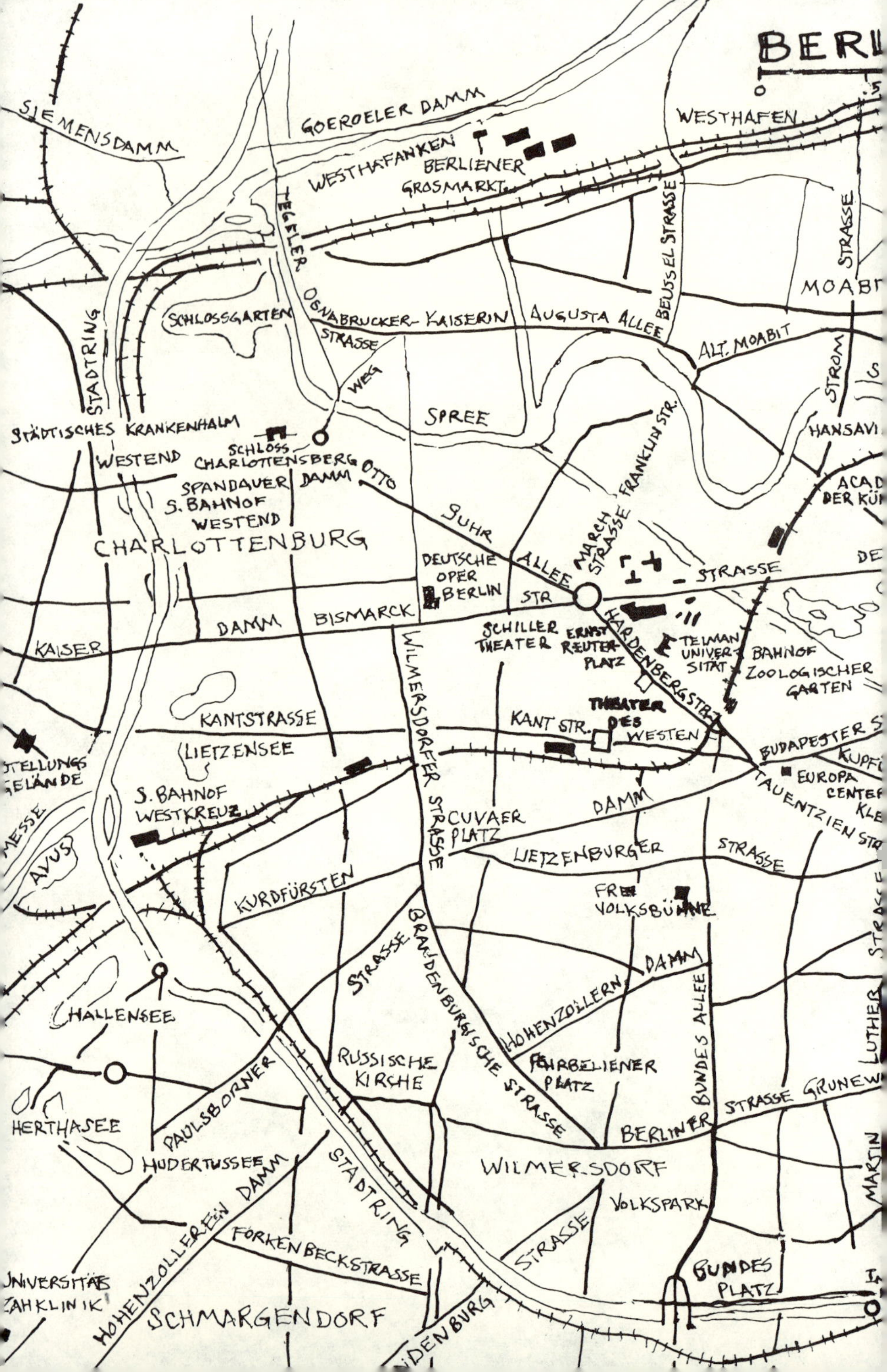
BERL
SIEMENSDAMM
GOERDELER DAMM
WESTHAFEN
WESTHAFANKEN
BERLIENER
GROSMARKT
TEGELER
BEUSSEL STRASSE
STRASSE
MOABI
STADTRING
SCHLOSSGARTEN
OSNABRUCKER-
STRASSE
KAISERIN
AUGUSTA ALLEE
ALT. MOABIT
STROM
WEG
SPREE
HANSAVI
STÄDTISCHES KRANKENHALM
SCHLOSS
CHARLOTTENSBERG
WESTEND
SPANDAUER
DAMM
OTTO
FRANKLIN STR.
S. BAHNOF
WESTEND
SUHR
ALLEE
ACAD
DER KÜ
CHARLOTTENBURG
MARCH
STRASSE
STRASSE
DEUTSCHE
OPER
BERLIN
STR
DAMM
BISMARCK
KAISER
SCHILLER
THEATER
ERNST
REUTER
PLATZ
HARDENBERGSTR.
TELMAN
UNIVER
SITÄT
BAHNOF
ZOOLOGISCHER
GARTEN
WILMERSDORFER
STRASSE
KANTSTRASSE
KANT STR.
THEATER
DES
WESTEN
LIETZENSEE
TELLUNGS
GELÄNDE
BUDAPESTER S
KUPF
EUROPA
CENTER
KLE
S. BAHNOF
WESTKREUZ
DAMM
TAUENTZIEN STR
MESSE
AVUS
CUVAER
PLATZ
LIETZENBURGER
STRASSE
KURDFÜRSTEN
FREI
VOLKSBÜHNE
STRASSE
BRANDENBURGISCHE
STRASSE
DAMM
HOHENZOLLERN
HALLENSEE
HOHENZOLLERN
FEHRBELIENER
PLATZ
BUNDES ALLEE
LUTHER
STRASSE
RUSSISCHE
KIRCHE
PAULSBORNER
HERTHASEE
STRASSE
GRUNEW
BERLINER
HUDERTUSSEE
WILMERSDORF
MARTIN
DAMM
STADTRING
VOLKSPARK
FORKENBECKSTRASSE
STRASSE
HOHENZOLLEREN
UNIVERSITÄTS
ZAHKLINIK
BUNDES
PLATZ
SCHMARGENDORF
DENBURG